Law Librarianship in the Twenty-First Century

Edited by
Roy Balleste
Sonia Luna-Lamas
Lisa Smith-Butler

The Scarecrow Press, Inc.
Lanham, Maryland • Toronto • Plymouth, UK
2007

SCARECROW PRESS, INC.

Published in the United States of America
by Scarecrow Press, Inc.
A wholly owned subsidiary of
The Rowman & Littlefield Publishing Group, Inc.
4501 Forbes Boulevard, Suite 200, Lanham, Maryland 20706
www.scarecrowpress.com

Estover Road
Plymouth PL6 7PY
United Kingdom

British Library Cataloguing in Publication Information Available

Library of Congress Cataloging-in-Publication Data

Law librarianship in the twenty-first century / edited by Roy Balleste, Sonia
Luna-Lamas, Lisa Smith-Butler.
    p. cm.
 Includes bibliographical references and index.
 ISBN-13: 978-0-8108-5881-7 (alk. paper)
 ISBN-10: 0-8108-5881-9 (alk. paper)
 1. Law libraries. 2. Law libraries—United States. I. Balleste, Roy. II. Luna-
Lamas, Sonia. III. Smith-Butler, Lisa.

Z675.L2L38375 2007
026'.34—dc22

2006026915

∞™ The paper used in this publication meets the minimum requirements
of American National Standard for Information Sciences—Permanence of
Paper for Printed Library Materials, ANSI/NISO Z39.48-1992.
Manufactured in the United States of America.

I dedicate this book to four individuals. To my mother, Ana Milagros, who has always given me the greatest gift there is: the belief that anything is possible. To my wife, Melisande, who always stood as the solid foundation from where my work sprung into fruition. To my father, Manuel, who instilled in me the love for science and science fiction. To my good friend Billie Jo Kaufman, associate dean for Library Information Resources and professor of law at American University, Washington College of Law, the one who introduced me into the world of academic law librarianship and inspired me to write in this field.

R. B.

To Tony and Christopher, who selflessly allowed me to spend an enormous amount of time away from them on professional activities. Thanks to all of you who have supported and encouraged me to do more than I thought I could ever do, especially St. Thomas University School of Law, which made it possible for me to be able to contribute to my profession; Roy Balleste, for asking me to be part of the great idea behind this book; and to Gordon Russell, associate dean, director of the Law Library and Information Services at Charleston School of Law, for always believing in me, feeding me unbelievable ideas, and pushing me to never be afraid of trying new things.

S. L. L.

For Victoria and Frank—you make everything possible and in memory of my father, P. Walter Smith, who shared his love of the law and libraries with me.

L. S. B.

Contents

Foreword

For many professors in the field of library and information science (LIS), law librarianship has been treated as a stepchild. This can be attributed in part to the field's traditional adherence to its analytical rigor based upon specialized subject-specific indexing, abstracting, and digesting schemes devoted to the need to access the case law that is the foundation of the American legal heritage. Library schools often ignored the discipline, depending on postgraduate subject-specific supplementation of the library science graduate's generalized knowledge, most usually accomplished through the student's acquisition of a law degree. In the days when law librarianship was a skill practiced almost exclusively in academic and law school settings, this was an adequate direction.

Today, though, as the following collection of materials and essays indicates, the divide that existed between information access in the legal environment and that which existed generally in libraries has become pedagogically insignificant. Electronic storage of documents, Boolean searching methods, and the steady evolution away from reliance on print resources are circumstances that have served to make law librarianship today a branch of twenty-first-century librarianship rather than a branch of the study and practice of law, as it probably was best characterized in the past. These days, library school education is more relevant to the law library practitioner than in the past.

The field of law librarianship remains a special and important one, with its own vocabulary and with its rich, almost unmatched, print heritage nurtured for many years by publishers, lawyers, law professors, and, yes, law librarians. It is also unique in that it has a dual goal that many other special library fields do not. Its service component is not just to the specialists in the field—that is, lawyers and judges—but to the public at large as well, because we are all affected by and bound by the law. Access to the law is critical if modern society is to avoid indulging its natural tendencies toward totalitarianism. Franz Kafka's defendant's problem was that he never knew what the law was that he was accused of violating. A law that is "an ass" is at least made more tolerable (and reformable) if its content can be understood. The role of providing public access to the law is a critical one for librarians.

The rigors of the law librarianship specialization are touched on in detail. Roy Balleste, a graduate of our MLS program at the University of South Florida, is well equipped with his background in emerging technological fields to have put these materials together and organized them in a useful and logical way. This collection should be helpful in meeting a need for materials for those involved in teaching law librarianship. Lisa Smith-Butler and Sonia Luna-Lamas added their skills, joining him in the compilation and development of this project.

Professor Berring, in his brief history of the profession of law librarianship included in these essays, concludes with a touch of pessimism regarding the long-term prospects of the discipline through the twenty-first century, wondering whether law librarianship will survive or change before our eyes to become something considerably different from what it is now. There is some basis for a gloomy outlook, and certainly the law librarianship profession at the beginning of the twenty-first century bears little resemblance to its nature at the end of the nineteenth, but the materials in this book suggest a bright future and continuing relevance for this important branch of the library profession. It is one that library educators should strive to ensure is filled with LIS graduates, enjoying that level of knowledgeability and competence in the field that will continue to justify its existence through service both to the legal profession and to the public that is affected by our country's laws.

Vicki L. Gregory, professor and director
School of Library and Information Science, University of South Florida
Tampa, Florida
March 2006

Preface

The title of this textbook reflects a new age in law librarianship. A hundred years ago, little had been written about the management of law libraries and their contributions to the legal profession. Since then, there has been a gradual but rapid growth of articles and books on various aspects of law librarianship. Today, law libraries exist at an important time in history. It is a time of great challenges, uncertainty, and rapid evolution. The introduction of the Internet and the continuous development of other technologies have created enormous tension in the library community. The world community has acknowledged the challenges that lie ahead in the information delivery arena. The United Nations World Summit on the Information Society, which was held in two phases, first in Geneva (2003) and later in Tunis (2005), expressed a desire and commitment "to build a people-centred, inclusive and development-oriented Information Society, where everyone can create, access, utilize and share information and knowledge." This is a tremendous challenge and an important goal in order to promote access and delivery of information around the world. This book is a small part in that all-encompassing effort.

The chapters set forth here are indicative of the universal role that law libraries continue to play in the legal profession. The book is intended to serve students in programs of library and information science. As in many other areas of library science, law librarianship continues to evolve. Since publication of the first law librarianship book, libraries and legal information centers have changed dramatically. Law librarians today must master legal materials while balancing them with an understanding of the latest technologies. Topics such as artificial intelligence and quantum computing will be addressed along with administration, consortia, collection development, and others as we consider their future impact on the profession. The world of law librarianship is entering an exciting time, one that will offers us an opportunity to shape the profession for the next century.

Roy Balleste
Sonia Luna-Lamas
Lisa Smith-Butler

Acknowledgments

This book would not have been possible without the generous support of great human beings and institutions that understand the importance of law libraries and their contributions to society.

First, we would like to thank the editorial and production staff at Scarecrow Press, Inc. In particular, we want to thank Martin Dillon, consulting editor, for all his help and guidance during the entire process.

We are indebted to the following individuals for their support and/or permission to reprint excerpts of their material: Pam Abbey, director of publications, the Estate of Carl Sagan, Carl Sagan Productions, Inc.; Carol Yecies, head of Information Services, Nova Southeastern University, Shepard Broad Law Center; Ann Druyan, president, Carl Sagan Productions, Inc.; Joseph Harbaugh, dean and professor of law, Nova Southeastern University, Shepard Broad Law Center; Dr. Seth Lloyd, professor, Massachusetts Institute of Technology, Department of Mechanical Engineering; Frank Novak, head of Network Services, Nova Southeastern University, Shepard Broad Law Center; Pedro Perez, assistant for Collection Maintenance, Nova Southeastern University, Shepard Broad Law Center; Gally Perry, vice president, Financial and Legal Affairs, Oddcast, Inc.; Jason Rosenberg, information systems administrator, Nova Southeastern University, Shepard Broad Law Center; Dr. Matthew Sellars, research fellow, Laser Physics Centre, Australian National University; Stephan Sobchak, head of computer services, Nova Southeastern University, Shepard Broad Law Center; Roy Tennant, user services architect, California Digital Library, University of California; Dr. Richard Wallace, chairman of the board and cofounder, the A.L.I.C.E. AI Foundation; and

Dr. Anton Zeilinger, codirector, Institute for Quantum Optics and Quantum Information, Austrian Academy of Sciences.

We are also indebted to the following institutions for permission to reprint excerpts of their material: A.L.I.C.E. AI Foundation; the Estate of Carl Sagan, Carl Sagan Productions, Inc.; and Oddcast, Inc.

We owe a great debt of gratitude to our contributors. This project would not have been possible without the tremendous efforts put forth by our peers: Robert C. Berring Jr., Walter Perry Johnson Professor of Law, School of Law, Boalt Hall, University of California, Berkeley; Jennifer Bryan, assistant librarian and lecturer in law, Indiana University School of Law, Bloomington; Dr. Vicki L. Gregory, professor and director, School of Library and Information Science, University of South Florida; Karl T. Gruben, law library director and associate professor of law, St. Thomas University, Miami; James S. Heller, director, law library and professor of law, William & Mary School of Law; Anne Klinefelter, associate director of the law library and clinical professor of law, University of North Carolina School of Law, Chapel Hill; Roy M. Mersky, Harry M. Reasoner Regents Chair in Law and director of research, The Jamail Center for Legal Research Tarlton Law Library, The University of Texas at Austin School of Law; Mary Rumsey, foreign, comparative, and international law librarian, University of Minnesota Law School; and Tracy L. Thompson, executive director, New England Law Library Consortium.

Finally, we express our gratitude to all others who have helped in any way during the drafting of this text.

Roy Balleste
Sonia Luna-Lamas
Lisa Smith-Butler

Introduction

Recently I addressed two librarian groups, the American Association of Law Libraries (AALL) Computer Services Interest Section (CIS) and attendees of the summer Center for Computer-Assisted Legal Instruction (CALI) conference.[1] At both of these gatherings, I talked about the future of law librarianship. The title of my presentation at the CIS gathering was "The Future of Law Librarianship: There Is None," and at CALI, "Look, Ma, No Books!" Both presentations were meant to sound controversial in order to encourage discussion and thought beyond the everyday issues facing the profession.

In this introduction, I am excited about the opportunity to provide some insight into opportunities for a career in law librarianship. To me, there is nothing controversial about the future of law librarianship. The profession is increasingly important and interesting, but there are matters that need to be considered when one enters the field. In 1980, Virginia Wise of Harvard Law School and I contributed a chapter, "Law Librarianship," for the publication *Special Librarianship: A New Reader.*[2] We wrote that law occupies a unique position in American society and that the complexity and rapid changes in the legal profession generated a new specialization of experts on legal information sources. When the first meeting of the American Association of Law Libraries was held in 1906, there were twenty-six members. There were 2,000 in 1980, and now there is a membership of over 5,000. The stated purpose of our article was to provide an introduction and an invitation to the profession of law librarianship.

We attempted to answer the questions: Why become a law librarian? What does a law librarian do? What are the qualifications needed to be a law librarian? What are the opportunities for professional growth? To answer these questions, we turned to the consideration about the importance of law in contemporary society.

Law is a method of peaceful revolution that affects everyone on a daily basis. It determines what time you get up (statutorily imposed by daylight savings time), what you eat (Food and Drug Administration regulations), and whether your sleep will be undisturbed by a burglar (sanctions of the common law of crime). These are exciting opportunities; whether a law librarian is doing research for an attorney involved in a products liability suit that ultimately results in a defective item being removed from the market, is helping to draft a statute that requires seat belts, or is finding a piece of information that tips the vote in an important Supreme Court case, law librarians can affect the quality of our society in a tangible way. Since September 11, 2001, important principles are at stake, including the right of law enforcement officials to use the Patriot Act to demand library records in counterterrorist investigations.[3]

The legal and law librarianship professions are constantly changing. Intelligent and well-educated persons are needed to keep up with the volume of legal material being generated, the increased access to information resources, the complexity of the digital information age, and the impact of information technology (IT) on library services and activities. Thinking back on my career, I remember when I entered the profession in the 1950s, "chip" meant a piece of wood, "hardware" was found in a general store, and "software" was not even a word. Reading library literature, I am reminded that currently there is a new library vocabulary, suggesting new intellectual opportunities for law librarians: podcasting, licensing contracts, copyright clearance centers, and open URL link resolvers. Additionally, there are evolving collection management strategies: consortia, resource sharing, preservation, conservation, document delivery services, and e-books. Law librarians must know how to integrate bibliographic knowledge with technical, reference, and instructional proficiency.

Law libraries of the future will look very different from our prototypical law library today. I foresee a time when a large percentage of academic law libraries will maintain a basic collection of primary materials and will contribute to funding a regional collection for secondary resources and for regional jurisdictions. Some libraries may be bookless. One of the main libraries on the University of Texas campus has been converted to a multi-department information center.[4] At the same time that the university is creating the bookless information commons, it is entering into consortium arrangements with other public and private universities within the state of Texas to develop a digital library of the institutions' work product.[5] Google announced in December 2004 that it was indexing all or part of the book collections of several major research libraries, and indicated that the company hoped to create a virtual card catalog of all books in all languages.[6]

If, as I predict, the law library of the future will, in the majority of situations, contain only a core collection of hard volumes, librarians and IT professionals will continue to be expected to enable access to an increasingly wide variety of interdisciplinary and international materials. The role of the law librarian as an instructor will be more demanding, and the role of the librarian and computer specialist as a creator of resources that serve the particular and very specialized needs of his or her institution's user group will expand as well.

What are the problems within the profession? Newly appointed academic law library directors are less likely to have tenure status. The title of assistant or associate dean of information or technology places law librarians in the same category as career services administrators or admissions directors. Library budgets are shrinking; salaries are often lower than in secular organizations. Law library professionals are more frequently put in the position of fighting for every dollar. An American Library Association (ALA) task force in 2002 collected data and reported its findings, and among the important issues facing academic law libraries were topics similar to those in law librarianship: recruitment; education and retention of librarians; impact of IT on library services; creation, control, and preservation of digital resources; chaos in scholarly communication; and funding.[7]

Issues in scholarly and legal publishing are creating concern about publisher mergers, increasing concentration of legal journals in the hands of a few publishers, and the effects of price escalation on law library budgets. Privatization of information troubles law librarians.[8] Government Printing Office and the Federal Library Depository Program proposed a budget for fiscal year 2006 that provides for electronic dissemination of 95 percent of the documents currently distributed to depository libraries, but as Victoria Trotter, the outgoing president of AALL reported,[9] the budget does not provide funding requests for authentication, permanent public access, or preservations mechanisms so important to the successful adoption of an electronic government information model. The guidance and input of the library community is increasingly important in assisting these government agencies to make these documents available to the public through documentary libraries.

So, is there a future in law librarianship? To rebut my own statement that "there is no future in law librarianship," the profession is increasingly important and the future is bright with tremendous prospects for those with degrees in library science, law, computer science, language, management degrees, and other specialized credentials. The challenge to emerging and veteran law librarians is to take a hard look at what we are doing and how we are doing it. There is a need to educate new law librarians and to reeducate existing librarians with skills and knowledge to meet the challenges of the profession and to ensure a proactive approach to services.

As you read the articles in *Law Librarianship in the Twenty-First Century,* I am confident that you will be struck—as I was—by the extraordinary changes and advances in our profession. There are magnificent opportunities for a new generation of law librarians. The work of a law librarian is indispensable in our legal and educational system. And perhaps the best incentive to be a law librarian is the satisfaction of knowing that one's work is stimulating, exciting, and challenging.

An added incentive is in earning the gratitude of one's constituencies. My friend, the Honorable Justice Michael Kirby, justice of the High Court of Australia, expressed his appreciation for the profession in his welcome to participants to High Court Symposium:

> I take this occasion to say thank you to all librarians who have been such special friends, colleagues and guides in my professional life: a warm appreciation. We should say it loud and say it often. Through you, I express the gratitude of generations of judges. Your work is indispensable. In the complexities of life it will become more so. It will change in delivery. It will be enhanced by technology. But it will always be there and essential to the idea that human beings can attain the noble goal of equal justice under the law for all.[10]

Roy M. Mersky, professor
Harry M. Reasoner Regents Chair in Law and director of research
Jamail Center for Legal Research
The University of Texas at Austin School of Law

NOTES

1. American Association of Law Libraries annual conference, San Antonio, TX, July 18, 2005, and CALI annual conference, Chicago, IL, June 10, 2005.

2. (with Virginia Wise) "Law Librarianship," in *Special Librarianship: A New Reader* (Metuchen, NJ: Scarecrow Press, 1980), 306–14.

3. Alison Leigh Cowan, "At Stake in the Court, The Use of the Patriot Act to Get Library Records," *New York Times,* September 1, 2005.

4. "Packing Up the Books," *Chronicle of Higher Education,* July 1, 2005.

5. "At Year's End, Facts at Your Fingertips," *Austin American Statesman,* July 13, 2005.

6. "Libraries Concerned about What Next Chapter Will Be," *Austin American Statesman,* July 24, 2005.

7. "Top Issues Facing Academic Libraries: A Report of the Focus on the Future Task Force," *College and Research News* 63, no. 10 (November 2002).

8. Lee C. Van Orsdel, "Antitrust Issues in Scholarly and Legal Publishing: Report on an Invitational Symposium in Washington, D.C.," *College and Research Libraries News* (May 2005): 374–77.

9. Victoria Trotter, "Marching On . . .," *AALL Spectrum* (March 2005).

10. "A Law Librarian's Love Affair," *Australian Law Librarian* 4 (Summer 2004): 7–11.

Chapter 1

A Brief History of Law Librarianship

Robert C. Berring Jr.

Describing the history of law librarianship is no simple task. First one must define law librarianship. Does it refer to anyone who works with legal materials? Does one have to work in a law school library? Are law firm and court librarians a separate group or part of the same professional cadre? Is a library school degree necessary to qualify? Must one have a law degree? Are law librarians different from other librarians?

There is no definition of law librarianship that cannot be disputed or contested. Given the nature of the law, perhaps this is as it should be. To locate the heart of the profession of law librarianship, a number of pathways can be consulted. The American Association of Law Libraries (AALL) provides an institutional framework for studying the profession. Biographical glimpses of those men and women who played crucial roles in its development could be equally enlightening. Probing the line that separates law librarianship from the more general profession of librarianship could also be fruitful. One could also study the institutions for which law librarians worked. Law schools, courts, law firms, and membership libraries could provide an avenue for examination. As with so much in life, the question of how to organize the discussion proves crucial to the dimensions of the discussion itself.

In the end, I chose an organizational principle that included the above factors and then added other criteria. This approach includes the factors enumerated above but also approaches the profession of law librarianship by looking at the way that the content, format, and the research practices of legal information have shaped the profession. Instead of following the money, we will follow the legal information.

Law librarianship has always been closely tied to the nature of legal information. The form in which legal authority is published and the ways in which it has been used have dictated the dimensions of the profession from the start. No matter in what setting a law librarian worked, her or his duties were formed by the information that she or he was manipulating. The special nature of legal information and legal authority brings this home with emphasis. Legal researchers search for statements of the positive law. This differs from most social science research where one searches for guidance or opinion. Legal researchers believe that they can find the truth.[1] When one combines this with the undeniable fact that the law has a profound impact on American society, the importance of legal information is clear. Further, legal information sources are arcane and highly specialized. Using legal information as the touchstone, we can center our discussion on five eras of legal information: the classic period, the setting of the stage, the field as it matures through the growth of law school libraries, its depth and expansion into law firm libraries, and the current questions facing legal librarians.

Before beginning, this caveat is issued: What follows is no more than an overview of the history of law librarianship, and a brief and highly subjective one at that. Fortunately for the reader who wishes to delve deeper into the questions at hand, 2006 is the centennial anniversary of the AALL. In conjunction with this celebration, the 2006 annual convention of the AALL will focus on the history of the association. Throughout the year, the *Law Library Journal* (LLJ) will feature articles outlining AALL history, the reminiscences of past leaders, and biographical sketches of historical figures. This chapter is being written before much of this material appears but the upcoming material promises to provide a mother lode of source material for anyone who wants to study the issue in greater depth.

Even before the centennial celebrations began, a great deal of scholarly work had been done on the history of law librarianship. Professor Frank Houdek of the Southern Illinois Law School is both editor of LLJ and the coordinator of many of the historical projects. Professor Houdek also edits a loose-leaf publication entitled *The AALL Reference Book: A Compendium of Facts, Figures, and Historical Information about the American Association of Law Libraries*. It began publication in 1994 and is updated regularly. It contains a comprehensive bibliography, a complete time line on the progress of law librarianship, and numerous sources that provide information about law librarianship. Anyone who wishes to dig deeply into the history of law librarianship should start here and should contact Professor Houdek. The best research advice is to go to someone who knows and cares about the subject. No one surpasses Professor Houdek on either count.[2]

THE CLASSIC ERA: FROM JANITORS TO SCHOLAR LIBRARIANS

Law libraries began as rather modest enterprises. The United States is a common law jurisdiction. In common law jurisdictions, judges write opinions that resolve disputes between parties. In theory, these opinions do not represent the judge's personal decision. Instead, they represent the judge's written statement of the existing law as applied to the facts of the particular case. The distinctive feature of common law systems is that these judicial decisions are viewed not as interpretations of the law but as the law itself.[3] They become legal precedent and are called "primary authority." How these judicial opinions rise above the status of representing the personal opinions of the judge and reach to the level of articulated legal principles is a thorny question. It has been debated for decades by the best legal theorists, with no answer yet in sight. Despite the debate, the fact remains that judicial opinions are the foundation of common law. Such opinions can be cited in the future as statements of the law. Lawyers spend many hours in law school mastering the skill of using such precedent via analogy and logic.

From the earliest days of the American republic, the publication of judicial opinions was at the core of legal research. This perspective continued well into the twentieth century, with legal researchers believing that one only needed to read cases to understand the law. While treatises existed to explain both the common law and foreign law, particularly the law of Great Britain, the heart of any law library, at this time, was its collections of judicial decisions.

At this time, the legal researcher's problem lay in obtaining copies of the judicial decisions. The number of decisions was small enough that a practitioner could read each case in his jurisdiction, plus most federal cases and perhaps English cases as well. Most of his interpretation was done inside his head or in his notebooks. A good law library consisted of a collection of judicial reports and little more. While a handful of practitioners assembled more extensive libraries, the finest repositories were in law school libraries and in the libraries of private subscription societies. Even these collections did not call for the skill set being developed by the nascent profession of librarianship. Judicial opinions were issued in series and came with their own indexing and abstracting systems that precluded the need for cataloging and classification. These libraries needed simple maintenance, not professional attention. Indeed, one of the earliest references that I have found to a law librarian comes from a history of the Harvard Law School Library, which explains that in the middle of the nineteenth century the librarian was usually a student, assisted by a janitor.[4] Tasks were minimal, especially since some professors preferred to buy materials themselves and keep them in their offices. These small law libraries did not produce a profession. Such collections need a caretaker, not an information professional.

By the end of the nineteenth century, the great libraries at law schools like Harvard, Yale, and Columbia, and at the great subscription law libraries like the Social Law Library in Boston, the Jenkins Library in Philadelphia, and the Library of the Association of the Bar of the City of New York, were preparing book catalogs and growing, but law librarianship was not yet needed.

SETTING THE STAGE: THE EXPANSION OF LEGAL INFORMATION

As the twentieth century progressed, the world of law was swept by a number of powerful forces. The Brandeis Brief serves as a famous marker of one important change. The Brandeis Brief is considered by many in the legal community to be a turning point in the use of nondoctrinal authority in legal argumentation. Louis D. Brandeis represented the state of Oregon in *Muller v. Oregon*, 208 U.S. 412 (1908), a case involving the constitutionality of state restrictions on women's working hours. The *Muller* Court reached a unanimous decision in this landmark case, upholding the statute, justified on the basis of the state's special interest in protecting women's maternal functions. Rather than the traditional theoretical format, Brandeis instead wrote his brief using only a few pages on the doctrinal test of the law's constitutionality, spending the remainder on data supporting the law as a "reasonable" regulation. In his 113-page brief, Brandeis compiled empirical data from hundreds of medical, economic, and sociological journals to illustrate the impact on women of working long hours. Not only was the brief persuasive in *Muller*, it became a landmark of its own and is a frequently used model for nonlegal arguments in presentations to the courts. This type of brief became commonly known as a "Brandeis Brief."

The success of the Brandeis Brief led legal researchers to look outside the world of judicial decisions and into the world of social science. While the Brandeis Brief is only the most famous marker of this change, the pressure to look to sources outside of traditional judicial reports built. Several sources applied this pressure. The change resulted in the need for law libraries to hold new types of material. Selecting and acquiring books and serial publications became important, as did the cataloging and classification skills of librarianship. Reference services became more than just directing researchers to the right case reporter or digest. The whole world began to open up.

In addition, the growing number of materials found in libraries pushed legal information to a critical mass. At some point, researchers can no longer hold in memory all of the information that they need. Primitive organizational schemes that once worked in a smaller information universe break down. New information systems become necessary. The stage is set for the professional field of law librarianship to emerge.

THE PROFESSION MATURES:
ACADEMIC LAW LIBRARIES TO THE FORE

Great law libraries grew in the middle of the twentieth century. Elite law schools like Harvard, Yale, Columbia, and Michigan built huge collections of materials. More important, the profession of law librarianship grew beyond the small band who founded the AALL into a much larger group. A. J. Small had founded AALL while acting as the curator of the Iowa State Law Library.[5]

Those early days were characterized by small numbers and a variety of nascent law libraries. State and court libraries were central players. Great collections could be found at libraries maintained through cooperative societies of lawyers such as the Law Library of the Association of the Bar of the City of New York and the Social Law Library in Boston. The Los Angeles County Law Library, supported by filing fees from court cases in California, was a leader as well. Many such libraries have histories that start well before this time period. It was at this point that they were required to expand their collections dramatically. While subscription law libraries initially were at the very forefront of the law library world, they could not compete with the ambitions of the law schools. Supported only by membership dues or filing fees, subscription law libraries could no longer lead the way. That mantle would fall to academic law libraries. At this point on the time line, academic institutions began investing in their legal libraries.

The law library had long been held to be crucial to a law school. Dean Christopher Columbus Langdell, the man who founded the modern version of the Harvard Law School, is credited with designing the law school curriculum that continues to be employed today. He introduced both the Socratic method and the case approach to legal education. Langdell believed in the primacy of the law library. Since Langdell believed that judicial opinions were the soul of the law, he felt that the law library was the laboratory of the law. Legal researchers reading judicial opinions were like scientists conducting experiments. Of course, Langdell conceived these ideas in a world where the law library consisted mostly of sets of judicial reports, but his influence ran deep. It paved the way for the modern academic law library to hold pride of place at the heart of the law school that it served.

Law schools began to compare the size of their law libraries as indicators of institutional quality. Bigger was best. An arms race of acquisitions began. Law school faculty and deans would watch for the results of the annual American Bar Association (ABA) survey to see what law schools had the highest volume count. While the elite schools competed to have the largest collection of books, the ABA and the American Association of Law Schools (AALS), the agencies that accredited law schools, promulgated standards as to the minimum collection that a law school must maintain. Eventually the ABA and the AALS would require that the director of the law library be made a member of the law school faculty. Other requirements, including the ratio of librarians on staff in comparison to faculty to be served, evolved in the accreditation process.

The middle of the century also saw great figures emerge to guide law librarianship. Mentioning influential figures is a chancy enterprise as the list is never complete, but several names from the middle of the twentieth century demand mention. Each of these individuals represents a great body of work and a large number of people. If you are to understand the nature of law librarianship, they are names that you must know.

Miles Price at Columbia Law Library trained several generations of law librarians and helped guide the profession into its adulthood. With his protégé Harry Bitner, he authored a text on legal bibliography that served as the bible for law librarians for decades.[6] At Yale Law School, Frederick Hicks brought a scholarly heft to law librarianship. Hicks published books on legal research as well as on substantive topics. His ideas on legal research are relevant even in the days of the Internet.[7] Rosamund Parma, the longtime director of the law library at Berkeley's Boalt Hall School of Law, was a pioneer. As the first female president of the AALL, she is one of the few individuals who served two years in the office. William Roalfe, director of the law library at the University of Southern California, conceived of the Roalfe Plan, a road map for making the AALL a true professional organization. This crucial step made all that followed possible.

Arthur Beardsley, at the University of Washington School of Law, began a program to train lawyers to become law librarians, inventing the master's of law librarianship (MLL) in the process. The program was subsequently taken over by Marian Gould Gallagher, who trained more law librarians than anyone else and established a great network of professionals. Her program, carried on today by Penny Hazelton, continues as a vital source.

Mike Jacobstein, who spent the bulk of his career at Stanford, and Roy Mersky, who became famous as the long-tenured director of the law library at the University of Texas, were both influential in many ways. Jacobstein trained under Miles Price while Mersky spent his first years working at Yale. Together they produced a book on legal bibliography that was the main text for legal researchers for many years.[8] These two men collaborated on more than two dozen titles and their influence reached far beyond their own libraries.

For several decades Professor Mersky turned the University of Texas Law Library into a training ground for law librarians that, while smaller than the University of Washington program, produced many high-profile law librarians. At one time he could point to the fact that the law library directors at Harvard, Stanford, Berkeley, and more than two dozen other law schools were all trained in his apprentice system.

Morris Cohen, who had the rare distinction of serving as director of the Harvard Law Library and then the Yale Law Library, picked up the intellectual mantle of Frederick Hicks and produced scholarship of the first order. Professor Cohen's writings were hugely influential.[9]

In 1961 Elizabeth Finley was the first law firm librarian to be elected president of the AALL and demonstrated that law firm librarians were ready to move into leadership. William Murphy, longtime librarian of the law firm Kirkland and Ellis in Chicago, served as patron saint of the AALL executive offices in Chicago. Antoinette (Babe) Russo served as the executive director of the AALL during its period of growth. Everyone knew Babe. Julius Marke, longtime director of the New York University Law Library, wrote widely on both substantive law and law librarianship. He was also a pioneer in understanding the importance of copyright law in legal information. Each of these individuals was crucial to the growth of law librarianship in the mid to late twentieth century.[10]

All but one of the figures mentioned above had law degrees. As law libraries grew and as legal education expanded, it became common for the director of the law library to hold a JD degree. Eventually it would become a requirement for accreditation. This development was a recognition that legal materials were so specialized that the normal skill set of a librarian would not be sufficient, particularly for librarians working with attorneys and others in public contact positions. To function as the director of an academic law library and eventually to serve as a reference librarian in such an institution, it was decided that one needed the kind of subject expertise that could only be gained by being a law school graduate. This skewed the profession towards a more scholarly bent. A quick glance at the *Law Library Journal*, the official publication of the AALL, would show that it resembles an academic law review. Law librarians at law schools identified with legal information and with the legal institutions that they served. Academic libraries served as the model and set the tone for law librarianship deep into the twentieth century.

LAW FIRM LIBRARIES AND THE AGE OF THE PRIVATE SECTOR

During the last third of the twentieth century, legal culture in the United States underwent profound change. Law firms became larger and larger while the practice of law became more and more like a corporate enterprise. Where once a law firm of thirty was thought to be large and most law firms limited their practice to one city, this gave way to law firms boasting dozens of offices and employing numerous, sometimes more than a thousand, lawyers. This shift occurred alongside a dramatic change in the world of information.

Legal information had benefited from highly sophisticated research tools in the world of print. Pioneering legal information systems were created by the West Publishing Company and the Shepard's Company. Law had the most advanced print systems of information tracking and delivery in the information delivery systems of the world. One company, West Publishing Company, dominated this world. Staffed by a cadre of lawyers and devoted both to serving the legal profession and making money, West Publishing Company brought experience and deep expertise to its business. The many smaller legal publishers shared the same characteristics. Each was run by people who were lawyers, law librarians, or men (and they were all men) who had grown up in and around legal literature.

Sophisticated print systems were built around the primacy of judicial opinions and were closely integrated with the work of law schools, leading to one seamless information universe. However, law firms often maintained impressive libraries of these print sources. Though law firms largely confined themselves to collecting judicial reports and statutes, leaving the gathering of the burgeoning social science works regarding law to the law schools, law firm collections could be substantial. Large law firms prided themselves on architecturally striking law libraries, sometimes building the entire office around a showpiece collection of books. The book collection was not just a gathering of legal information; it was also a statement about the quality of the law firm. When printed books ruled the world, a showplace library spoke to the intellectual heft of the law firm. Larger law firms might employ a law librarian to oversee such a collection, but in all but the grandest firms, the librarian had often been little more than a secretary assigned to watch over things.

This began to change. Just as law school librarians sprang from a root system of janitors and student librarians, law firm libraries grew from collections of books whose stewardship was in the hands of legal secretaries. As the practice of law saw the development of ever-larger law firms, the information needs of these firms grew. No longer just collections of judicial decisions, statutes, and a few form books, law firm libraries became sophisticated collections. Law firm librarians very early developed interlibrary loan capabilities that allowed them to combine the power of their collections. The increasingly sophisticated research needs of lawyers in these large firms demanded increasingly sophisticated law librarians to assist them. The explosive growth in the number of lawyers and law firms made law firm librarianship a growth industry. While some law firm librarians had law degrees, most did not. Law firms needed professionals who could work with information and find them what they needed.

In the early 1980s, a law firm librarian, still living in the pre-Internet world of paper, came to speak to my Advanced Legal Research class at Berkeley. When a student asked for an example of a piece of information that she could not find, the librarian replied, "There is no piece of information that I cannot find. You might not be able to pay for it, but if you can, I can find a way to get it." Her bravado stunned the students but I saw it as a simple truth. Academic law libraries had the bigger collections but law firm libraries were more nimble and service oriented. Because the lawyers who employed them were part of profit-making enterprises and responded to clients, they demanded fast turnaround times and accurate performance.

When a professor asks a reference librarian in a law school to locate an obscure article, there is normally no immediate deadline staring the professor in the face. As an academic, she might understand that it might take a few days to obtain what she needed. By contrast, when a partner in a law firm demands a piece of similarly obscure information, the law firm librarian goes on red alert. A client who is paying by the hour cannot be kept waiting, nor can a court or agency be asked to be patient. The information may be needed now. No excuses are accepted. That sort of incentive leads to a different level of performance.

The pressure of the private sector and the demands imposed by market forces compelled law firm librarians to hone research skills and become skilled managers of information emergencies. Before long, academic law libraries had the biggest collections, but the law firm libraries were leaders in innovation. Many academic law librarians can share harrowing tales of new professors, hired out of positions in law firms, who arrive at the law school expecting the same level of service the law firm librarians provided, and having a hard time learning the new truth. When the budget for searching for information is not provided by a paying client, but instead is funded out of a fixed academic budget, priorities change. Where once the law school libraries could put the budgets of county and court libraries to shame, now law firms were ready to invest in information in ways in which the law schools could only dream.

Since law librarians had always been wedded to legal information, they had to follow it into the digital world. The digital revolution came to law librarianship in the last two decades of the twentieth century. Lexis and

Westlaw, each a full-text database of judicial opinions, statutory material, administrative sources, and secondary materials, changed the face of legal information. Both Lexis and Westlaw (LW) were pioneers in automated searching. Each invested massive amounts of resources in training law students to use their systems by providing deeply subsidized access, in-person training and support, and innovative marketing. LW forced law librarians to become computer literate, and they did.[11] In a shadow play of the paper world, LW first took root in the law schools as a generation of students came to rely on digital information, but it flowered in the law firm environment. LW knew that the money to be made was in the private sector, so they trained law students to use the systems, and then focused on working with researchers in law firms.

Law firm librarians were ready. As ever, they followed the needs and requests of the lawyers who employed them. When the Internet came on the scene and LW migrated to more sophisticated platforms, law firm librarians were there to meet it. Because LW had worked to create a base of users who would use Boolean searching and digital systems instead of the old book-based tools, the Internet opened up whole new worlds. Suddenly law librarianship was turned on its head. Where academic law libraries with their large collections of books and highly trained staffs had once been the gravitational center of the profession, now law firm libraries that could innovate and had the resources to buy newer and more sophisticated databases took over. The students arriving at law school at the end of the twentieth century were computer-savvy searchers who cared little for the giant collections of paper materials in the library. They wanted access to databases and sophisticated search engines. In other words, they arrived at law school expecting the resources of the law firm environment.

By the end of the twentieth century, law firm librarians were the heart of the profession in many ways. By developing intranets, running their law firms' information and systems operations, and implementing knowledge management systems, law firm librarians were moving the ball forward. This is not to say that academic law libraries stagnated. They too responded and changed, but the real energy was in the private sector. Once again, if one follows the money, one finds the cutting edge of development.

It is a fortunate fact that the law firm librarians continued to see themselves as members of the same profession as the academic law librarians. There were several points where the AALL almost sundered over this issue. For decades, AALL had been dominated by those from the academic side and some law firm librarians felt that they should break away. But the moments of crisis passed. The AALL formed Special Interest Sections (SISs), which allowed the different stakeholders to each have an autonomous entity and yet still remain united in an umbrella organization.

In the AALL of the twenty-first century, law firm librarians play a central role both in leadership positions and in numbers of members.

CURRENT QUESTIONS

Where does law librarianship stand in 2006? Where does it go from here? In recent decades, some law firm librarians have gravitated toward the Special Library Association, feeling that they have more in common with librarians who work in other private sector and specialized environments than they do with their academic counterparts. Some academic law librarians feel that their interests now differ so much from those of their colleagues in the private sector that they should put energy into working with the American Association of Law Schools, the professional association that serves law schools. The AALL's solution of creating SISs to prevent a split between academic and firm librarians is limited. Added to this is the possibility that law librarianship might be absorbed whole by the larger field of librarianship.

Some feel that the term "librarian" should be abandoned in favor of a term that reflects a professional who manages knowledge by working with information, systems, and databases. The profession of librarianship has struggled to find its identity and its place at the table in the information economy. Although that is a question for another day, it affects the very foundation of law librarianship.

The conglomeration of the legal publishing industry could have significant consequences for the field of legal librarianship. The traditional legal publishers were once conservative bastions of highly specialized information, managed by individuals with significant expertise, who knew and understood not just the books but what was in them. Today, these publishers are part of large international information conglomerates. The West Publishing Company, which had always been owned entirely by certain employees, went public and is now part of the Thomson empire. When West was a closely held corporation, it could make decisions based on the long term and upon its understanding of legal information. A publicly traded company, however, owes responsibility to its shareholders and must keep its eyes fastened on the bottom line. Most of the small legal publishers have been absorbed into either the Thomson/West camp or that of Lexis, which is owned by Reed Elsevier, the English-Dutch information conglomerate. Reed Elsevier also looks to its bottom line and sees legal information as one of its products. Will legal information soon be indistinguishable from the other commodified information that inundates all of us?

It is important that the field of law librarianship does remain cohesive. Law librarians, no matter what the specifics of their situations, have a great deal in common, enough to overcome the centrifugal trends set out in the previous paragraph. Law librarians have fought to protect the integrity of information and keep it available to the public. The Washington office of the AALL, pioneered by Professor Robert Oakley and carried on by the indefatigable Mary Ellen Baish, has a seat at the table of national information policy. By combining the intellectual power and contacts of academic law librarians with the financial power of law firm librarians and the influential position of court and county law librarians, law librarians can continue to occupy a unique position together. In the information wars, the law librarians wear the white hats. Can the profession survive and prosper? The answer to that question will be part of the future. For the sake of legal information and those who use it, I hope so.

NOTES

My thanks to Sarah Angel, Boalt Hall class of 2007, for assistance and admirable advocacy of the comma.

1. Legal information in the form of positive statements of the law represents a special kind of cognitive authority. The late Patrick Wilson's *Second-Hand Knowledge: An Inquiry into Cognitive Authority* (Westport, CT: Greenwood Press, 1983) provides an excellent discussion of this issue.

2. The AALL Publication Series, now past seventy volumes in length, includes numerous titles that can offer perspectives on law librarianship as well as guides to its practice. Of special interest is Laura Gasaway and Michael Chiorazzi (eds.), *Law Librarianship: Historical Perspectives*, AALL Publication Series, no. 52 (Littleton, CO: Rothman, 1996). This volume contains perspectives from all points of view on the profession and its roots and its editors are two of the leaders in contemporary law librarianship. For a glimpse of personal perspectives on law librarianship from a variety of viewpoints presented in the form of oral histories, see Marjorie Garson et al. (eds.), *Reflections on Law Librarianship*, AALL Publication Series, no. 29 (Littleton, CO: Rothman, 1988).

3. Common law systems all have roots in the legal system of the United Kingdom.

4. See *The Centennial History of the Harvard Law School: 1817–1917* (Harvard Law School Association, 1918), p. 98: "The librarian had generally been a member of the School, who occupied a room in Dane Hall, and received a trifling compensation in addition to his room rent and tuition. It is not any part of his duty to spend any of his time in the library; still less to exercise any authority or supervision over those who used it. The janitor had certain duties to perform in reference to the library but it was not his business to exercise authority."

5. A. J. Small, "Reflections," *Law Library Journal* 24, no. 12 (1931) gives a short first-person view of the AALL's early days. It took almost twenty years before an academic law librarian was elected president (Frederick Hicks) and more than fifty years before a law firm librarian (Elizabeth Finley) would be so chosen.

6. Miles Price and Harry Bitner, *Effective Legal Research* (New York: Prentice Hall, 1953). There were many subsequent editions.

7. Frederick Hicks's *Men and Books of the Law* is one of my favorite titles in legal literature. Professor Hicks discussed the great books of the law with descriptions of the book, its author, and why it is important.

8. J. Myron Jacobstein and Roy M. Mersky, *Fundamentals of Legal Research* (Mineola, NY: Foundation Press, 1980). This text, which was taken over from Prof. Erwin Pollack, was for a time known as *Pollack's Fundamentals of Legal Research*, edited by Jacobstein and Mersky. It has gone through many editions, added junior authors, and spun off a paperback abridgement, *Legal Research Illustrated*.

9. *How to Find the Law* remains the masterwork of legal bibliography. It too has seen numerous editions and junior authors. Prof. Morris Cohen's massive *Bibliography of Early American Law* is perhaps the greatest single achievement of modern legal bibliography.

10. "The American Association of Law Libraries: A Selective Bibliography," contained in the AALL reference books cited above, lists articles and tributes to all librarians mentioned here. Rather than pepper the page with multiple citations, I refer to the existing source.

11. As one who started in the profession in 1975, I experienced the changes taking place.

Chapter 2

Working at the Law Library: A Practical Guide

Karl T. Gruben

There are three types of law libraries: state, court, and county; firm or private; and academic. While each has its own peculiarities and idiosyncrasies, they are all similar and are named differently primarily because of the clientele they serve. The state, court, and county law libraries generally serve courts of all varieties; the firm or private law libraries serve law firms or corporations; and the academic law libraries are associated with a law school.[1] Some libraries fulfill multiple functions,[2] but most fill only one role and serve the main clientele of that particular law library. The differences that arise among these law libraries are because of the different clientele, each of which has a different aim and use for legal materials.

Academic law libraries have a mission to preserve the law and the legal materials associated with it and, to that end, contain collections that are generally larger than those of the other types of law libraries. They must also fulfill their academic mission, often purchasing ephemeral law school materials that the other types of law libraries do not purchase. These would include materials such as case books and study aids. Academic law libraries also are "collecting for the ages." As such, they retain superseded materials, such as older editions of treatises, superseded pocket parts from treatises and statutory materials, and long runs of periodicals.

All academic law libraries have collection development policies that spell out what they should be purchasing. For example, if not spelled out in the policy, the academic might not purchase ephemera such as course case books and study aids. Financial considerations and the advent of electronic serials and books have caused many academic law libraries to review their collection policies such that they might only get a serial title once, rather than in the multiple film, fiche, paper, and electronic versions

15

that exist.[3] Additionally, academic law libraries often purchase materials that seem to be outside the general purview of a law library but which are purchased for the research needs of the faculty.[4] This is due to the inter-disciplinary nature of legal scholarship that has come about in the past twenty or so years. Law professors incorporate many works from outside what might be termed "mainstream" law sources, delving into history, sociology, and, lately, statistical research.[5] I think it is important to recognize the American Bar Association's supervision of the academic law library pursuant to chapter 6 of the Library Resource Section of the Accreditation Guidelines, which requires a specific number of law librarians based upon the size of the student body.

State court and county law libraries and law firm law libraries generally do not purchase the ephemera of case books and the like, because they do not have a clientele demanding it. They usually have smaller collections that are called "working collections."[6] Firm libraries generally do not maintain large back runs of periodicals,[7] generally keep only the current editions of treatises, and retain pocket parts for limited materials such as the local statutes. State, court, and county law libraries fall somewhere in between the academic and firm libraries in their retention policies, depending on their locale and mission.

Firm and state, court, and county law libraries, however, have large quantities of "practice" materials that the academic law library does not likely possess.[8] In fact, some practice materials are defined for such small local jurisdictions and practice specialties that huge law libraries such as those at Harvard and Yale, whose collection development policies direct them to purchase almost everything that is in the law or law-related fields, are unlikely to purchase them, while the much, much smaller state, court, and county or law firm library often acquire them. Such materials include form books, specialty treatises penned by experts in the specialty, and checklists. Because practicing attorneys are big on not having to reinvent the wheel, they like checklists that have prepared the way for their depositions and cross-examinations, particularly of expert witnesses. These smaller libraries purchase materials primarily based on demand from their clientele. Contrast this with the "collection development policies" of the academic law libraries.[9]

And so you will begin to discern that collection development, as it relates to different kinds of law libraries, is very dependent on the clientele served. Academics purchase materials that would seldom appear in a state, court, and county or law firm library and vice versa. All types have a lot of materials in common, however, but generally academic law libraries (and some of the larger state, court, and county and firm law libraries) have collections that are historical in nature and aimed more at the academic study of the law, while the state, court, and county and firm libraries are aimed at the actual practice of law, much as one would imagine.

Where do you, the new law librarian, fit into this picture? Much depends on where you enter. It is highly unlikely that you will enter an academic law library anywhere but at the lowest level, perhaps even at a nonprofessional level.[10] Academic law libraries, in general and due to the small size of the staffs, do not have an employment "track" where you may advance, other than by sheer happenstance. Typically these academic libraries have been around for many years and have loyal and dedicated staff members. State, court, and county law libraries often have the same types of employees—loyal, dedicated, and long term. Often, to move up, you have to move out as midlevel and higher openings occur due to retirement. There is more about "out and up" later in the chapter. Because law firms, upon reaching a certain size, often decide to create a law librarian position or lose a librarian due to a round-robin effect,[11] there is sometimes more movement in that job market.

THE DUAL DEGREE

If you possess a law degree along with your MLS, you will most likely enter a public services position as a reference or some other form of public services librarian. Public services positions, as one would imagine, deal with the public—here mostly faculty and students, though the occasional *pro se* patron or practicing attorney will come by. It is not mandatory that you possess a JD to work in public service, or even reference, but most of the reference staff members have dual degrees and most jobs advertised for such positions list that as either highly desirable or required. Jobs generally not requiring dual degrees, but which are in public services, would include collection maintenance, circulation, and audiovisual (AV) services. Some law libraries place an electronic services librarian in public services, some in technical services. The provision of audiovisual services is often a function of the law library in a university setting and performing or managing AV services does not require a dual degree. Jobs in collection maintenance, circulation, and AV services usually provide experience in personnel supervision that other public services jobs, such as an entry-level reference job, do not. Supervisory experience is often the best stepping-stone to midlevel management jobs with their attendant higher salaries.

MOVING AROUND IN YOUR LAW LIBRARY

Perhaps the best introduction to a law library would be a tour through all the departments. Indeed, some law libraries consider this the best way for new employees to learn the requisites of law librarianship and how those parts and pieces fit all together. Many of the large academic law libraries require all their new staff members to work around the various jobs in the law library to become acquainted with how things work. To this end I would recommend that, if you are hired for a specific job and your new library does not provide such a training program, you advocate for moving around, at least at the beginning, and doing other jobs. If you start in a public services job, you might work a few hours a week in circulation to see what kinds of problems and questions arise at what is often the main point of contact between the law library and the students. From there, you might want to move to AV to provide services to faculty and students. Skills in organization are of high value in AV services, as there are often conflicting demands during peak class periods. Stack and collection maintenance is a high priority in a law library[12] but, unfortunately, one with a high level of boredom. Shelf-reading is tedious at best but must be experienced to be believed. Shelving and shelf-reading, however, can lead to the discovery of treasures and a knowledge of the collection that cannot be matched. The shelver must be awake and on the lookout for materials, notice how materials relate to each other through the call number system,[13] and find out what materials appear to be used. Knowledge of materials can lead to better reference service and can assist in the acquisition of new materials.

Let us suppose that you will begin your tour from the back offices (technical services, as it is often called) to the front (public services). Starting in technical services will give you the basic knowledge needed to understand how the law library is put together, as you will see all the pieces that come in, why those pieces arrive, and how they are arranged. Then, we will continue the tour through the public services areas. I will use a mythical midsize law library containing many units that may not be present as standalone units in many smaller law libraries (AV services, for instance) but which may be present and which require some introduction.

MOVING AROUND IN TECHNICAL SERVICES

The Mail

Sorting and distributing the mail—each piece of which must be handled and directed to the appropriate staff member—and observing the vast array of materials that flow, like a ceaseless river, into the law library can be a mammoth job. Large manuals can, and have been, written about the handling of the day-to-day mail; your new institution might have one of these manuals. Perusal of such a tome is advised (and may be required). Each institution has its own procedures for handling the mail, but most include some form of opening, stamping a date on the envelope or the cover of whatever piece was received, and distributing the pieces to the appropriate person or workstation. Box mail—that mail received mainly from publishers and shipped inside some form of corrugated container—will need to be opened. Many institutions retain shipping boxes for reuse with other items, such as interlibrary loan shipping, or to return unwanted items to the publisher. Be sure you know your policies.

Processing

From the mail you might move on to processing what has been received. Processing involves checking the pieces into a receiving system[14] and dealing with any anomalies that arise, such as missed issues, odd issues, and pieces received out of sequence. When items are not received after a specified amount of time, you will be instructed in the fine art of "claiming." Claiming is an art because it will vary from one publisher to another and consists of telling the publisher or producer that you have not received a particular piece of some subscription and please to ship it pronto. While some publishers are very quick to respond to claims, others are not. The art lies in knowing how, and when, to claim with individual publishers. Claim too quickly and you will get the brush-off that it is "in the mail"; too late, and the piece will no longer be available. If you are lucky, your institution will use a jobber (a company that serves as a middleman between the library and a vendor) for your serial pieces and a great deal of the dirty work can go to them; unfortunately, no jobber can handle everything serial.[15] It is here, too, that you will learn the nefarious tricks of the publishers, such as sending supplementation for items that have been long discontinued; sending items that are claimed to be "on standing order" or "related to such and so" publication; and including items that have never been ordered but are shipped and billed along with a large number of other items. These will all need to be checked against the library's integrated system, and those items that are suspect will then need to be looked at by someone with the authority to decide whether to retain the item, which takes up valuable staff time. Generally, these missent items will be returned to the publisher for credit against the bill, which often takes a long time to be credited and resolved. Sometimes the reviewer will be enamored with a title and allow it to be purchased, thus illustrating one of the reasons publishers will send out such items.[16] Remember, above all, two things: (1) you stamp it, you bought it—so don't get too carefree with that property stamp; (2) keep your paperwork in good order to settle billing problems. Acquisitions personnel must, above all things, be organized—and if you are processing and lose needed paperwork, woe betide you at the hands of the acquisitions staff.

Once checked in, the pieces received in the mail are processed for the shelf with stamping, tagging, labeling, and security stripping. New monographs might arrive preprocessed from a jobber such as Yankee Book Peddler, Ebsco, or Blackwells, already bearing a label with a call number and, depending on the level of processing your institution is willing to pay for, need only to have the cataloging data reviewed, be security stripped, and shelved.

Acquisitions

Next, to see what generates all this incoming mail, you should go through acquisitions. Depending on your library, you will most likely deal with either a blanket book plan or a slips plan. Large law libraries don't want to take the time to select each item that falls into a subject area, knowing they will want everything published in that subject. Blanket plans take care of this and are available through large monographic jobbers such as Yankee Book Peddler or Blackwell. In addition to these plans, the jobbers offer something for the smaller law libraries called a "slips" program. Using a slips program, the library will set up a profile with the jobber of Library of Congress (LC) classification numbers. The jobber has relationships with many publishers and receives a prepublication notice or notice that something is published. The jobber then prepares a slip of paper (some are single slips, some are multipart) with basic bibliographic data and the LC classification number, and sends the participating libraries the slips corresponding to the profiles previously developed. Public services types cull through these slips and select those book titles they want to purchase. This selection process on the part of the librarians requires a thorough knowledge of the collection and of the collection development policy, so any selection work you do in your beginning job is most likely to be reviewed by someone higher in the job food chain.

Once selections have been made, the acquisitions staff processes those selections for presentation to the jobber for purchase. This often includes an automated system the jobber has, so there is no passing to and fro of paper pieces but, rather, the simple flow of electrons. Purchase through a jobber eliminates multiple bank checks[17] to different publishers and streamlines the work, pushing the tedium onto the jobber. In addition, because jobbers can purchase many copies of the same item (because they are dealing with many different libraries and not just law libraries, purchasing the same materials) they can receive, and pass along to your law library, a discount off the list price of the books ordered.

At the point the items are ordered from the jobber, the acquisitions person puts some form of notice into the integrated library system so that when the piece arrives there is no hullabaloo of running around asking people to remember why something is coming, who it is for, and so on. Failure to follow this procedure almost always results in the loss of productivity and, sometimes, the purchase of unwanted material. The system might be as simple as a card file (usually what is found in a one-person library) or, if an automated system is available, an abbreviated record might be placed therein, indicating the placement of the order.[18]

Most law libraries also purchase materials outside the jobber programs since no jobber can handle everything published. This purchasing process is particularly difficult when dealing with foreign publishers. Often the publishers do not speak English or, if so, their command of English is often about as good as yours is of their language. In addition, it may be necessary to find some method of payment for the foreign publisher who often will not take your word for it that you will pay him, if he will only send you the book now. While a credit card often takes care of the method of payment, it is sometimes difficult to prove that a payment has been made when the foreign seller claims nonpayment. All of these issues fall into the hands of the acquisitions personnel and you will learn valuable lessons: that ordering a book does not necessarily mean that the book will arrive any time soon, if at all, and that payment might be made without receiving the end product of that payment.

A fact of life is that publishers have shortened their press runs and, while they try to predict how many copies will be needed, they sometimes underestimate that number and the latecomer might have to wait for republication, which can take a long time, if ever. Some publishers try to gauge the need for their items by sending out prepublication notices and soliciting prepaid orders.[19] This can cause problems for both the publisher and the purchaser when the author does not follow through in a timely fashion.[20] Many pages have been written about the acquisitions process, so suffice it to say that here your tour of duty is, in the main, to get the gloss of the process and its attendant problems.[21] You will only need the details if you are going to work full time in acquisitions.[22]

Cataloging

Catalogers are, in general, a precise lot. A great deal of the tedium of cataloging and classification has been taken out of the job through the use of bibliographic utilities such as the Online Computer Library Center (OCLC) and Research Libraries Group (RLG), both of which provide uniform cataloging data, mostly from the Library of Congress. There is still room for flair by the cataloger, however, in that many collections have a need for the insertion of individualized materials into a classification scheme, or the desire to put certain materials in a place that the Library of Congress would not place them. If you have only had training at the graduate school level and no practical experience, you will certainly not be given the ability to insert data, other than under the strict supervision of one who knows what to do. Watching, though, can be very instructive to a public services type, as you learn the various fields of the machine-readable cataloging (MARC) record and how those fields may be searched in your institution's online public access catalog (OPAC). Note in particular the policies that the library follows for different types of materials and which MARC fields are used and which are not. This gives you more of an idea of what is searchable by the general public. Often there is a paraprofessional who does base-level cataloging—the insertion of MARC records into the local database, later checked by a librarian—which frees the professional librarian to do more technical processes, such as the addition of subject headings or additional tracings. Each library has its own rules. Be sure you learn what your library's policy is with regard to additional subject headings and tracings.

If you are lucky, you will be around when there is an upgrade to the integrated system. If not while you are there, you should inquire about any future upgrades and try to be present when they are done. Upgrades entail their own special problems for technical services since an upgrade sometimes has unanticipated results, such as eliminating the customizations made for the institution. Learn what the problems inherent in an upgrade are, as you might spot problems that need correction while using the systems in the future. If the system is shared with other libraries on campus, participation—even if only as an observer—will also give you an opportunity to visit with librarians from the other libraries that you otherwise might not get to know.

This book has a chapter on technical services. The level of description there is much more inclusive of what happens in the technical services department of a major law library and I would advise you to read that chapter a couple of times if you are planning to work in public services. No, you did not misread: read the technical services chapter *twice* if you are going to work in public services. That way you will not appear to be completely ignorant of the vital processes that take place "in the back office" of the law library. What goes on out front is hectic and sometimes loud and often confusing. What goes on in the back makes what goes on in the front much easier.

MOVING AROUND IN PUBLIC SERVICES

Once you have finished touring the technical services side of the law library, the "back office," you should move to the "front office" side, public services. Let's begin our tour through public services by starting where they check resources in and out: circulation services. This is typically operated by student employees, both law and undergraduate, under the supervision of a circulation manager or supervisor, not typically a librarian.[23] This is interesting because it is usually the primary focal point of the law library, as almost every student and faculty member will come into contact with a circulation employee. These employees, then, need to be highly trained in the policies and procedures of the law library and what to do when their knowledge of those policies and procedures does not cover a circumstance. They especially need to learn when to refer a problem to a higher authority.

The job is one of using the circulation system, often automated, to charge out and discharge in the materials of the law library. There are usually a number of different types of materials, each with its own period of available circulation. For example, items from the general collection might circulate for two weeks. Those items from the general collection that are volumes from a multiple-volume set, however, might not be allowed to circulate at all.[24] The items from the reserve collection circulate for twenty-four hours while those from the course reserve collection only circulate for four hours and those from the reference collection do not circulate at all.

Generally this is not as complicated as it might seem, since an automated circulation system is set up to include all these multiple variations. When the final record for the item is inserted in the integrated library system, the period of circulation is set. When the item is "wanded" or the bar code is read, so long as the items are noted in the system in the correct category, their periodicity is not a problem. It is the good circulation staff member, however, who recognizes that a particular item has not been properly categorized and draws it to the attention of a supervisor or superior.

Circulation staff is often used to check the shelves and pull items for faculty and students and to perform what is usually called "stack maintenance." Stack maintenance is the catch-all phrase used for three functions carried out by circulation staff: shelf-reading, cleaning, and reshelving. Shelf-reading is a highly tedious but necessary part of working in a library of any kind. Mistakes are often made when items are reshelved. Materials are sometimes deliberately misshelved, as well. Generally the circulation supervisor divides the library into areas of equal amounts of shelving. Each staff member in circulation (and sometimes other staff members in the law library as well, depending on the law library) is responsible for examining each piece on the shelves and determining whether it is in the right location, particularly with regard to call number order. If an item is misshelved, it is essentially lost in the general mass of the collection. Deliberate, concerted shelf-reading does not solve the problem (people, after all, do make mistakes), but as problems occur they can be corrected on a regular basis.

Cleaning the shelves is often a part of stack maintenance. While it might not seem like it, libraries are fairly dirty places. Think, if you will, about a carpeted space that is trod upon by a many different people, each of whom carries into the space a different amount and type of dirt. In addition, carpet begins to break down the day it is installed and creates a host of small fibers which are scattered, daily, into the air space of the library. While vacuuming removes some of the larger pieces of waste material, unless it is a highly filtered vacuum, the smaller particles are merely moved around and often land on the books and shelves. It is a good idea for the circulation supervisor to assign cleaning areas to each employee, as well—and these might correspond to the shelf-reading areas. The employee may find that the monotony of shelf-reading can be eased by alternating it with shelf-cleaning. I have found that the use of disposable paper products, along with a good dusting agent moistener, allows the employee to place the dirt on the paper and place it in a waste receptacle, rather than merely move it around. It is, however, a never-ending battle.

Finally, the circulation staff is often the group who keeps the law library open late into the evening. You can begin to see why these positions are usually held by student workers, as what could be better than sitting at a desk in the evenings, earning money for essentially reading your homework or working on a paper? Good employees understand that all stack maintenance tasks assigned must be accomplished first, but a good supervisor will usually not assign more than a couple of hours a shift of stack maintenance; too much more than this and errors will be made. There will also be rush times when students pile up at the desk, wanting to remove materials for classes or overnight, so all desk personnel will be busy serving patrons. Many times in the evening, however, there is little more to do than make sure someone is not trying to sneak something out past the security system, or to find staples for an empty stapler. It is then that the good studying can be accomplished; good supervisors realize this and allow it to happen after the maintenance work has been accomplished.

Interlibrary Loan

Interlibrary loan (ILL) is often a part of public services. It is divided into two parts: borrowing and lending. Most academic and state, court, and county law libraries (and a few firm libraries) use the OCLC interlibrary loan system,[25] which allows a search of the OCLC catalog records system and the placement of a request to borrow into the OCLC electronic ILL software system, Clio. A library willing to lend will respond to the system and mark the request to prevent multiple libraries from responding. This speeds the interlibrary loan process up immensely over the old days of paper forms and the use of the U.S. Postal Service to deliver both the forms and the borrowed and returned items. The system is highly sophisticated and allows the borrower to request that items be filled from certain categories of lenders first, before the request is placed with other lenders. Such a prioritization allows the borrower to take advantage of cooperative and network relationships that provide lower (or no added) costs to the borrowing library, if the item is filled "within the network" of cooperating libraries.[26] Otherwise, there is often a fee for ILL from non-network libraries—usually fairly reasonable at about $15 to $25. If that fee can be avoided, however, it makes ILL more desirable.

The lending piece is fairly easy: the employee checks the OCLC system several times a day for requests placed to the library. Since the OCLC system has cataloging records of what the potential lending library owns, the request will seldom be for an item that the library has never held. If, upon checking the shelves, the item is found, the lending library enters a system response that the item will be filled. If, in the interim while the shelf is being checked, another library has responded, your ILL employee will be unable to respond and your item will have to be returned to your shelf. If you decide to loan it, the item is checked out to the borrowing library using the library circulation system, packed for shipping (along with any documentation the library uses to identify the item as an ILL piece), labeled, and shipped out to the borrower.[27] The entire system is fairly efficient and usually has only a modest cost.[28]

Suffice it to say that you, in your rotation of duty, will most likely not be allowed to do any record keeping in the Clio system until you have been thoroughly trained. Watching to get the general "flow" of things, however, can be highly instructive and will give you a good idea of how the system works and how long it takes to receive items—particularly when dealing with the U.S. Postal Service. Additionally, you should inquire about "good" lending libraries and "bad" lending libraries. Some libraries are understaffed and take some time to respond to requests; as a result, those libraries receive fewer requests than they otherwise would. Others do their best to respond as quickly as possible and, consequently, do more volume.[29] Responsible libraries usually have a fairly balanced ratio of borrowed items to lent items. It is better, in many instances, to be a net lender rather than a net borrower, as net borrowing indicates some need to beef up the collection. ILL statistics can also give acquisitions librarians an idea of where their collection needs additions.

Audiovisual

While not in all law libraries, often the law library staff will be responsible for providing AV services to the library clientele. This will be more likely in an academic environment, but state, court, and county libraries often provide such services (and it is not beyond the realm of possibility that a firm library will do the same). AV services can be demanding. Multiple events will often occur simultaneously and staff will not be sufficient to cover everything. The smart staff will endeavor to make the plug-in and switch-on connections for equipment in the rooms (LCD projectors, VHS and DVD players, and sound systems) as uniform as possible. Uniform equipment connections make it more likely that, with a little user education, the connections to needed equipment can be made by the end user, thus freeing the AV staff for more technical work. For other services, such as recording services, individual personnel will most likely be needed on site to man the equipment. If multiple services are required at the same time, often the camera or recording equipment can be started and left running while the staff member goes on to the next event. AV services require an organized person to direct the operations with a good technical knowledge of equipment to run and, moreover, to troubleshoot problems with malfunctioning equipment. Typical services include connecting computers to LCD display projectors; connecting audio equipment to record or reproduce sound; connecting video equipment to display video; using video cameras to record sessions, and the like. Because there will generally need to be more than one person making connections, assisting end users, and troubleshooting problems, the AV group is definitely a good place to learn management and personnel supervisory skills.

Electronic Services

The electronic services librarian (ESL) position does not exist in every library. Someone, however, does the work and it may be that in your library the work will be divided among several people. In the modern law library, many of the products and services are offered to patrons as electronic versions. A serial title, for example, may be available variously in paper format, a microform format, or in an electronic format. No matter the format, someone must make that product available to the end user. Paper formats are easy to use, usually grouped by title or subject or arranged by call number, and their location may be found through the online public catalog. Users are familiar with paper products and, once directed to the location or call number, can find what they need with ease. Microform formats are a bit more difficult, mainly because the equipment to view and print them is difficult to use. Nonetheless, the concept is familiar: physical location, something to identify it, get it out, and view and print from it.

The location of the electronic item being sought, though, is not "physical" in the normal sense of the word since it cannot be seen with the naked eye, though it is physical (not to get too metaphysical) in the sense that it exists as electrons in time and space. The location of the product can only be "seen" by using a personal computer and high-speed access to a network. Someone must construct something that allows the user a "place" to go to see electronic products and that is the job of the ESL.

Typically many of the electronic products are accessible in a couple of ways: through hyperlinks in the online public access catalog or through a custom-built Web page with similar hyperlinks. The ESL will usually work on the second access method, while the first method is produced by the technical services staff catalogers. The Web page must be built to certain standards, sometimes dictated by a larger entity in the organization, such as an information technology (IT) department or a main library, but the ESL must use those standards to standardize access to a multitude of products that are not always easily categorized and arranged. Luckily, electronic products allow the links to them to appear in many areas at once, thus placing materials with multiple subjects in several subject areas at the same time. A quick click on the link and the user is on the way to the material.

Electronic serial products produce unusual problems as the institution may have multiple electronic points of access to the product, all with different pricing. For instance, a periodical title may be available through Lexis or Westlaw,[30] through two or three different repackagers, and through a subscription to the hard copy that allows the institution access to the product electronically as part of the subscription.[31] The job of the ESL is to produce the links in such a manner that the cheapest item is set before the user first. The cost will vary for every institution, depending on the contracts with the electronic providers. Tools are available to provide a price-differentiated list, such as the combination of a federated search engine and a link resolver. Federated search engines should allow a user to run one search across multiple full-text databases. The results are presented to the user in the form of multiple links, through a link resolver, to products available from within the institution. The order in which these products are shown is dependent on an algorithm developed by the ESL, which should show the link with the lowest cost to the institution first in the list.

For example, a law firm library will probably not want to direct users to Lexis or Westlaw for serials that are available on HeinOnline;[32] going to Lexis or Westlaw will incur a charge for each use—and these can be substantial charges for firms—while the HeinOnline service is a flat-fee product and every use drops the overall per-item cost. Lexis and Westlaw, however, are more likely to have the current issues of periodicals first, as HeinOnline takes longer to make them available. The way to use the tools to present items in a cost-efficient manner is an intellectual problem for the ESL, which may be solved in a multitude of ways—all highly dependent on factors present in the institutions' contracts and cost schedules.

A Reference Time

Though we have seen that there are many different jobs in the public services area, many librarians and educated lay persons think of public services as consisting solely of reference. As such, reference librarians are not on the reference desk eight hours a day, five days a week. Usually only three to four hours of each day are given over to providing reference services in a typical week. The balance of the time is spent working on other law library services, such as selection of materials, creating pathfinders, working up or reworking websites, creation of bibliographies on special subjects, and interaction with other library staff members concerning the location of materials and services and cataloging records.

Because of their professional status, most librarians have an office of some sort. The modern office, however, has changed from that of the traditional one person–one office with a closable door. Offices in academic law libraries vary, but many times a "cube farm" has been developed for the junior staff members, where one large room is shared by several reference staff members using modular furniture to create a personal space. Don't worry, it's not just you; it is a sign of the times and a desire to maximize the use of space available. The individual office is often the rarity, rather than the rule. Those having managerial or supervisory roles, though, often require a private space for counseling the supervised staff.

Reference positions, when advertised for a law library, generally require a dual degree: the possession of a master's in library science, the MLS or its equivalent, and the juris doctorate, the JD. I say generally because, as stated above, one does not have to have a JD and MLS to do reference. Much of the reference currently done in a law library is not necessarily legal in nature; a great deal is directional in nature and nonlegal.[33] Legal reference often requires the interpretation of citations,[34] location of cases using the briefest of information, and, occasionally, some interpretation of what a case or statute means.[35] While the JD will introduce the student to the language of the law and some of its peculiarities, the basics are nothing that a good student cannot learn on his or her own. More complicated questions are aided, however, by the depth of knowledge in a subject area that can only be obtained through intensive study, such as is required for the law degree. Mediation, arbitration, and negotiation are also good skills to have, as the law library reference desk is often the place where grammar questions are settled between faculty members.[36]

MOVING UP IN YOUR LAW LIBRARY AND OUT OF IT

Everyone wants to advance—well, almost everyone. There are some who are perfectly happy (and they may be the happiest ones) to take a reference job, a cataloging job, an acquisitions job, and stay in it for years and years, and there is nothing wrong with that. Such employees develop skills, such as a "sense of reference," far beyond the skills of those who move from job to job. However, there is usually a limit beyond which a law library will not go in the pay for a specific position. That is, salaries get capped at a certain level. To make more money, it is often necessary to move up.

Large law libraries have some sort of track for advancement. Thus, an entry-level reference librarian might have the opportunity to move to one or even two higher levels of reference service, often dependent on time in grade or some form of performance evaluation and recommendation, totally within the institution. It might be that there are different midlevel management positions to which one can aspire. These often require some supervisory experience, as noted above. If you want to move to these, you should position yourself accordingly when you enter the profession.

A glance at some statistics about law libraries reveals that in academic law libraries there is an *average* of 8 librarians, 3.5 librarians in private/firm law libraries, and 2.1 librarians in government libraries.[37] These are exceedingly low numbers upon which to develop a career track. It is sort of a good news/bad news situation: there isn't going to be much of a career track but you can probably find a job where you will be the head honcho. The test is whether you want to be the head honcho of an outfit that would hire you.[38]

If you are lucky enough to be hired into one of the largest of the academic, private, or government law libraries, you will be able to advance from position to position, gaining skills that will serve you well in the next position. A typical progression in public services (and this would be an ideal progression) is from reference librarian to head of reference to head of public services to associate director to director. Though highly unlikely, you might even be able to accomplish this all in the same institution.

The reality is that you will most likely have to move from institution to institution, perhaps moving up one notch in an institution before moving to another. Again, it isn't you; it is merely the nature of a specialized profession that there isn't always the ideal career path. All along the way you will have to contend with family issues, location issues (some areas are prohibitively expensive to live in for married, single-income families), and job issues. A work life in which one deals day-in and day-out with attorneys or law students is not always ideally suited to low blood pressure and a relaxed lifestyle. So if you choose law libraries as a career, be prepared to move out to move up.

THE ROAD TO MANAGEMENT

Reference is not the best job in which to obtain required skills in supervision and management. As stated above, often the nonreference public services and the technical services jobs have a better "track to management" than do the reference jobs. The American Bar Association requires the director of an academic law library to hold both law and library science degrees. In the past, because this is also a requirement for reference positions, the reference job became the stepping-stone to a directorship. Now, however, the number of technical services librarians and nonreference public services librarians who are moving toward directorships is increasing. It is my contention that the "all-around" librarian who knows all the facets of both public services and technical services is the better director.[39] The better you understand the workings of your machine—the modern law library—the better the machine will be maintained and will work for you and your clientele.

Entire courses are devoted to management and management skills, so I will only encourage you to develop some basic skills while you are in school. There are probably courses offered in your library school. You should take them—all of them, if possible. If you must pick and choose, take courses that emphasize personnel management and budgeting. Managing people is a skill required, eventually, of every librarian. It is only through the direction of the efforts of others that all the jobs in the law library are accomplished efficiently, thoughtfully, and professionally. The application of the properly motivated and skilled person accomplishes necessary tasks more easily than one person trying to do every task himself or herself—the common mistake of the tyro in management skills.

Some of the hardest issues with which you will deal in your law librarianship career will involve personal interaction with people. These may be coworkers or library patrons and even institutional support staff from outside the law library. Your ability to handle the situations that arise from these relationships is critical to the perception of how you are doing "your job." If you are adept at handling people, that perception will be positive. If you are unable to handle people on your own or, after a certain amount of time, attempt to do so and fail, your chances of advancement are lowered. It is best to start slowly, know your boundaries, and, where necessary, seek guidance from someone of higher authority or experience.

A position that requires you to supervise students is an excellent place to learn supervisory skills. Students are usually tractable and interesting and they generally know less than you do. Unfortunately, if you are new in the business, they will approximate your own age and might possibly rebel against any authority you might try to exercise. Supervision is best done lightly. Recall that, when riding a horse, the reins are not pulled tight, as the horse will come to a complete halt. Rather, hold them lightly, allowing the horse to think he is going his own way and deigning to carry you along for the ride, all while you nudge him in the correct directions.

Unfortunately, much of the clerical work done in libraries is incredibly boring and repetitive but highly necessary. Consistency is the watchword in a library and its failure is the general cause for misinformation. If at all possible, vary the tasks given clerical staff such that they do not burn out on one task and start to make errors due to inattention. Shelf-reading, for instance, requires a great deal of concentration but does not engage the intellect. In addition, because the majority of items will be in the correct order, the worker will start to think that everything is in order and begin to skip over segments of the assigned shelving. Shelf-reading is best done in small segments of an hour or less. This means that you need to have other tasks to assign to clerical workers so they may keep busy. This means that you have to be organized and have tasks ready to assign. When doing so, be fair—don't overload one student with dusting all the time while others frolic at the circulation desk; remember that no one (not even you) is able to focus and work diligently all the time—some slack must be given (see the horse analogy above). Successful supervision of small groups of students will result in recognition by your superiors and the addition of newer, and hopefully more interesting, tasks to supervise.

Budgeting is the anathema that will follow you all your professional life. Making choices about how to spend money is what drives all law libraries in whichever directions they move: Do we spend more on personnel? Do we buy more books? Do we stop buying so many paper books and invest in electronic books? What databases do we buy? All are questions you will face, and quickly, as you move into the professional world. They are not easy questions and the answers are often vague and uncertain—but they require some answer or the law library comes to a halt. In the beginning you will not have much of a connection to the budgeting process of the law library. I encourage you to find out as much as you can, as it should not be a secret process. As you progress, you might be given a small piece of the budget to control—purchasing reference materials, for example—and to handle money in small steps. The advice is to learn skills while you have the time to do so and the sums are small.

In addition to knowing about supervision and budgets, a good librarian exercises self-discipline and is a self-starter.[40] If you have both these qualities, you will receive good evaluations and better work. Procrastination is a curse. The ability to start an assigned task and see it through to completion is highly regarded. Even more highly regarded is the ability to see a task that needs to be done, start it on your own, and follow through to completion. Here, however, some caution must be exercised to avoid falling into a trap for the unwary. Sometimes what a beginner sees as "needed doing" will be a task that is being left for a purpose. As an example: suppose you are doing some shelf-reading to get ready for an ABA accreditation inspection[41] and come across a large section of casebooks that have never been processed but are taking up an inordinate amount of room. You take it upon yourself to get them carted up and taken to technical services for cataloging and processing. What you may have actually run across is a "place filler" to hold empty shelving. In academic libraries, the perception of nonlibrary deans and faculty[42] is that empty shelving is an indicator that a library has too much space—and such space may be taken from the library and used for more useful purposes such as offices and classrooms. Actually, properly run libraries will have a great deal of unused shelf space, mainly because they are planned to last for many years.[43] Deans and partners and library board members, however, have a much shorter viewpoint than do librarians.[44] So be careful when you think you find "something that needs doing" to be sure you are right.

PRIVATE OR FIRM LAW LIBRARIES

Most law librarians in law firms work in small operations. Some law firms might be huge, such as the firms represented in the American Lawyer 100 (commonly referred to as the AmLaw 100), but their library operations are generally not, tending more to the "one-person library" than to a heavily staffed one. Here the librarian does it all, from ordering the books to checking in and routing the mail, to learning how to program in HTML because the IT guy who knew how to do that left or doesn't have the time or actually doesn't know how. There is a lot of room for growth in firm law libraries and plenty of potential to show the attorneys working in the firm what a gem you really are. It is, however, a great deal of work and the individual doing that work must be able to multitask, doing several operations at the same time, or at least carry the stage of several tasks in his or her mind, because the various tasks will arrive at the least expected moment. Let me explain by giving a short "day in the life" of the firm law librarian as an example.

8:00 a.m.—Arrive at work and clear off the table(s) of materials left out by the attorneys working during the preceding evening (it's the twenty-first century and they don't use many "books" so it might not take even fifteen minutes).[45]

8:15–8:30 a.m.—Go to your desk, which might be a desk in the open area of the library or, if lucky, a desk in a small enclosed area with a door, and fire up the PC to check your e-mail. Find several queries from the younger attorneys about what materials your library owns as well as requests from them for materials you don't own. Most of what you do not own will be available from HeinOnline, Lexis, or Westlaw (computer-assisted legal research services) but some will require you to borrow from other law libraries. You find one question from a senior partner requiring you to do some research. Respond to the quick answers and start work on the others. It is sometimes easier to get the small stuff out of the way unless there is a time bomb of a request that requires a great deal of effort in a short time frame. Discerning this is an acquired skill, and the phrase "but you didn't say it was urgent" will buy you little sympathy, particularly from a senior partner whose every whim is ASAP.[46]

8:30–9:30 a.m.—Work on the little "document delivery" projects that came in late e-mails of the day before. Printing from Lexis, Westlaw, and/or HeinOnline should satisfy some requests. Others will have to be obtained from the local public law library or elsewhere. Check your local union lists of periodicals or go to the online catalogs of the institutions where you do your business and organize your field trip for the afternoon.

9:30–11:30 a.m.—The mail arrives! You will often feel a thrill about new mail, as it will bear fruits of past labors: ILL materials, newly ordered books and reprinted articles, bills, and the like. Spend an hour sorting, checking in, and routing the mail and an hour on the new arrivals, checking them against your files to be sure you ordered them,[47] then stamping and processing them, and putting them into the interoffice mail to be delivered to the appropriate attorney—or putting them on the shelves in the library. It is often good public relations to physically take a volume to its intended recipient, as face time with lawyers is usually a good thing, particularly when you are bearing gifts.

11:30–12:30 p.m.—Lunch. Eat lunch, preferably out of the office. You will be tempted and, often more than you will like, sometimes required to eat lunch at your desk while you perform some librarian magic. At all possible times, eat away from your office. It will keep you fresher for your job later on.

12:30–1:00 p.m.—Office raids. You will generally need to seek permission from your managing partner for this search and seizure, but they are usually willing to grant it, particularly if they have not been able to look at something because it's missing. Once permission is obtained, office searches make the firm librarian's job smoother. Notify your attorneys in advance that you are going to go through offices looking for materials that have been removed from the library but not checked out. The mere notification will result in a number of items

being returned in the office mail. The hard-core malfeasants, however, will never cough them up without a struggle and it's best to get
the materials while the malfeasants are off to lunch.

1:00–2:30 p.m.—Right after lunch is usually a good time to push off for
   your field trip. You might want to vary your lunch schedule to go to
   libraries when they are not on a lunch schedule, eating later and going out afterwards so you are not fighting with every other employee
   in the area for valuable library services over the lunch period. This
   might be moved to one of the first things done during the morning or
   the last things done in the afternoon, arriving a bit late or leaving a
   bit early to go work outside the office, a lot depending on your com-
   mute and whether it takes you to or close to other libraries in the
   area.[48]

2:30–3:00 p.m.—Read e-mails that came in over lunch and during your
   field trip. Respond to those and provide the services necessary, such
   as computer-aided legal research (CALR) searches and document
   provision.

3:00–5:00 p.m.—Work on long-term projects and finish up the daily requests that come in.

What's missing from the time line above? Reading journal literature; attending continuing legal education (CLE) or law library association meetings;[49] talking on the telephone with clients and other librarians; attending firm meetings regarding human relations policies and precedent and
budgeting; and reading mountains of e-mail, both client related and informational, that you skipped while looking for the projects of the day.[50]
E-mail is a grand way to contact other law librarians in other parts of the
country. Many law librarians subscribe to listservs such as lawlib or acq-
1, which carry e-mail traffic concerning issues relating to your job. These
listservs are excellent for bouncing odd reference questions off a host of
experienced law librarians. Often you will find that there is really nothing
new in the world, just things that are new to you.

STATE, COURT, AND COUNTY LAW LIBRARIES

Many of the things accomplished on a day-to-day basis noted above apply to the law librarian in the state, court, or county law library, as well.
They have a slightly different clientele than do the firm and academic law
libraries—the *pro se* patron, the practicing attorney, the public prosecutor
and defender, and the judge—but the provision of basic legal research services remains the same. The state, court, and county law librarians, however, often have an outreach mission to the general public. They educate

the public about the law, lawyers, and the legal process. To this end the state, court, and county law librarians prepare tours of historic legal buildings and exhibits of bits of legal history such as photographs and exhibits relating to famous cases. Finally, the state, court, and county law librarians prepare research aids to assist the "do-it-yourself" *pro se* patron in accomplishing specific legal tasks, often working in tandem with a local court clerk's office to do so.[51] Such works assists persons without the means to hire legal assistance to make their way through the morass of the law. Many times the assistance needed is how to fill out forms or how to file legal papers. Sometimes the *pro se* patron needs to find the correct forms to accomplish something as simple as a name change, and sometimes something as complex as a divorce. The state, court, and county librarians can assist this process, and reduce their workload, by preparing comprehensive help pieces, though always keeping in mind the difference between legal reference and practicing law.

In addition, the state, court, and county librarian also has a potential client not possessed by the other types of law libraries: the prisoner. Because state, court, and county law libraries are public law libraries, they are generally imposed on for legal research assistance by those incarcerated and to provide copies of specific citations. Many of the state's highest appellate court law libraries also receive requests from prisoners for copies of the transcripts of the imprisoned. The transcripts are poured over by the prisoners, looking for any irregularity that might be used to set them free. Unfortunately, many of the requests for service are futile and often incomprehensible because, in general, the prisoners may not know what they are looking for or how to ask for it.

Rather than be besieged by a hail of requests, the library providing this sort of service should institute a payment plan whereby the prisoner will send funds to the law library to pay for copying. The law library should also inform prisoners of the following: that they will only fill requests for specific citations or very easy reference questions;[52] that the prisoner has ascertained the prison institution regulations relating to copies; that they will copy only as staff time allows; and that they demand cash up front or a prepaid account for the provision of copies. Provision of copies of legal materials to prisoners can be personally rewarding but it can also cause disruption in the primary mission of the state, court, and county law library unless strictly controlled.

SPECIALIZED SERVICES OF THE LAW LIBRARIAN

"The librarian performs miracles." "How did you do that?" "Where do you find this stuff? This is great!" "Thanks, thanks, thanks." These are things I have heard said about law librarians from their patron base—their clients, if you will. These clients say these things because the law librarian has developed specialized skills at manipulating databases or other information sources to provide what seems like magic to the layperson. The magic is not so specialized, nowadays, since many people can get into databases, but most people are too busy doing what they do best—here, it's practicing law—to truly learn the ins and outs of good IT. Specialized services include things like

- Smart Current Index to Legal Periodicals (CILP)—a current awareness service for law reviews, providing a subject-customizable listing of the tables of contents of new law review articles. It is modestly priced for law firms and very modestly priced for academic law libraries.
- Dialog databases—this database aggregator provides the access to a host of databases that allow the librarian to provide lists of publications written by expert witnesses, the market share of an industry to show anticompetitive tendencies, and journal articles in scientific and business areas for attorney education in a field outside the law.
- People finders, helping you to find deadbeats and witnesses.
- People information—allowing you to find information about the assets people own, including property and moving vehicles such as cars, boats, and airplanes.
- Company information—showing who and what companies are and whether they have good credit ratings and, very importantly, whether it is likely they will be able to pay a fee if they engage the services of your firm.
- Geographic information—showing just how far an address is from the courthouse, allowing the attorney to subpoena someone.
- Ephemeral information—assisting you to determine whether the moon was actually shining that night or was it dark and rainy, thus preventing the testifying witness from really seeing what he or she is testifying was seen.
- Client development—depending on the size of your law firm, you may be the only person in the firm who can provide information about potential clients. Large law firms have a host of people who scan the news and search databases to cull information relevant to landing new clients for the firm. Smaller firms do not and this work is often done by the attorneys themselves—attorneys who have neither the expertise nor the time to do such work. If a partner is going to go pitch the firm to a potential client, you can truly impress if you put together a company dossier with pertinent information about the company or individual in question, what they do, and whether they are a good credit

risk. Lexis and Westlaw have client development products that are very useful (though costly), so you might trade some of your time and skill to provide a similar product at a lower price.[53]

- Conflicts—sometimes the law library becomes heavily involved in conflicts. Conflicts are not fistfights but, rather, a term of art indicating a relationship of your firm with another party such that you cannot be hired as counsel. In highly simplified terms, let us say your firm wants to be hired to do some work for Company A but also represents Company B, which has a pending law suit against Company A. Legal ethics rules would usually prevent your firm from representing Company A and, if in error your firm started representing Company A, serious repercussions could result in the loss of income and your firm's good name. Librarians are often able to ferret out complex company relationships that would baffle others, by using a variety of paper and online resources. "Conflicts" is a shorthand term for pointing out the ramifications for such "conflicts of interest" when a law firm begins to take on the representation of a new client. Often, the conflicts in a small firm are handled by one person who has other duties. In large firms there are hosts of people devoted to keeping the firm out of a conflicting interest situation.

CONCLUSION

So, we have gone through the various jobs in the law library, advocating that you try to go through each one when you begin your career. You will learn more about your new institution, you will meet your new comrades, and you will learn more about law libraries in general. Once you see all the parts, the whole makes more sense. You also have seen a brief description of most of the professional jobs in the modern law library, which should give you some idea of whether you would want to work there. You have gotten some idea of what the workday for a law firm librarian will be like. Finally, there is a list of what makes a law librarian special— the various specialized services that can be given to faculty, judges, and practicing attorneys that will make the value of the law librarian worth his or her salary.

NOTES

1. There are, as well, three flavors of law schools: state supported; private or affiliated with a private college or university; and standalone. They are all, however, generally run along the same lines.

2. One prime example would be the joint governance structure existing between the Duquesne University Law Library and the Allegheny County Law Library.

3. In my own institution, for example, we recently made the decision to drop microform copies of legal serials if we held that serial in hard copy and it was also available to us electronically. In some cases we found that we had access to as many as five different forms of some serial titles.

4. It has been said that the academic law library truly exists for the research needs of the law faculty and that the students are merely the funding mechanism, but that probably goes a bit too far.

5. Witness the title of the 2006 American Association of Law Schools annual meeting: "Empirical Scholarship: What Should We Study and How Should We Study It?" See the 2006 *Proceedings of the American Association of Law Schools*.

6. There are notable exceptions, such as the Los Angeles County Law Library. LA County, as it is known, is one of the largest law libraries in the United States and is well known for its collection of foreign legal materials, unusual for a county law library but necessary in the high-stakes legal world of Southern California.

7. In the law firm environment, space is money. Although a few firms own their own buildings, most rent space and space can run into the hundreds of dollars per month per square foot in the denser metropolitan areas such as New York City and San Francisco. While it is generally cheaper in the less dense areas, it can still run into the mid-double digits. It is prohibitively expensive to retain materials on-site when they can be obtained elsewhere or stored off-site.

8. That is, they will not unless they are of the caliber where the collection development plan calls for the purchase of nearly everything published in the legal field that comes on the market. This would be the law libraries on the magnitude of Harvard, Yale, Georgetown, and the University of Texas. Even these law libraries, though, cannot have everything and interlibrary loan is used quite extensively between law libraries.

9. But this is not to say that law firm libraries and state, court, and county law libraries do not have collection policies. Many will use a collection development policy to justify what they purchase and to control costs by not purchasing things that are not necessary. Take a look at the following articles for more information: James S. Heller, "Collection Development and Weeding à la Versace: Fashioning a Policy for Your Library," *AALL Spectrum* 6, no. 5 (February 2002): 12–14; Karen Silber, "Every Library Is Special and So Is Its Collection Development Policy," *AALL Spectrum* 4, no. 4 (December 1999): 10–11; Jonathan A. Franklin, "One Piece of the Collection Development Puzzle: Issues in Drafting Format Selection Guidelines," *Law Library Journal* 86, no. 4 (Fall 1994): 753–80.

10. My first job out of library school was as a documents receiving clerk in the federal Government Documents Collection at the Texas State Library. That clerical job gave me the entrée to my first professional job eight months later, as a cataloger, reference, and government documents specialist at the Texas State Law Library. Nothing will hone your skills so much as doing the clerical jobs with your mind alert and your eyes open; you will gain a better understanding of how things are done and, perhaps, how they can be done better. Systems analysis can be used at any point in any job, but only if you can see the details.

11. Firm library openings are usually caused by someone up the food chain, such as the director of a law firm library, leaving for retirement, whose job is filled by someone from a smaller firm, and that job is filled from someone at a smaller firm, and so on. An entry-level job would most likely be in one of the smaller firms.

12. I hate to bring it up but in highly competitive law schools students often "hide" materials from one another. That is, they will scope out a class and the syllabus, then head to the collection to remove materials that might be of assistance to fellow classmates and move them to another location out of call-number sequence. An active stack maintenance program can foil such evildoers.

13. Difficult as it may be to believe, technical services staff can make mistakes. Shelvers find those mistakes when they shelve materials, such as mislabeled items and incorrect (or seemingly incorrect) call numbers, where the call number does not match the item or the area. These can only be caught if the shelver is awake and paying attention. Do you see some supervisory issues arising from your circulation through different departments, yet?

14. Most modern libraries have an integrated library system (ILS) of one form or another that integrates a serials system and online public catalog into one, hopefully seamless, whole. Serial items arriving in the mail are generally checked into the serials system.

15. For instance, some publishers refuse to deal with a jobber. Commerce Clearing House, a large tax, business, and law loose-leaf publisher, does not sell its serials to jobbers for redistribution. Thomson/West—a large legal publisher—is the same.

16. Another reason I believe the publishers are "fishing" for someone to retain an unrequested item is the practice, upon being confronted with the offending piece and requested to send a postage paid return label, of telling the law library to "just keep it—it's cheaper for us if you don't return it."

17. Issuing a check costs an institution money. That cost will vary depending on the bank involved, the types of retention policies, the cost of the staff issuing the check, and other factors such as storage, retrieval, and accounting services. I have found costs varying from $1.50 to $10 per check (run a general Internet search on the cost of issuing a check and look at the results) and have had comptrollers at places where I work quote me figures as high as $20 per check, over the life of the check. It stands to reason that if you can reduce the number of checks issued, you will reduce your costs of doing business and save money for the place where you work. Some institutions are very high tech and will also engage in electronic data interchange (commonly known as EDI, which is a standardized data exchange of information that eliminates a great deal of paperwork) and wire transfers (transfers of funds between banks such that the purchasing institution does not have to write a check at all).

18. Many times these sorts of records in the public access catalog are suppressed for the general public, mainly to prevent confusion and anxiety at the public services desks. After many years I continue to be amazed that users (and I include librarians and, with no small amount of embarrassment, myself), no matter how large the typeface, stop reading after they get to the part that tells them what they want. That is, after seeing the title they go to the reference or circulation

desk and ask where it is, not noticing that the record is prominently noted "On Order." Depending on the user's level of sophistication, he or she might not accept even this notation, requesting the public services person to "go to the back to see if it has come in yet"—something that is not a problem in the one-person library since the front and the back are manned by the same person. In a large library, however, tracking down a book "in the back" could take as long as an hour, due to the complexity of the processing that takes place.

19. An initial problem for most academic and state-owned institutions is that prepayment is usually prohibited; payment can only be made for items in hand (though this rule can sometimes be "bent" if there is a discount for prepayment sufficient to sway a comptroller).

20. When I was working at a firm library we once prepaid a book order that took two years to be filled. We really did want the publication and were not getting stiffed by the publisher, who was at the mercy of an already overcommitted author. We were in the good company of many other firm law libraries in the United States, but two years is a long time to wait.

21. If you are interested, your library school probably has some course on acquisitions, or if you want to learn on your own, take a look at Liz Chapman, *Managing Acquisitions in Library and Information Services*, 3rd ed. (New York: Neal-Schuman, 2004). Although U.K. oriented, it is a good take on the process. Another is Audrey Eaglen, *Buying Books: A How-to-Do-It Manual for Librarians*, 2nd ed. (New York: Neal-Shuman, 2000).

22. Public services types would do themselves a great service by learning to use the institution's catalog to ascertain whether the library already has something or not. Acquisitions people should act as the secondary checker, not the primary checker, of whether an institution already owns something.

23. As with most rules, this one is proved by the exceptions. Count the number of law libraries in the United States and you will have some idea about the number of different ways a law library can be staffed. Certainly, in some law libraries, circulation services can be supervised by a librarian. It is not necessarily a "librarian" type of function, however, since a great deal of what is described is clerical by its very nature: cleaning, reshelving, charging, and discharging books. It is a "management" area, since there are a number of staff members working there, so a librarian might be in the position.

24. Why? Because these are typically loose-leaf volumes in nature, sometimes very difficult to replace if lost, and the set is often less valuable if a volume is missing from the set for upwards of two weeks. Nothing can be more frustrating to the researcher than finding the citation, in the index to a set, to a specific part of the set and discovering that "piece" is missing. Well, one thing is more frustrating: finding that the volume with the index is missing.

25. OCLC uses a third-party-developed interlibrary loan software called Clio. Please be aware that RLG uses a different piece of software, called RLG's ILL Manager (which, interestingly enough, interfaces with OCLC's system), but the general concept and process is the same as that of OCLC's.

26. For example, the South Florida area has the South East Florida Library and Information Network (SEFLIN), whose members have agreed not to charge each other fees for lending. There is also a courier who makes the rounds among the

SEFLIN member libraries, delivering loans and returning borrowed items. While there is a fee for SEFLIN membership, the value of this feature, among others, makes it highly desirable to participate. For example, if a library borrows fifty items per month (a modest borrowing rate for an academic law library) at an average cost of $15 handling per item, the library will spend $9,000 per year on fees alone, not counting postage charges. Cutting this number in half is highly desirous.

27. Many libraries are now using Infotrieve's Ariel to send materials. Ariel is a software piece that, along with a scanner, PC, and high-speed data line, allows the user to scan a document or portion from a book into an image file, and send that scanned document to a requestor. This eliminates the need to pack, label, and ship materials and the resulting time delay, as well as any postal charges. This is very useful for journal articles since journals are usually not circulated. If Ariel is not used, then the journals are usually photocopied and mailed. Scanning does require about the same amount of time as photocopying, so no savings in staff time is made using Ariel.

28. The cost of interlibrary lending, of course, varies from library to library depending on a multitude of cost variables. The Association of Research Libraries (ARL) has conducted studies of the costs associated with interlibrary loan, giving libraries a benchmark of average costs. Such benchmarks allow libraries to compare their costs to averages to see if they are in line. One study, performed in 1998, indicated that the total average cost of a mediated interlibrary loan transaction was $27.83 for a research library and $19.33 for a college library (Mary E. Jackson, "Measuring the Performance of Interlibrary Loan and Document Delivery Services," *ARL: A Bimonthly Newsletter of Research Library Issues and Actions*, no. 195 [December 1997], available at www.arl.org/newsltr/195/195toc.html). ARL conducted a follow-up study in 2004. In the intervening years, the ILL systems developed unmediated interfaces (user-based systems, rather than those mediated by staff). The 2004 ARL study (Mary E. Jackson, *Assessing ILL/DD Services: New Cost-Effective Alternatives* [Washington, D.C.: Association of Research Libraries, 2004]) indicates that the unmediated costs have decreased substantially from the mediated costs of the 1998 study, summarized in "Assessing ILL/DD Services: New Cost-Effective Alternatives," *ARL Bimonthly Report*, no. 236 (October 2004), available at www.arl.org/newsltr/236/illstudy.html.

29. Thus vividly illustrating the adage that no good deed goes unpunished, no bad deed unrewarded.

30. Lexis and Westlaw are two computer-assisted legal research databases that are quite comprehensive in nature. They are competing services owned, respectively, by Elsevier and Thomson, two foreign public companies. Both contain a host of primary legal materials as well as secondary materials published by their own companies. There is a great deal of overlap in the primary materials, but the secondary sources do not overlap as much.

31. A good example is the Haworth journals; they are available through a couple of repackagers and through direct links for subscription to the hard copy.

32. HeinOnline is a product put out by William S. Hein & Co., commonly referred to as Hein. Hein started as a reprint house, providing reprints of legal serials. It also publishes a large quantity of legislative history compilations and individual monographs in the legal fields. It produces the "green slips" service for

acquisitions of legal materials. Before 2006 it also jobbed the books; a recent notice indicated, however, that it no longer intends to provide this service. HeinOnline is a ten-year-old venture that reproduces law review and other serial titles as PDF files via online access. The genius of HeinOnline is that, in general, it goes back to the initial volume of the serial, while its competition, Lexis and Westlaw, do not. In addition, Hein has recently made the *Federal Register* available back to volume 1, issue 1—a mammoth undertaking but one long overdue in the legal information industry.

33. Directional reference is directing people to where *things* are, such as facilities within the library (Where is the media department? Where is the bathroom?), as well as the location of materials (Where are the state reporters and the state statutes?). General nonlegal reference consists of queries such as would arrive at the reference desk of any library (What is the capital of . . . ?; Who is the president of . . . ?; What is the address and how should I address the ambassador to Burkina Faso?). Business nonlegal, though, is one of the fastest growing segments of reference, particularly in law firm libraries. Business nonlegal reference would include things like market share and competitive intelligence questions.

34. Usually extremely old citations—only the newest of law students will inquire as to the meaning of a citation to the National Reporter System. Immediate access to Bieber's work (Doris M. Bieber and Mary Miles Prince, *Bieber's Dictionary of Legal Abbreviations: Reference Guide for Attorneys, Legal Secretaries, Paralegals and Law Students*, 5th ed. [Buffalo, NY: Hein, 2001]) is exceedingly useful for interpreting ancient citations.

35. Great care must be taken in interpretation not to run afoul of the unauthorized practice of law statutes, particularly with the *pro se* or general lay patron. A great bibliography of articles about unauthorized practice is Paul D. Healey, "Pro Se Users, Reference Liability, and the Unauthorized Practice of Law: Twenty-Five Selected Readings," *Law Library Journal* 94, no. 1 (Winter 2002): 133–39.

36. This also happens a great deal in law firms where it is usually the attorney and longtime secretary who are arguing about tenses and punctuation. Such debaters are usually highly educated people and it is best to try to avoid such arguments, giving the aggrieved parties the appropriate Strunk & White or Fowler's and, particularly, Bryan Garner, *A Dictionary of Modern Legal Usage*, 2nd ed. (New York: Oxford, 2001) or Bryan Garner, *The Elements of Legal Style*, 2nd ed. (New York: Oxford, 2002).

37. Table 11, "Average Number of Professionals per Library (FTE)" in *AALL Biennial Salary Survey & Organization Characteristics* (2005); and Item 20.2, Full Time Equivalent Professional Librarians in the American Bar Association's *Law Library Comprehensive Statistical Table Data from the Annual Questionnaire*, which gives the specific numbers of professional law librarians in each academic institution.

38. As Groucho Marx opined, "Please accept my resignation. I don't care to belong to any club that will have me as a member." *Columbia World of Quotations* (1996) as found in www.bartleby.com/66/19/38119.html.

39. It is, of course, by happenstance that the purveyor of this advice has worked in both technical services and public services, as well as all three types of law libraries.

40. Remember these two words as, when you supervise personnel, you will be able to use them either to the advantage or detriment of the supervised employee when you complete his or her performance evaluation.

41. The American Association of Law Libraries' annual meeting of 2000 had a program titled "The ABA Reaccreditation Visit: Process and Preparation," July 16, 2000. Two presentations at that meeting resulted in documents posted to the Internet site of the Association's Academic Law Libraries SIS. The first is Donald J. Dunn, "What to Expect When the ABA Site Evaluator Arrives—and Perhaps a Bit Before . . ." and the second is a bibliography compiled by Leslie M. Campbell and Ellen Platt, "The ABA Reaccreditation Inspection Visit: Process and Preparation," with both available at www.aallnet.org/sis/allsis/abavisit/index.html.

42. And this would be true for firm partners and court judges, as well.

43. It is wasteful to move and remove and move volumes yet again, because not enough space has been left for the growth of a collection. In general, when a library has only 15 percent of growth space remaining overall, it is time to plan to weed the collection heavily or add more shelving.

44. While it will vary from institution to institution, members of library governing boards are usually elected or appointed for a fixed term of years. Deans, by nature of their contentious jobs, have a general "life expectancy" of four years.

45. If you are lucky, you will have a student or part-time employee to assist in the more mundane tasks, such as this one. However, you will have to demonstrate that you are worth such an investment—because hiring someone is more than just paying him or her a wage; there are a multitude of costs appended to an employee besides his or her pay, including unemployment taxes, Social Security taxes, and health care (if lucky). Such ancillary benefits can rise to as much as one-third more of the straight salary.

46. As Soon As Possible (leaving out the word "humanly" before possible— senior partners are not interested in what is not capable of accomplishment by mere mortals—they just want results).

47. It has been said above but bears repeating, some publishers are, through inadvertence, sloppiness, or malice, trying to get you to buy stuff you did not order. Remember—if you stamp it, you bought it. Be sure to check your "on order" files to be sure the books and materials you receive are the books and materials you ordered.

48. Be careful leaving early or arriving late. Office politics might cause you to avoid this as persons leaving early, even when on a good-cause mission, are sometimes frowned upon as shirkers. How are they to know that you are doing valuable work outside the office? Often, however, leaving during the day and returning heavily burdened is a good thing, demonstrating that you have been working hard. Perception is often much of the battle for status.

49. Become a joiner. You should join, at a minimum, your local law librarian group, if one exists, and your regional chapter of AALL. If no local group exists, you should join whatever local librarian group is available. If there are none, you should start one. Librarians are social creatures and enjoy each other's company, sharing experiences and tips. At some point you should also join the national association, the AALL, as this is the premier tool for education for law librarians.

50. E-mail is a good delivery mechanism for keeping up with Internet-related topics, as well as current happenings in the law library world. Professional list-servs will allow you to contact law librarians from other parts of the country. A list of the listservs offered as part of the AALL are listed at www.aallnet.org/ discuss/list_index_sis.asp. In addition to those listservs officially sponsored by the American Association of Law Library units is Law-Lib. Law-Lib is the oldest law library listserv. To subscribe to Law-Lib, send an e-mail to listproc@uc-davis.edu. In the body of the e-mail, write "subscribe law-lib first name last name" without the quotes.

51. The clerk's office has a vested interest in helping the law librarian, as the time needed to assist the *pro se* patron in filing court cases can be reduced.

52. Otherwise the law library will receive long, nonsensical recitations of facts, real and fanciful, requesting in-depth research services.

53. Note here that the price is really not lower; you have traded your valuable time in place of paying someone else (like Lexis or Westlaw) to provide a product. Your client, however, will see it as a lower cost because the firm will be paying you whether you furnish the information or not.

Chapter 3

Administration

Lisa Smith-Butler

Since the mid-1990s, law library administration has changed significantly.[1] The increasing development and use of technology as well as an expanding global economy have resulted in an explosion of information resources and a corresponding need to access this information immediately from any place. Blackberrys, Treos, and PalmPilots are some of the new tools that allow library users to access the library at any time, from any place. These changes in patron behaviors have created corresponding changes in the services provided by libraries as well as the formats of their collections. Full-text electronic retrieval of primary and secondary sources of law, once a futurist vision, is now a daily occurrence for most law faculty, law students, and attorneys. Everyone is now connected. Responding to these changes, law libraries in the academic, firm, and county settings[2] have expanded the scope of their activities. Academic law libraries are frequently responsible for providing technology services[3] in addition to traditional information services. Firm libraries, in addition to traditional library services, are often now responsible for conflict checks and records management within the law firm.

In this changing environment, law libraries are reaching out and creating relationships with other organizations in order to expand their services and survive. Once a well-defined concept, autonomy within the academic law library setting as required by ABA Standard 602(a) is now in flux,[4] allowing the academic law library to accommodate a multidisciplinary approach to legal education.[5] Exploding patron interests and reduced budgets are forcing law libraries to develop strategies to increase patron services while holding the bottom line steady. To accomplish these conflicting goals, academic law libraries are partnering with local public, academic, and other law libraries, joining and creating consortia,[6] adding value to the services that they provide, and increasing the services offered. Firm libraries also have been affected by these trends. Intimate working relationships exist within local legal communities, allowing firm librarians to work closely with their counterparts in rival firms. These close relationships enable firm librarians to quickly obtain information needed by their patrons. County, court, and state law libraries are also being affected. Since many resources are now on the Internet,[7] legislatures are either drastically reducing funding for county and state law libraries or closing them altogether. As funding dries up[8] among county and state law libraries, many of their collections and services are absorbed into local public libraries.

Traditionally law library administration has been concerned with the process of acquiring and cataloging a collection, making this collection accessible to patrons, providing staff to assist patrons with information retrieval, and preserving the information for future patrons.[9] While all of this still occurs, library automation has vastly reduced the time and labor needed[10] to accomplish these tasks. Consequently, law library administrators and their staffs have expanded their services to meet the information and technology needs of today's patrons.

WHAT IS LIBRARY ADMINISTRATION?

A well-organized law library functions quietly but effectively, acquiring, processing, and distributing information to its patrons—while a disorganized library lurches from crisis to crisis, never resolving any of its issues. To function effectively, library administration needs to work through numerous issues. Reduced or flat budgets, loss of space, changing job descriptions, and additional responsibilities are just a few of the issues facing law library administrators today. Carefully crafted mission statements allow law libraries to effectively plan while retaining flexibility, an essential characteristic necessary for the future.[11] Organizational structure determines working relationships within the library while affecting relationships with various patron constituencies. Collection development affects budget and space constraints. Add responsibility for technology to this existing mix, and you will understand what today's law library administrator deals with on a daily basis. Responses to these issues create a road map, making it easy for fellow and future travelers to follow.

A mission statement is essential.[12] Some view mission statements as faddish; however, they are important as a road map. While brief and to the point, a good mission statement forces a library to focus on its services and patrons while analyzing its mission in relation to the greater organization to which it is attached. If the two don't match, conflict is inevitable. Mission statements highlight the direction into which the law library intends to head. According to Dean Richard A. Danner, a mission statement should answer the following five questions:

What business are we in (or should we be in)?
Who are our customers (or who will they be by the end of the plan period)?
What products or services do we provide (or should we be providing)?
Who are our competitors?
What competitive advantages do we have (or should we develop)?[13]

Once a mission statement exists, strategic planning is next.[14] To accomplish the library's mission as defined, general-purpose goals are created. To achieve the goals, objectives that are easily identifiable and measurable are then added. Finally, strategies are developed to help libraries accomplish these objectives, meeting their goals.

Mission statements and strategic planning also reflect the organizational structure of a library. In terms of structural organization, academic law libraries traditionally were organized into departments by function—for example, technical services, public services, and administration.[15] If technology now falls under the umbrella of the library, where do computer services, Web development, video conferencing, and audiovisual services fit within the organizational structure? Are there now additional departments within the academic law library: administration, technical services, public services, and computer services? If so, do technology professionals and the librarians interact and under what conditions? How do their relationships affect the relationships throughout the organization? Should librarians also learn how to handle basic technology questions and issues at the reference desk? Should technology staff learn how to conduct a reference type interview in order to more effectively diagnose and service patrons' computer issues?

While generalizations are possible, each library must ultimately design its organizational structure to best fit its people, its mission, and the larger organization that it serves. Choices of organizational structures include a flat organization, a traditional hierarchy, or a team-centered approach.[16] While flat organizational structures work effectively with smaller staffs, they become unwieldy in larger organizations. In larger organizations, it is too time consuming for everyone to report to the director. In the past, traditional hierarchical structures were effective to train departmental heads to become directors—but this approach is less appealing to newer generations of law librarians as well as older librarians who have no interest in heading an academic law library.[17] Newer approaches attempt to mimic what often actually happens at work, that is, a team-oriented approach in which various members of the library work together to achieve specific goals and tasks. Each member then assumes responsibility for ensuring that tasks are accomplished.[18] Whatever organizational structure is chosen, it should be clearly defined and understood by all. An organization chart that is adhered to[19] is essential for everyone.

In terms of structure, it is most important that individuals who work together effectively communicate with each other and see that the library's work is completed. Conflict and disagreement are inevitable. How this conflict is handled determines relationships both within and outside of the library. Colleagues should be able to effectively discuss differing opinions and perspectives without allowing their viewpoints to disintegrate into personal attacks.[20]

Relationships with others outside the library are vital. At an academic law library, there are relationships with the dean, the law faculty, the law library staff, law students, the wider university community, alumni, local attorneys, and finally the general public. All of these groups have differing needs.

In an academic law school setting, the law library director usually reports to the dean of the law school. The director is responsible for managing a materials budget; building and shaping a library collection; creating and maintaining information services for faculty, staff, students, and the public; managing a staff; and oftentimes managing technology resources for the law school. In order to accomplish these tasks and satisfy the various constituencies, management and leadership skills are essential.[21] Management skills see that the library functions smoothly, providing order and consistency in operational functions, while leadership skills allow a leader to motivate staff to adapt and become comfortable with change.[22] To effectively lead and manage the information and technology resources of a law library, it is imperative that relationships be forged with the dean, the library staff, the faculty, and law school administrative colleagues.

To work effectively with the law school dean, it is essential to understand the dean's work style, vision, goals, objectives, and pressures.[23] Working effectively with the dean requires the law library director to problem solve, bringing suggested solutions along with problems to the dean's office. Keep the dean informed; surprises are unpleasant. Discover whether the dean wants daily, weekly, semimonthly, or monthly reports and updates. Learn whether the dean prefers details or anecdotal reports. Ultimately, the dean wants to be reassured that the law library director has details under control, is ready to resolve any problems that arise, manages money and staff effectively, eases administrative burdens, and helps the dean maintain a positive image of the law school.

Managing staff effectively is essential. In order to effectively lead staff, listen. People want to be acknowledged. They want directors to hear their ideas and concerns. They want attribution and praise for their successes.[24] To learn what is going on within the library, walk the floors, visiting all departments and library staff. This allows a director to observe and provides an opportunity to informally exchange greetings and ideas.

Problems and problem employees exist and present challenges. Once someone comes to the director with a problem, the director must decide how this problem will be resolved, communicate this, and then follow through. If the director thinks the issue is exaggerated and does not constitute a problem, he or she should say so. If the director intends to take steps to resolve the problem, the employee should be told what steps will be taken and be updated as needed. Conflict is inevitable. If handled properly, it can be productive, allowing employees to share and explore divergent perspectives. If handled badly and left unresolved, it festers, destroying morale.[25]

Keep library staff updated as to their performance. Catch people doing excellent work, tell them the work is excellent, thank them, and then tell the dean or managing partner.[26] Meet with staff several times a year to keep them updated about performance.[27] Keep a file with notes from others as well as your own observations to use when preparing performance reviews. Make expectations about performance very clear. "Do your best" might not be the best directive if the director and the employee have different perspectives as to what constitutes the employee's best. If performance issues arise, make sure employees understand precisely what is expected in terms of behavior and performance. If corrections, discipline, or reprimands are needed, this should be done in private and in person rather than via e-mail or the telephone, if at all possible.

Some employees will never be satisfied or happy. If you inherited one of these, be very clear about what behaviors will and will not be tolerated. When interviewing and hiring, "select out the negative, maladjusted, trouble-making faultfinders who derive little satisfaction in anything about their jobs."[28]

Relationships with faculty, students, and other law school administrators are essential to effectively do the job. Again, walk the floors, visiting individuals in their own environment. Talk to faculty, students, and staff to find out what their technology and information needs are. Again, listen. Promptly respond to faculty, administrator, and student requests, even if telling them no. Annually survey the law faculty and law students to learn what services are working and which services need tweaking. Attend faculty workshops, presentations, and luncheons. A director's support is noticed and appreciated; as an added benefit, you will learn of any information or technology concerns that exist. Establish relationships with other library and technology directors on campus. Ideas and occasionally resources can be shared.

Alumni and local attorneys are also important. Services can be provided to these two constituencies in a manner that benefits both the law library and the law school. Providing access to continuing legal education (CLE) tapes for alumni and local attorneys can often reap financial rewards in the forms of donations, gifts, or bequests. Another service of use to local alumni and attorneys includes providing them with a room within the library in which to do research. Consider providing access to word processing equipment and electronic subscriptions.[29] Document delivery can be provided to local area attorneys too.

SERVICES

Frequently the law library is responsible for providing both information and technology services to its patrons. After consultation with the appropriate individuals,[30] decide what services will be provided. Once that decision is made, be certain that excellent service is being provided.

Some of the traditional library information services that can be provided include current awareness updates; research assistance with information retrieval for scholarship, classes, and class preparation; preparation of subject bibliographies and research guides to assist faculty and students with information retrieval; and training and technology assistance for faculty and students.[31]

With a liaison program, the above services can be effectively and efficiently organized. Traditional liaison programs match individual librarians with individual faculty members. Once matched, the librarian will handle the faculty members' interlibrary loans (ILLs), research requests, handle requests for special lectures on research topics, and set up current awareness resources. This process also assists the faculty in discovering new materials for their research needs, introducing new electronic resources, and training research assistants.

There are numerous resources to help faculty maintain current awareness. Faculty should have their own RSS feeds (Really Simple Syndication, a format that sends headlines to news aggregators and libraries), Westclips, and Lexis alerts in their subject areas. Tables of contents from journal pages can be downloaded with the University of Washington's CILP,[32] which is distributed electronically. Smartclips can be set up in CILP so that faculty are alerted whenever articles in their subject area are published. Blogs can be used to disseminate current information about what is happening in the library, in the law school, and in the legal community. Create your own library blog to accomplish this. Once created, link it to Jurist's Paper Chase[33] and other blogs.[34] Create a Special Legal Bulletins page that provides links to recent, newsworthy legislation, cases, and articles.[35] Publish this information to faculty, staff, and students via e-mail alerts.

Interview faculty to learn what courses they teach and what their research interests are.[36] Set up Alerts or Westclips in the Index to Legal Periodicals as well as local newspaper databases on Westlaw or Lexis so that the librarian and the faculty member are alerted when a faculty member is cited or quoted. Offer the routing of journals as well as a photocopy/print service for faculty. Publish a monthly newsletter that provides information about the library's resources and lists recent faculty publications. Maintain the faculty publication list from each newsletter and then annually publish a bibliography of faculty publications. Publish research guides and subject-specific bibliographies as well. Distribute this material electronically via e-mail and on the law library's website.[37] Offer faculty guest lectures on specialized legal research topics. Train faculty, staff, and students to cost effectively use print and electronic resources in individual and group training sessions.[38]

Provide reference assistance to faculty, staff, students, alumni, local attorneys, and the general public if the public is included in the library's mission. Provide this assistance via several resources, including in-person reference service at a reference desk,[39] electronic reference service via e-mail, virtual reference service with chat and URL push functions,[40] and telephone reference services. Maintain reference and liaison statistics electronically to gauge the effectiveness of information services provided as well as determining staffing levels for appropriate times.

While discussing services, a twenty-first-century discussion of law libraries would not be complete without a discussion of technology services. Whether technology services are housed within the law library or in a separate computer services department,[41] law schools expect a network infrastructure that supports faculty, staff, and students as well as databases and Web pages that provide information about the school, its resources, classes, and region. Electronic classrooms and courtrooms with Webcasting, videoconferencing, simulcasting, and audiovisual capabilities are becoming the norm rather than the exception. Wireless networks, once unique, are now expected by students.[42]

In terms of network infrastructure, an internal law center network with servers that provides faculty and students with access to e-mail, word processing, databases, and the Internet is essential. Once this infrastructure is in place, a centralized help desk, located within the law school, is necessary to provide hardware and software support for patrons. In addition, most technology departments also support law school computer labs, building wide wireless networks, Internet service providers (ISPs) for faculty and students, and virtual private networks (VPNs) that allow the faculty's and staff's home computers to behave as though at work.[43]

Before applying to law school, prospective students expect to be able to chat live and online with the admissions director or with part of the admissions committee. Students expect to apply to law school online. Once admitted, students expect to register for classes online and obtain grades, class rankings, and transcripts via the Internet. They will rank faculty online; collaborate with one another via electronic message boards, instant message, and e-mail; submit assignments electronically; print wirelessly from within anywhere in the law school; review digital audio recordings/podcasting of classes; telecommute via videoconferencing for classes from distant clinics; and take exams and the final bar exam with their laptops, using secure computerized software.[44] They expect to research electronically and retrieve information resources from the library and the law school's website from any place at any time.[45] They expect to provide employers with electronic business cards that contain a resume, writing sample, and video clip of a presentation, mock negotiation, or Moot Court experience. They expect to search for and apply for jobs with online software as well. They expect to publish law reviews and journals online. If the library is in charge of technology, it is responsible for meeting the students' expectations.

Given these expectations, faculty expectations about technology services have increased.[46] Faculty teach in electronic classrooms that allow them to poll students within the class, show bits and clips of legal-related movies on DVDs, examine physical evidence via a document camera, project PowerPoints and statutory provisions via an LCD on an overhead screen, and connect to the Internet in order to answer questions that arise about a case or piece of legislation. To use these classrooms, they must be trained.

To communicate effectively, efficiently, and quickly with students, faculty use class distribution lists to e-mail students, post messages and assignments on electronic bulletin boards, and post syllabi on the website. To alert others of their specialization and interests, they also post their CV, bibliographies, and other documents on their website. Many want the ability to use their Web page to link to other websites. Digital video or audio recordings of class preserve lectures for students while a digital photobook, password protected, allows professors to view photos of their students by class.

Information access from any place at any time is important for a law center's faculty, staff, and students. To achieve this, many law libraries provide an easy proxy server that authenticates students and faculty, allowing them to access and retrieve electronic information resources[47] from anyplace. An intranet allows faculty and students to retrieve passwords and documents while away from the office/school. Web design and maintenance for the various law school departments, such as admissions, alumni, career development, faculty, library, and student affairs, provide crucial information to faculty and students about these departments.

Should technology be housed in the law library or exist as an independent, separate department? Again, it depends on the law school's mission and organization. Given how closely intertwined library and technology concerns are,[48] many schools are now housing technology within the law library. Reference librarians are learning to respond to frontline technology queries while computer professionals develop service skills to better assist patrons.

COLLECTION DEVELOPMENT

One of the intellectual challenges of a law library director includes collection development. Collection development varies from library to library. Some libraries have a collection development librarian while others use a collection development committee that is composed of various professionals. A law library's collection should support the needs of its primary patrons. In an academic setting, those patrons are the law students and the law faculty. This means that the law library should provide a core collection of primary sources of law, indexing and finding aids, updating tools, secondary sources, treatises, and monographs to support the law school's curriculum and the faculty's research and scholarship needs.

In order to comply with American Bar Association (ABA) Standards,[49] a law library must have a written collection development policy that is periodically reviewed and updated.[50] Along with the collection development policy, a collection retention policy, while not required, is extremely useful. Weeding is essential, and it is imperative that a library decide what will be kept and what will later be discarded because libraries have limited shelf space. This means format (microform, print, or electronic) becomes a consideration in collection development. Microforms and electronic collections reduce the need for shelf space. Once electronic collections are introduced, access versus ownership, discussed in a later chapter, becomes an issue. While some new electronic products are being sold in a manner similar to the sale of print products, many electronic resources continue to provide access only rather than ownership.[51] This format is changing collection development as well as the job of the acquisitions librarian.

Presently the annual *ABA Report* requires both the volume and title count of academic law libraries. Many believe that the volume count provides an inaccurate measurement of the breadth and depth of a law library's collection. Counting also raises other issues. Can electronic titles be counted? If so, how are they measured? As academic law libraries move into the twenty-first century, many directors and staff are discussing the need to more accurately measure a collection and determine if it does indeed support a law school's curricular, research, and scholarship needs.

In addition to space considerations, there are numerous other reasons to buy electronic resources. Electronic serial subscriptions coupled with an easy proxy server allow law faculty and students to access primary and secondary sources of law at any time from any place. If a law school has a mandatory laptop program for students, electronic resources, if not limited to a certain number of simultaneous users, can literally put a resource in every patron's hands.

To develop this collection, a number of tools exist. Hein's green slip service[52] and Yankee Peddler's Gobi yellow slip service[53] alert librarians of new monographic and serial titles being published. Annual publications such as *Legal Information Buyer's Guide and Reference Manual*[54] and *Recommended Publications for Legal Research*,[55] as well as *Law Library Journal's* quarterly column "Keeping Up with New Legal Titles" also assist librarians working with collection development. There are also other collection development tools available.[56]

BUDGETING

Given the size of most law library budgets,[57] budgeting is an essential skill needed by a law library director. All academic law schools must annually file a report with the ABA. Included within that report is a library report that lists, among other things, library expenditures by the following categories:

- serials
- online resources
- monographs
- ILL expenses
- bindery expenses
- preservation expenses
- computer bibliographic expenses
- computing equipment
- equipment repair and purchase
- postage, telephone, paper, and office supplies
- travel
- professional dues and memberships
- all other expenses

Budgeting is a critical issue in today's environment. Costs of legal serials have often seen double-digit increases in the past twenty years[58] while most law library budgets have either increased modestly or stayed flat. In order to remain within budgets, most law libraries are now taking a long, hard look at their collection and making choices.[59]

To stay within budget, review library and technology (if within one's purview) accounts by account number as well as vendor on a weekly basis. Annually review serial subscriptions by vendor.[60] When reviewing these subscriptions, check not only the updating costs but also verify the name of the requestor of the item. Cancel items that are appropriate for cancellation. As technology has made the online or virtual library more of a reality, firm libraries have been quick to remove many print resources, relying primarily on electronic resources. While academic law libraries have moved more slowly with regards to print, academic law library directors are reviewing print legal serials and canceling duplicative print coverage. They are also reviewing decisions to pay for resources in both print and electronic formats. Many academic law libraries are moving from print Shepard's to online updating services such as KeyCite or Shepard's.

With electronic access via Lexis, LoisLaw, Westlaw, VersusLaw, and official government sites on the Internet, law libraries are asking crucial collection development and budgetary questions.[61] Should print Shepard's be maintained? Should every print digest be continued? If not, which digests should be discontinued? Should the library continue to carry print law reviews or discontinue current coverage since many are now available online? Is it necessary to consult legal research instructors before making such a decision? Should print statutes for all fifty states be continued or will a combination of print and online statutory provisions suffice?[62] These are some of the questions the director must ponder.

The law library director also needs to annually compile and justify a materials budget to the dean, managing partner, or a board of trustees.[63] To help justify rising costs, there are several resources to consult, including the *Price Index for Legal Publications*,[64] which allows the director to review serial costs by title or type of publication.[65] Other resources[66] that discuss price increases are also available.

POLICIES

A law library director is also expected to implement policies and procedures.[67] These policies are created in conjunction with the dean, law faculty, and librarians with the goal of seeing that the library functions efficiently and provides faculty and students with teaching, learning, research, and scholarship support. If technology or records management is included, these need to be satisfactorily handled as well.

In addition to crafting and creating law library policies, the director needs to enforce any institutional policies as well. Frequently there are institutional policies[68] covering various legal topics such as the Americans with Disabilities Act,[69] the Family Medical Leave Act,[70] Title VII prohibited employment practices,[71] overtime,[72] and workers' compensation.[73]

Finally, a director needs to be familiar with an institution's disciplinary actions, employee grievance process and procedure, and prescribed ethical standards of conduct as well as promotional, reclassification, and raise policies. These are all issues with which the director will eventually grapple.

TEACHING AND FACULTY RESPONSIBILITIES

According to the ABA Standard 603 for Approval of Law Schools, the law library director, except in extraordinary circumstances, is to hold a faculty tenure/tenure track slot.[74] As a practical matter, this means that the law library director must also satisfy service, teaching, and scholarship requirements in addition to seeing to the administration of the law library. Some law libraries also provide tenure for all librarians. If this is true for a library, librarians must also fulfill scholarship, teaching, and service requirements in addition to handling the day-to-day responsibilities of their jobs.

Service requirements can be fulfilled with law school, university, and law library committee work. Volunteer to serve on law school and university committees. Offer to serve law library organizations at the local, regional, and national levels.[75]

In terms of teaching, some law schools require that legal bibliography be taught by the law school librarians while others utilize legal research and writing instructors. In addition to teaching legal bibliography, law library directors usually teach an advanced legal research course.[76] Sometimes the director is given the opportunity to teach a substantive legal course. Seize this opportunity if it occurs. The director, working with other librarians, may also be responsible for training first-year students to use Westlaw and Lexis.

Scholarship is essential. Write about topics that are of interest. Maintain a notebook or electronic folder with articles that catch the eye. Volunteer to speak at meetings and turn those topics into articles. Offer to edit a newsletter. Opportunities to write will be plentiful.

CONCLUSION

The law library director wears many hats: colleague, administrator, technologist, teacher, and researcher. In order to effectively run a law library, the director needs leadership, management, budgeting, planning, teaching, researching, listening, writing, and technology skills.

To implement his or her vision of the library and technology center, the director needs to effectively market[77] the library's resources and services in order to attract patron attention and resources. Prepare brochures, handouts, manuals, newsletters, and bibliographies. Invite faculty and students to attend training and informational sessions. Draft an annual report,[78] sharing it with the dean, managing partner, or trustees. Invite feedback[79] from patrons. Listen. Ask what patrons want and need. Trying to accomplish these tasks and answer these questions creates law library directors.

NOTES

1. Kathleen M. Price, "Rededication Symposia: Evolving Technology and Law Library Planning: Technology and Law Library Administration," *St. John's Law Review* 70 (Winter 1996): 145–61.

2. Susan Westerberg Prager, "Expectations of the Twenty-First Century Law Library for the Support of Faculty Scholarship: Law Library and the Scholarly Mission," *Law Library Journal* 96 (Spring 2004): 513–24. See also "The Value of a Public Law Library," *State, Court, and County Law Libraries, American Association of Law Libraries*, www.aallnet.org/sis/sccll/pdfs/Sccllguide2.pdf (accessed January 2, 2006).

3. Carol Bredemeyer, "What Do Directors Do?" *Law Library Journal* 96 (Spring 2004): 317–23.

4. "Standards for Approval of Law Schools," *American Bar Association*, www.abanet.org/legaledu/standards/2005–2006standardsbook.pdf (accessed January 2, 2006).

5. James G. Miles, "Leaky Boundaries and the Decline of the Autonomous Law School Library," *Law Library Journal* 96 (Summer 2004): 387–423.

6. According to the American Association of Law Libraries' website, there are presently nineteen law library consortia. See "Consortia," *American Association of Law Libraries*, www.aallnet.org/chapter/consortia.asp (accessed January 2, 2006).

7. There appears to be widespread belief that all information is now accessible via the Internet. See Michelle Wu, "Why Print and Electronic Resources Are Essential to the Academic Law Library," *Law Library Journal* 97 (Spring 2005): 233–56. For a list of government information that is permanently available in electronic format, see "State by State Report on Permanent Public Access to Electronic

Government Information," *American Association of Law Libraries*, www.11 .georgetown.edu/aallwash/State_report.pdf (accessed January 2, 2006).

8. Florida's County Law Libraries are facing draconian budget cuts after the filing fee structure was changed. See Florida Statute '939.185 (2005). See also Robert Riger, "The Florida Saga Continues," *State, Court & County Law Libraries News* (Winter 2005): 7–8; and Meredith Hobbs and Greg Bluestein, "State Law Library May Be on House's Chopping Block," *Fulton County Daily Report*, March 29, 2005, p. 1 for information about closing the public's access to the State Law Library of Georgia.

9. Richard A. Danner, "What Are Law Libraries For?" *Law Librarian* 30, no. 4 (December 1999): 211–15.

10. A. B. Veaner, "Paradigm Lost, Paradigm Regained? A Persistent Personnel Issue in Academic Librarianship," *College and Research Librarianship* 55 (1994): 389.

11. Thomas Friedman, "How Companies Cope," in *The World Is Flat: A Brief History of the Twenty-First Century* (New York: Farrar, Strauss, & Giroux, 2005).

12. Virginia J. Kelsh, "The Law Library Mission Statement," *Law Library Journal* 97 (Spring 2005): 323–34.

13. Richard A. Danner, *Strategic Planning: A Law Library Management Tool for the 90s* (Dobbs Ferry, NY: Glanville, 1991), 10. See the later edition, Richard A. Danner, *Strategic Planning: A Law Library Management Tool for the 90s and Beyond*, 2nd ed. (Dobbs Ferry, NY: Glanville, 1997).

14. Danner, *Strategic Planning*, 1st ed., 12. See also Donald E. Riggs, *Strategic Planning for Library Managers* (Phoenix, AZ: Oryx Press, 1984).

15. Roy M. Mersky, "Administration of Academic Law Libraries," in *Law Librarianship: A Handbook*, ed. H. Mueller and P. Kehoe (Littleton, CO: Fred B. Rothman, 1983).

16. For a thorough discussion of library staff organization, see Martha J. Dragich, "Organizational Structures in Law Libraries: A Critique and Models for Change," in *Law Library Staff Organization and Administration*, ed. Martha J. Dragich and Peter C. Schnack (Littleton, CO: Fred B. Rothman, 1990).

17. Jonathan A. Franklin, "Why Let Them Go? Retaining Experienced Librarians by Creating Challenging Internal Career Paths: Introducing the Executive Librarian," *Law Library Journal* 88 (Summer 1996): 352–81.

18. Herb Cihak and Sue Burch, "Leading Your Law Library Staff: Four Principles of Effective Leaders," *Virginia Libraries* (July 1996): 18–19.

19. If the circulation manager reports to the head of public services, the manager should first address complaints or issues with the head rather than going around and above this position directly to either the associate director or director. Only if the circulation manager and head of public services are unable to resolve the issue should the conflict be taken to the next level.

20. Kenneth W. Thomas, "Conflict and Conflict Management: Reflections and Update," *Journal of Organizational Behavior* 13 (1992): 266–74.

21. Jean M. Holcomb, "Learning to Lead: Debunking Leadership Myths," *Law Library Journal* 97 (Spring 2005): 729–34 discussing Michael Feiner, *The Feiner Points of Leadership: The Fifty Basic Laws That Will Make People Want to Perform Better for You* (New York: Warner Books, 2004).

22. Holcomb, "Learning to Lead," 730–31. According to Holcomb, Feiner defines management skills as those involving planning, budgeting, problem solving, and resource allocation while leadership skills are defined as relationship building, coaching, feedback, and direct communications.

23. Janis Johnston, "Managing the Boss," *Law Library Journal* 89 (Winter 1997): 21–29.

24. Stephen R. Robbins, "Truth 36: Hearing Isn't Listening" and "Truth 63: Beware the Quick Fix" in *The Truth about Managing People . . . and Nothing but the Truth* (London: Prentice Hall 2003), 106–8, 195–97.

25. Rachel Singer Gordon, "Managing People: Communication and Leadership" in *The Accidental Library Manager* (Medford, NJ: Information Today, 2004). See also John Lubans Jr., "On Managing: Disagreeing Agreeably," *Library Administration & Management* 19 (2005): 36.

26. Gordon, *The Accidental Library Manager*, 135.

27. Robbins, *The Truth about Managing People*, 162–64.

28. Robbins, *The Truth about Managing People*, 13.

29. Examples of some electronic subscriptions that permit walk-in patron access include HeinOnline, LexisNexis Academic Universe, and Westlaw Patron Access.

30. Most academic law libraries have a library committee to which faculty are appointed. At some institutions, this committee is simply advisory while at other institutions, the committee actually makes policy. According to ABA Standard 602, "the dean and director of the law library, in consultation with the faculty of the law school, shall determine library policy." See "Standards for Approval of Law Schools," *American Bar Association*, www.abanet.org/legaledu/standards/chapter6.html (accessed January 23, 2006).

31. For a description of two deans' perspectives about the services to be provided by the law library in the twenty-first century, see Mary Kay Kane, "The Law School Library Director of the Twenty-First Century: What Deans Think: Technology and the Law School Librarian of the Twenty-First Century," *Law Library Journal* 95 (Summer 2003): 427–29; and John Makdisi, "The Law School Library Director of the Twenty-First Century: What Deans Think: Improving Education Delivery in the Twenty-First Century: The Vital Role of the Law Librarian," *Law Library Journal* 95 (Summer 2003): 431–34. For a faculty perspective, see also Robert M. Jarvis, "Expectations of the Twenty-First Century Law Library for the Support of Faculty Scholarship: What Law Professors Will Want from Law Librarians in the Twenty-First Century," *Law Library Journal* 96 (Summer 2004): 503–6.

32. "Current Index to Legal Periodicals," *Marian Gould Gallagher Law Library, University of Washington School of Law*, http://lib.law.washington.edu/cilp/cilp.html (accessed January 17, 2006).

33. "Jurist: Legal News and Research: Paper Chase," *University of Pittsburgh School of Law*, http://jurist.law.pitt.edu/paperchase (accessed January 17, 2006).

34. "Legal Blogs," *The Law Library & Technology Center of the Shepard Broad Law Center, Nova Southeastern University*, nsulaw.typepad.com/novalawcity (accessed September 9, 2006).

35. "Special Legal Bulletins," *Law Library & Technology Center*, http://www
.nsulaw.nova.edu/library_tech/library/services/bulletins.cfm (accessed September 9, 2006).

36. Sheri Lewis, "A Three-Tiered Approach to Faculty Services Librarianship in the Law School Environment, *Law Library Journal* 94 (Winter 2002): 89–100.

37. "Library Publications," *Law Library & Technology Center*, http://www.nsulaw
.nova.edu/library_tech/library/publications/index.cfm (accessed September 9, 2006).

38. For an excellent and concise work on developing legal research skills, see Nancy P. Johnson, Robert Berring, and Thomas Woxland, *Winning Research Skills*, 5th ed. (Eagan, MN: West, 2002).

39. Rhea Ballard-Thrower, "A Day in My Law Library Life: If Only the Desk Could Talk," *Law Library Journal* 89 (Spring 1997): 161.

40. With chat reference, a librarian responds to text messages received from a patron. The librarian is then able to push URLs/Web pages to the patron to respond to his or her query. QuestionPoint, by OCLC, is an example of a chat reference service. An additional benefit of this service is that it usually provides a transcript of the chat between the librarian and patron. "24/7 Reference Services," *QuestionPoint*, www.questionpoint.org/ (accessed January 18, 2006).

41. Marie Wallace, "Profile in Partnering: An Interview with Barbara K. Geier," *Law Librarians Resource Exchange (LLRX)*, www.llrx.com/extras/interview.htm (accessed January 17, 2006).

42. For a preview of technology services provided by law schools, see Colleen Gareau, "Top of the Technology Class," *National Jurist* 14, no. 4 (January 2005): 20–23. See also Billie Jo Kaufman, "Taking the Wireless Route at NSU," *Spectrum* (November 1999): 12–13.

43. For a discussion of the function of a VPN, see "VPN Setup," *Help Desk, Office of Information Technologies, Nova Southeastern University*, www.nova.edu/help/internet/vpn/index.html (accessed January 17, 2006).

44. Software that secures laptops for computerized exams include ExamSoft, www.examsoft.com, and Software Secure, www.marketwire.com/mw/fram_multimedia?prid'75214&attachid'158027 (accessed January 17, 2006).

45. For an interesting discussion of the GenX and millennial generations currently shaping and driving technology expectations, see John C. Beck and Mitchell Wade, *Got Game: How the Gamer Generation Is Reshaping Business Forever* (Boston, MA: Harvard Business School Press, 2004).

46. For an early discussion about how technology would influence law professors, see Peter W. Martin, "How New Information Technologies Will Change the Way Law Professors Do and Distribute Scholarship," *Law Library Journal* 83 (Fall 1991): 633–40.

47. I am referring to electronic serial subscriptions to products such as BNA, CCH, Matthew Bender, RIA, and others. See "Online Resources," *Law Library & Technology Center*, http://www.nsulaw.nova.edu/library_tech/library/resources/index.cfm (accessed September 9, 2006).

48. Richard A. Danner, "Redefining a Profession," *Law Library Journal* 90 (Summer 1998): 315–56.

49. See "Standards for Approval of Law Schools," ABA Standard 606c, *American Bar Association*, www.abanet.org/legaledu/standards/chapter6.html (accessed January 23, 2006).

50. To see examples of collection development policies, visit "Law Library Collection Development Policies," *American Association of Law Libraries*, www .aallnet.org/sis/tssis/committees/acquisitions/colldevpolicies/libtype.htm #academic (accessed January 17, 2006).

51. Diane Altimari, Brenna Louzin, Kermit Lowery, Lisa Smith-Butler, and Lorna Tang, "Negotiating License Agreements Reaccessed," paper presented at the annual meeting of the American Association of Law Libraries, Seattle, WA, July 2003, 91–122.

52. See "Electronic Greenslip," *William S. Hein Company*, www.heingreen slips.com/ (accessed January 18, 2006).

53. See "Gobi," *Yankee Peddler*, www.gobi2.com/ge2_Login.asp (accessed January 18, 2006).

54. Kendall F. Svengalis, *The Legal Information Buyer's Guide and Reference Manual* (Littleton, CO: F. B. Rothman, 1967–2005).

55. Oscar J. Miller and Mortimer D. Schwartz, compilers, *Recommended Publications for Legal Research* (Littleton, CO: F. B. Rothman, 1988–2005).

56. Other tools include *Law Books in Print Online*, ed. Merle Slyhoff (Dobbs Ferry, NY: Oceana, 2005); and American Association of Law Schools, *Law Books Recommended for Libraries* (Littleton, CO: F. B. Rothman, 1967–2005).

57. Jane Hammond, "Library Costs as Percentage of Law School Budgets," *Law Library Journal* 80 (Summer 1988): 439–45.

58. Kent Milunovich, "Issues in Law Library Acquisitions: An Analysis," *Law Library Journal* 91 (Spring 2000): 203–15.

59. Laura N. Gasaway, Bruce S. Johnson, and James M. Murray, *Law Library Management during Fiscal Austerity*, ed. Roy Mersky (Dobbs Ferry, NY: Glanville, 1992).

60. Aspen, BNA, CCH, Hein, Lexis, Matthew Bender, RIA, and West are vendors publishing a large number of legal serial titles.

61. ABA Standard 606 indicates that the law library is to provide a core collection of accessible materials through either ownership or reliable access. Interpretation 606-2 states that the collection should be an "appropriate mixture" of formats and further indicates that a "single format" may violate Standard 606. See "Standards for Approval of Law Schools," *American Bar Association*, www.abanet.org/legaledu/standards/chapter6.html (accessed January 23, 2006).

62. Several articles and bibliographies attempt to address these issues. See Paul E. Howard and Renee Y. Rastorfer, "Do We Still Need Books? A Selected Annotated Bibliography," *Law Library Journal* 97 (Spring 2005): 257–83. See also Penny Hazelton, "How Much of Your Print Collection Is Really on Westlaw or Lexis-Nexis?" *Legal Reference Services Quarterly*, no. 1 (1999): 3–22; and Gordon Russell, "Re-Engineering the Law Library Resources Today for Tomorrow's Users: A Response to How Much of Your Print Collection Is Really on Lexis-Nexis?" *Legal Reference Services Quarterly*, no. 2–3 (2002): 29.

63. See the appendix to this chapter as an example of a budget justification submitted to a law school dean. Ultimately, this justification will be submitted to a university president.

64. American Association of Law Libraries, *Price Index for Legal Publications*, 2nd ed. (Chicago, IL: AALL 2005).

65. Publications are divided into the following categories: academic and commercial periodicals, court reporters, citators, codes, digests, newsletters, loose-leaf services, and supplemented legal treatises. See "Price Index," *American Association of Law Libraries*, www.aallnet.org/members/price_index.asp (accessed January 24, 2006).

66. See "Serials Prices 2001–2005 with Projections for 2006," *Ebsco*, www.ebsco.com/home/printsubs/serialspriceporjec06.pdf (accessed January 22, 2006); and Brenda Dingley, "U.S. Periodical Price Index: U.S. Periodical Prices 2004," *American Library Association*, www.ala.org/ala/alctscontent/alctspubsbucket/alctresources/general/periodicalsindex/2004-PPI.pdf (accessed January 22, 2006).

67. At Nova Southeastern University, Shepard Broad Law Center, Law Library and Technology Center, we have several written policies, including a General Library Policy Manual, a Collection Development and Collection Retention Manual, an Information Services Policy Manual, a Technical Services Policy Manual, and an Emergency Procedures Manual. See also Carol Bredemeyer, "What Do Directors Do?" *Law Library Journal* 96 (Spring 2004): 317–23.

68. As an example, see the policies of Nova Southeastern University, at www.nova.edu/cwis/hrd/emphanbk (accessed January 22, 2006).

69. See the Americans with Disabilities Act of 1990, 42 U.S.C. '12101 (Washington, D.C.: Government Printing Office, 2000) and Supp.

70. See the Family and Medical Leave Act, 29 U.S.C. '207 (Washington, D.C.: Government Printing Office, 2000) and Supp.

71. See Equal Employment Opportunities Unlawful Employment Practices, 42 U.S.C. '2000e(2)–(3) (Washington, D.C.: Government Printing Office, 2000) and Supp.

72. See the Fair Labor Standards Act, 29 U.S.C. '207 (Washington, D.C.: Government Printing Office, 2000) and Supp.

73. Workers' compensation is based on state rather than federal law. As an example of a workers' compensation statute, see Florida Workers' Compensation, Florida Statute '440.01 (2005).

74. American Bar Association, *Standards for Approval of Law Schools*, www.abanet.org/legaledu/standards/chapter6.html (accessed January 29, 2006).

75. For a list of law library organizations, see "AALL Chapters," *American Association of Law Libraries*, www.aallnet.org/chapter/chapters.asp (accessed January 29, 2006).

76. Ann Hemmens, "Advanced Legal Research Courses: A Survey of ABA-Accredited Law Schools," *Law Library Journal* 94 (Spring 2002): 209–36.

77. Barbara Bintliff, ed., "Marketing Toolkit for Academic Law Libraries," *American Association of Law Libraries*, www.aallnet.org/sis/allsis/Toolkit/ (accessed January 26, 2006).

78. See Roy Mersky, "The Jamail Center for Legal Research 2000–2001 and 2001–2002," *University of Texas,* http://tarlton.law.utexas.edu/annrep/2002.pdf (accessed January 26, 2006); and "Cornell Law Library Highlights: July 2002—July 2003," *Cornell Law Library,* www.lawschool.cornell.edu/library/INFORMATION/ highlights/2003.htm (accessed January 26, 2006).

79. Dwight B. King Jr., "User Surveys: Libraries Ask, 'Hey, How Am I Doing?'" *Law Library Journal* 97 (Winter 2005): 103–15.

APPENDIX TO CHAPTER 3 BUDGET JUSTIFICATION INTEROFFICE MEMORANDUM

**Budget Justification
Interoffice Memorandum**

TO: Dean and Professor of Law

FROM: Director, Law Library

DATE: December 2005

SUBJECT: 2006–2007 Budget Requests and Justifications

Account   **Consultants/Academic**
$_____ is budgeted to support and maintain Amicus Attorney software, licenses, and a consultant for the clinic law office program. This software trains law students working in the clinics to work with automated billing, document production, and billable hours.

Account   **Contract Services**
$_____ is budgeted for payment to XYZ Enterprises. This organization provides loose-leaf filing and updating on a monthly basis for the law library. This includes filing for BNA, CCH, and other loose-leaf publications as well as updating pocket parts in other publications.

Account   **Equipment Rental**
$_____ is budgeted to maintain office copiers and fax machines and provide servicing of the plants in the law library.

Account   **Supplies/Classroom**
$_____ is budgeted for maintaining erasers, whiteboards, and markers for study rooms as well as copying and any other related classroom expense when librarians provide special lectures for classes. Examples of special classes for students include *Locating Business Information Resources* for the business clinic, *Jump Start Your Clerkship*, and *Locating Ethics Resources*. Librarians also provide a research series for first-year students known as *Glad You Asked* and a series for faculty known as *Faculty Informs*. Librarians also handle student Westlaw and Lexis training, requiring supplies for these sessions as well.

Account   **Supplies/Office**
$_____ is budgeted for office supplies, copying, and printing for a staff of __ and approximately 1,000 students.

Account   **Supplies/Computer**
$_____ is budgeted to purchase various essential computer supplies such as disk drives, mice, batteries, keyboards, and power cords. These replace lost and/or broken faculty staff items.

Account   **Audio Visual Supplies**
$_____ is budgeted for power cords, tripods, video tapes, and CDs for the AV office, which frequently tapes professors' classes and is taping ___ sessions on a weekly basis. Special programs and events, such as the _____ Series, are also taped.

Account   **Supplies/Photocopy**
$_____ is budgeted to pay for copying charges incurred by the law library when requesting interlibrary loans from other libraries. With several new faculty members who are writing to attain tenure, we are using interlibrary loans more frequently.

Account   **Internal/Copying**
$_____ is budgeted to pay for copying by the University Copy Center in the event that the law library is unable to complete a copying project on time.

Account   **Internal/Printing**
$_____ is budgeted for printing of business cards for law library staff as well as library stationery by University Publications.

Account   **Repair and Maintenance**
$_____ is budgeted for repairing and maintaining various library equipment, including the fiche reader machine.

Account   **Equipment Service and Repair**
$_____ is budgeted for servicing the 3M law library entry gates as well as the Helix Universal Server upgrades and maintenance. This sum also includes a service contract for the compact shelving located on the _____ floor. The compact shelving maintenance contracts cost approximately $_____ last year. These agreements are essential as the cost to actually repair would be considerably more. This service is used frequently.

Account   **Phone/Fax Expense**
$_____ is budgeted to maintain ___ Nextel phones for _____ staff that need both a cell phone as well as a walkie-talkie to effectively communicate with each other both on- and off-site. It also includes three Blackberrys for the _____ in order to remain in contact with the office when traveling for business.

Account   **Postage**
$_____ is budgeted for law library postage expense.

Account   **Marketing/Advertising**
$_____ is budgeted to help promote the law library in various sponsored events such as the *AALL Excellence in Marketing Award* and *West's National Legal Research Teach In.*

Account   **Nonmarket/Advertising**
$_____ is budgeted to advertise vacant positions within the law library.

Account   **Computer Network**
$_____ is budgeted for computer network expenses. This includes monies paid to CompuServe, Solinet, and vendors for electronic resources. This is a substantial increase in this

account as we are beginning to pull away from print resources and are trying to acquire more electronic resources. To accomplish this, we have canceled several print titles and tried to hold the print serials budget (9030) at the same amount even though serials are increasing at a rate of 8 percent for 2005.

From this account, electronic resources for other departments are purchased, including:

$1,000.00 to CALI for Online Consortia membership;
$3,200.00 to West for a Job/Career database;
$3,000.00 for Live Chat software shared among _____ programs.

The law library's mission is to provide students with 24/7 access at any time, in any place. To accomplish this goal, we purchase a variety of electronic resources that allow students to dial up from home or the office at 2:00 a.m. and use library resources. Electronic resources allow us to serve our distance students in the _____ programs. Off-site JD students, spending a semester in another city, state, or country for their clinic experience, are also well and easily served with electronic resources.

Electronic resources help us train students for the changing world of legal practice that they will be entering where information is compiled, processed, and retrieved in electronic formats that allow data to be manipulated.

Electronic resources preserve shelf space, which is needed for the National Reporter Series, state codes, and case-finding tools, which are still maintained in print copy. Presently our shelves are at 68 percent capacity, and we want to conserve as much of this space as is possible for print copy items mandated by the ABA. Also, electronic resources allowing for simultaneous users permit us to serve multiple students at the same time whereas print copies serve only one student at a time.

Presently our electronic resources include (see also www.nsulaw.nova.edu/library/resources.cfm#research):

BNA Online, Selected Databases
CALI
Carilaw
CIS Congressional Indexes
Chronicle of Higher Education
Daily Business Review
Disability Compliance for Higher Education
Environmental Law Reporter
GDCS Autographics (electronic index to U.S. government
    documents)
HeinOnline
Journal of Refugee Studies
Law Trio Database
Lexis
LLMC Digital
LoisLaw
Matthew Bender
Oxford English Dictionary
RIA Checkpoint
Westlaw
UN Access
U.S. Congressional Serial Set

With some of the above titles, annual access (Westlaw
and Lexis come readily to mind) is being purchased
while with others, the electronic title itself, with an annual maintenance fee, is being purchased. Recently the
trend has been to allow the purchase of an electronic title
for a substantial sum and then require only an annual
maintenance fee. Recent electronic titles in this category
that would be useful scholarship additions to our collection include:

Gale/Thomson *Making of Modern Law* (See www.gale
    .com/tlist/moml.pdf for a complete title list.)
Gale/Thomson *Supreme Court Records and Briefs 1832–1978*
Public Documents Masterfile (See www.nellco.org/
    trial_documents/pdm%20brochure.pdf for more infor-
    mation about this resource.)
Wilson's Index to Legal Periodicals Restrospective: 1918–1981

Information about annual pricing increases for serials/periodicals in both print and electronic formats can be found at AALL's Price Index site at www.aallnet.org/members/price_index.asp.

Account   **Conference Travel**
$_____ is budgeted to allow _____ professionals to attend various conferences throughout the United States, speaking, publishing, and promoting _____. Conferences attended include AALL (American Association of Law Libraries), AALS (American Association of Law Schools), ABA Tech Show, Bricks, and Bytes, CALI (Computer Assisted Legal Instruction), Computers In Libraries, IUG (Innovative Users Group), SEAALL (Southeastern American Association of Law Libraries), and _____ ALL (_____ Association of Law Libraries). _____ paraprofessionals are also encouraged to attend local workshops to improve skills.

Account   **Administrative Travel**
$_____ is budgeted to allow the _____ to attend _____ Law Library Director meetings throughout the state as well as to attend committee meetings for various committees at the national and regional level. This sum also includes expenses of the _____ for traveling to conferences. Job candidates' travel expenses are also paid from this account.

Account   **Dues/Memberships**
$_____ is budgeted to pay the dues and memberships of _____professional staff members. Dues are paid to various organizations, including AALL, Attorney's Title Insurance Fund, _____ County Library Association, _____ Bar Association, IALL, IUG, NELLCO, SFALL, and SEALL.

Account   **Promotional**
$_____ is budgeted to provide luncheons and other events, marketing the law library and its services to other organizations and individuals. These include functions such as *Glad You Asked*, *Faculty Informs*, and *Jumpstart Your Summer Clerkship*.

Account   **Books**
$_____ is budgeted for the purchase of books in electronic, fiche, and print formats. This amount includes requests

from professors as well as collection development done by librarians with various tools, including Hein's green slips, Gobi Alerts, as well as *Recommended Legal Research Publications*. As new professors join the faculty and produce more research, the law library will increase its collection efforts to support expanded faculty research. Collection for new programs and courses _____ is also a necessity as are ongoing collection efforts for existing programs.

Account   **CD-ROMs**
$_____ is budgeted to create and purchase CDs for the law library _____ training project. Instructional laptop CDs are created and distributed to students. This account also includes pricing for software to be purchased in ASCIII format for Professor _____ to accommodate his needs.

Account   **Replacements**
$_____ has been budgeted to replace lost and/or damaged materials held by the law library.

Account   **Subscriptions**
$_____ has been budgeted to continue law library serial subscriptions.
Serials continue to be one of the largest expenses in any law library, and one of the most difficult to control. Since 1998, publishers have increased serial prices between 1.93 percent to 21.69 percent, depending upon the type of serial and year. Double-digit increases in serials are the norm for the 1998–2004 time frame. (See *AALL Price Index for Legal Publications*, 2nd ed., at www.aallnet.org/members/price_index.asp, which contains charts that list serial increases by publication type and year.) Since we began tracking this data in 2002, budget increases have been constant. To contain costs in this area, duplicate copies of the National Reporter System have been canceled so that we now hold only one copy of items in the National Reporter System. This copy allows us to teach first-year law students legal research of primary sources of law as well as comply with ABA holdings requirements.
    We review serials on an ongoing basis and have canceled serials that cost $_____ for the 2004–2005 year. In order to contain costs, ongoing reviews of serials are conducted on an annual basis. Cancellations continue with limited

cancellations of duplicative digest coverage. Approximately $_____ worth of digests were cut for the 2005–2006 budget year. Serials are reviewed on an annual basis, and decisions are made to cut as appropriate.

This amount includes all of the West National Reporter Series including *Supreme Court Reporter, U.S. Lawyer's Edition, Supreme Court Reports, Federal Supplement, Federal Reporter*, regional reporters, digests, state statutes, BNA & CCH print loose leafs as well as other continuations, such as law reviews for all law schools. Print Shepard's for Florida is also included in this. Thus this account provides for the primary sources of American law as well as case-finding tools, case updating tools, and legal treatises, loose leafs and encyclopedias. International serial material is also included.

Account   **Binding**

$_____ has been budgeted to continue binding over 200 annual law review subscriptions.

Total Requested $_____

cc: Budget Dean

Chapter 4

Public Services

Anne Klinefelter

Public services provide the face of the law library. Public services staff connect with library users both at the moment of need and in more anticipatory ways.[1] For many law librarians, public services is the most exhilarating, the most interesting, and sometimes the most frustrating role in the library, all because the library user drives the work. Although public services includes organizational, instructional, promotional, evaluative, and planning activities to meet anticipated library users' needs, much of public services is reactive, and the librarian or library support staff member must be ready to respond to all sorts of questions and requests.

"What do you mean I never returned that book?"

"I'm going to take this to my office. . . ."

"Can I come in when the library is closed?"

"I need a form for service of process in Mexico."

"Are you a lawyer?"

"I need corporate parent institution information on this company. And I need a conflicts check."

"The library is missing *Wood on Fire Insurance*—can you get it for me by tomorrow morning?"

"Can you give me a refund from the photocopier? How does the scanner work?"

"There was a Senate hearing today on this bill—can you get me a transcript by tomorrow?"

The background required for law library public services may include specialized knowledge of legal research tools and techniques or training with library systems ranging in complexity from replacing paper in the photocopier to manipulating an integrated online system. Interpersonal skills are invaluable, and public services staff benefit from both a natural enthusiasm for interaction and ongoing training in areas such as accommodating differing learning styles, using the reference interview to fully understand specific users' needs, handling complaints, and marketing the services of the library.

The public services umbrella can cover circulation, reference, and interlibrary loan (ILL) functions and present a variety of special issues. Public services are informed by users' needs and shaped by the other services in the library, such as cataloging, collection development, and information technology (IT) services. In smaller law libraries, one or two library employees may provide the full array of library services, so that public services are just one aspect of each library staff member's responsibilities. In larger law libraries, more specialization often separates public services from technical services, IT services, and administration.

The type of library and parent institution dictates the composition and scope of public services. Law libraries or legal information centers are present in private environments such as law firms and corporations as well as in governmental institutions ranging from the Law Library of Congress to state, court, and county institutions. Almost all law schools have libraries dedicated to supporting legal education, and public libraries usually have a law collection. Prisons sometimes have libraries, and various other law libraries, particularly those serving the public, provide document delivery services to prisoners.

The types of services can vary greatly, depending on the type of law library. In a larger law firm library, as in a larger academic law library, librarians may need specialized law backgrounds to support the research needs of busy attorneys or professors focused on litigation, tax, or foreign and international law. The level of service in different libraries varies to meet the needs of the parent institution. Law firm librarians may do the research for the attorney, while academic law librarians may recommend tools and strategies to the inquiring professor or law student. In court libraries, public services personnel address needs ranging from research for a judge to providing assistance to the litigant representing herself. In recent years, technology has had a great impact on law libraries, and different types of libraries have responded differently. In law firms, the librarian may have an entirely different job title, such as information resources manager, to align himself or herself with a shift toward electronic resources and away from a central location for research. In law firms, the information resources manager may be involved in checking for conflicts of interest in representing multiple clients, the management of the law firm's internal records, the creation of a knowledge management system, and monitoring the continuing legal education compliance of the attorneys. In court libraries, the public services librarian may see fewer attorneys than in years before legal databases provided reasonably priced access to huge amounts of legal materials. Academic law librarians in public services are teaching advanced legal research courses that help law students learn methods for comparing and evaluating research options that are likely to change rapidly throughout the students' careers as lawyers.

Whatever the type of law library, librarians and other library employees who perform public services create the public image of the library, and their work is likely to be the source of most of the library's compliments and, sometimes, complaints. Because of the interactive nature of most of public services, creativity, spontaneity, patience, and judgment can be as important as specialized training and knowledge. Experience, a commitment to service, flexibility, and a genuine interest in working with other people can contribute to the success of the librarian performing public services work. While some strategies for interaction can be taught, and knowledge of research options can always be expanded, a positive outlook is a powerful tool for overcoming barriers in the research process and for diffusing library users' frustration.

CIRCULATION DEPARTMENT

The circulation function of the law library is generally located at the central service point and is where library users come to check out materials. This area, sometimes called access services, is the place where all sorts of questions and comments are directed. This public service point is where many library users form their opinions about the library and where they share their opinions about the library and its services, so the circulation staff must be adept at using systems, applying policies, and redirecting requests and comments as appropriate. The public relations aspect of circulation work is critical, as the respect and appreciation users feel for the circulation staff is generally projected onto the entire library.

The Circulation System

In a larger library, an integrated online system (ILS) is a standard tool for identifying, locating, and checking out materials from the law library collection. This system may be used for circulation, reserve, and ILL. Such systems are complex, supporting or thwarting specific services, depending on both the system's capabilities and on the librarian's facility in using the system. A thorough understanding of the ILS is extremely useful to access services staff. In a smaller library, the circulation system may be more casual, and the librarian or library staff member may draw on a familiarity with the library users and their research interests to track down

missing items. So, when the user says, "I'm going to take this to my office
. . . " the circulation staff member may appropriately either require the
user to check out the material or may just thank the user and make a quick
note of who and what are leaving together—the difference determined
from the customs and needs of the institution. Whatever the level of technology, though, the circulation system is critical for maintaining order
and control over the library collection.

In law firm and corporate law libraries, a greater proportion of the library "collection" may be electronic, and circulation of books is less important than managing access to databases. In such settings, space for the
library is often limited, and attorneys use their own offices or other remote sites to do research from desktops or laptops, using centrally supported databases and websites. In these private law libraries, users drive
the system, and if a treatise is in high demand, the librarian is more likely
to purchase additional copies than to try to enforce shorter circulation periods. Some academic law libraries accommodate faculty in this way
when budgets allow.

Reserves, Stack Maintenance, and Special Collections

Some law libraries maintain a reserve collection for high-use items that
have limited circulation, and this function is often tied to circulation. The
reserve collection may be open to users for browsing or limited to access
by library staff. Stack maintenance, including loose-leaf filing and shelving, may also be handled by the circulation staff. As electronic resources
replace loose-leaf and other print materials in law libraries, the staffing
needs shift from filing and shelving to Web page, licensing, and computer
systems management—responsibilities that may reside in any number of
areas in a large law library.

The arrangement of the law library collection usually follows local cus-
tom, and the isolation of some materials reflects that library's users' interests. In academic law libraries, the Library of Congress cataloging
scheme tends to direct the arrangement of materials. In other libraries,
such a sophisticated system is not as important, since primary law publications are identifiable by jurisdiction and a date-related sequential serial
format. Areas of specialization, such as tax and foreign and international
law, are sometimes shelved separately. In academic law libraries, rare materials and copies of faculty members' publications may be kept in a special collection space with improved climate control and limited access.

REFERENCE DEPARTMENT

Law library reference services help library users locate legal information,
both at the moment of need and in anticipation of that moment of need.

While circulation staff draw on their connections with library catalog and sometimes stack maintenance experience to locate a known item, the reference staff are trained to identify materials and research strategies on a particular topic regardless of whether the library collection contains the needed material. This service requires a solid understanding of legal research options and the law itself. Many larger law libraries, particularly academic law libraries, require the reference librarians to hold both the graduate library degree and a law degree, so that the librarians can speak the same language as law professors and law students. A number of services grow out of reference and vary depending on the type of library and priority given to the particular category of library user.

The Reference Interview

The reference interview is a classic component of reference service. Good interview techniques help the librarian assist the library user. Frequently, questions that come to the reference librarian appear to be straightforward, such as "Where can I find the *Encyclopedia of Associations*?" If this resource is unavailable, the librarian might suggest other tools that contain the information the user is seeking. The librarian could follow up and ask whether the user is looking for a specific association. The answer to this question and subsequent dialogue could lead the user to a website for a particular association or to another resource with broad coverage of this association's interest. If the question came by telephone, the librarian might ask whether the researcher had access to a computer and to the Internet before suggesting alternatives.

A fine line exists between invading the privacy of the library user and gaining enough information to help him or her locate the needed information. The public services provider should take care not to respond simply, "We don't have the *Encyclopedia of Associations*," since the expressed user's need may mask a different goal. The researcher needs to feel comfortable knowing that the librarian is offering a service, not collecting personal information. There is a fine line between the follow-up questions, "Why do you want to know about this association?" and "What type of information on this association do you need?"

In the busy law firm or corporate environment, the reference librarian should be especially careful to get a full description of the information or item sought. These reference questions are often requests for the delivery of material or information rather than advice on research strategies. Deadlines and cost may be important pieces of information that shape the librarian's response. In the court library, reference librarians likely have the same need to clarify requests from judges. Reference librarians in academic libraries may also provide this level of service to law professors, and sometimes the reference interview is an ongoing process during the librarian's research. At times, discoveries lead to the need for further

clarification from the attorney, judge, or professor, and the request is re-
fined in response to uncovered information. When the information is elu-
sive and the librarian feels confident that the answer does not exist, the
professor or attorney should be consulted as quickly as possible to ask if
he or she would like the next best thing. When an attorney says, "What
do you mean there is no case on point in Florida?" the librarian might offer to find a case on the topic in a neighboring state. In some situations,
the answer may exist but only for a price, so the clarification needed is
how much can be spent on obtaining the information.

The form of communication also influences the reference interview. A
face-to-face discussion includes body language and the opportunity for
immediate back-and-forth discussion. Of course, the researcher may return for further explanation after confronting the offered resources, and
the librarian may need to follow up with the researcher as further questions develop. Telephone, e-mail, and chat reference are also options with
varying advantages and disadvantages. E-mail and chat reference, for example, provide full typed descriptions that can be easier to comprehend
than communications in conversation in person or by telephone.

Specialized Knowledge

Knowledge of legal research techniques is the basic tool that enables a
law librarian to provide a high level of reference services. In many academic law libraries and sometimes in other types of law libraries, the law
degree is required of reference librarians. The processes of legal research
and legal analysis inform each other, and a full legal education strength-
ens the reference librarian's ability to engage fully in these processes to
help users develop a research strategy or, if appropriate, to help the library user by performing legal research.

At all times, the lawyer must work with the most current information
because to do otherwise is to fail to represent the client properly and
could even be malpractice. Given the importance of legal authority in the
practice of law, legal research cannot be treated casually. Entire courses
address legal analysis and legal research, and entire books and sets of
books provide guidance on legal bibliography and legal research strategies. As publishers make more legal information available, attorneys and
other legal researchers rely on reference librarians to keep current so they
can compete in the adversarial legal system. For example, state administrative codes, state legislative history, and municipal codes are now much
more accessible than they were a decade ago. E-mail-based newsletters
covering particular legal topics are now fast replacing print options for
getting updates on a legal topic. Reference librarians can keep track of and
evaluate legal research options to support attorneys, judges, academic re-

searchers, and the general public. With this expertise, the reference librarian can recommend new tools and strategies to meet the needs of particular library users, such as attorneys in the law firm, judges in the court library, and professors in the law school library.

In addition to changes in legal publishing, reference librarians are well advised to keep current with major changes and certain trends in the law. For example, when a major piece of legislation is passed, reference librarians could produce or acquire key legislative history documents as well as key commentary and alert attorneys or professors working in this area. Legal trends such as the increase in administrative law and use of social science data also increase the types of resources reference librarians should be comfortable using.

Beyond ongoing learning about general legal research and trends in the law, the reference librarian may need to develop an expertise in a particular area of law and/or to have foreign language skills. For example, legal reference librarians may need to be savvy about medical or business research, or they may need to have a sophisticated understanding of patent or tax law research. In a law firm doing plaintiff or business work, a reference librarian may do a significant amount of business-related research such as identifying a corporate parent or acquiring copies of corporate filings. The trend toward globalization has made foreign and international law research an important area of specialization as well. Some larger law firms and law schools employ law librarians who have foreign language skills. Law librarians with expertise in a special area serve as resources for their colleagues as well as for the library users they serve through their own library. Many publish research guides in journals or on library websites, and some publish chapters or books on specialized legal research. Law library e-mail discussion lists are also a resource where experts share their knowledge in response to questions. When an attorney asks, "Where can I find a form for service of process in Mexico?" the reference librarian may draw on his own experience and knowledge, consult a research guide, or seek advice from colleagues with special expertise.

Law librarians build their understanding of legal research and of the law through formal education, professional development workshops, conferences, law and library publications, and through networking and collegial support.

Practicing Law and the *Pro Se* Patron

Law librarians in state, court, and county libraries and many academic libraries include service to the general public in their missions. This noble effort helps make the law accessible to all and helps to justify the expenditure of tax funds to support the library. The law librarian has special concerns in serving this group because of the risk of crossing the line from library assistance to practicing law. Numerous articles have debated the nature of this risk. While the danger may be overstated, reference librarians should take care not to offer legal advice, as this is the province of the licensed and practicing attorney. Reference librarians who have law degrees and who are licensed to practice law in the state in which they work may need to be particularly cautious in establishing that their services are offered as a librarian, not as a free attorney. After three years of law school and perhaps stressful bar examination experience, the licensed JD holder may be tempted to assert these qualifications at the reference desk. When a library user asks, "Are you a lawyer?" the proper response may be, "I am a librarian, and I do have a legal education that will help me help you use the library resources. What are you looking for?"

The library user who is representing herself in some legal matter or in litigation is referred to by courts as the *pro se* litigant. In law libraries the *pro se* patron may be fairly self-sufficient or may ask for a great deal of help. The reference librarian should take care not to interpret the law, only to provide instruction on finding legal information. The distinction can be quite tricky if a *pro se* litigant knows little about the law. Court opinions and court rules, legislation, administrative law, and persuasive secondary sources in federal and state jurisdictions may be needed, as might municipal law or institutional policies. Even identifying the relevant area of law for the patron could constitute legal advice, so the reference librarian must be cautious. Some libraries outline the boundaries of their services in prominent locations in the library and on the library's website in order to avoid misunderstandings and to discourage library users from attempting to obtain free legal advice from a law librarian.

Levels of Service

All law libraries have some policies, written or unwritten, about levels of service offered to different library users or categories of users. If the library has a fairly restricted community of users to support, the levels of support may be more a matter of user preferences than actual library policy. Academic and court libraries are likely to have the most stratified user communities. Law school libraries tend to provide a higher level of support to law faculty, and court libraries may devote most of their attention to delivering information to judges. Reference librarians may do fairly extensive research for law professors, either through a system of library-supervised law student research assistants or by the reference librarians themselves. Academic research for professors may focus on strictly legal points or might include historical or other law-related points such as, "What is the source of the phrase 'the devil is in the details?'"

In some situations, teaching the researcher rather than delivering the answer is the better approach. In academic law libraries, law students and other students are generally helped in this way, because research instruction is part of their legal education. Teaching at the point of need provides a golden opportunity to convey research methods when the student is most likely to internalize and remember the strategy. Reference librarians delight in sharing stories of the teachable moment, that time when the researcher is truly receptive to learning. Law firm librarians make judgment calls about when the moment is right for teaching and when simply delivering the answer is most helpful. Some attorneys are interested in learning about new resources, while others are content to have material retrieved for them. Personality, comfort with the resource format, and the time pressure of the moment are all factors that play into the attorneys' and other researchers' receptivity to instruction.

Levels of service are determined not just during the reference service interaction but also in the purchase and negotiation of electronic resources. In some large law firms, the cost of licensing a particular tax resource for the entire firm would be prohibitive, whereas licensing it only for the tax group is more feasible and meets the most important needs in the firm. Similarly, in law school libraries, some electronic resources are marketed only to law schools to the exclusion of faculty and students in other campus programs. At many universities, when a journalism student approaches the law reference librarian and asks for access to Westlaw, the librarian is likely to have to apologize and explain that this service is available only to current law students and faculty at the institution. When an attorney or student is excluded from access in these ways, the reference librarian should attempt to gain a limited-time exception for access or should provide guidance in finding alternative resources.

Technology

Technology continues to open the way for a variety of information delivery options that impact the method of providing reference services if not the very role of the reference librarian. The shift away from print toward electronic resources means that reference librarians have increased in importance as evaluators of options and as teachers of research methods. In some institutions, the reference librarian is increasing her publishing role, creating websites with research guides, and even providing feeds of breaking news from other sources.

Library users communicate with reference librarians through an ever-expanding list of options, moving beyond face-to-face and telephone conversations to e-mail reference, instant messaging, and blogs. Each form has advantages and disadvantages, and user groups are not consistent in their willingness to embrace each new option. Reference librarians find that they have many different delivery methods for their services, and they are continually reinventing the options in order to take advantage of the changing technology. Some law libraries attempt to offer off-hours reference service by providing their librarians with cell phones or by scheduling librarians to participate in deadline-sensitive projects and litigation. This option is more likely to be an expectation of law firm librarians where deadlines dominate.

Law firm librarians are using technology as a vehicle for expanding their job descriptions to include internal document management, knowledge management and other research activities such as checking to make sure a new client is not an adversary of another existing client, client development, and competitive intelligence using public records. Client development could mean identifying potential clients based on the firm's areas of expertise or identifying additional areas of legal advice that the firm might provide to an existing client, based on in-depth research about the client. Competitive intelligence could mean finding out more about competitor law firms, based on public records.

Marketing, Teaching, and Breaking New Ground

Law firm librarians are leading the way into new information management areas. Many lawyers and law librarians see the legal profession moving more toward a business model, where a greater percentage of billing is based on projects rather than by hourly rates and where both clients and attorneys shift allegiances from one firm to another much more than in the past. Law librarians are promoting themselves as information managers and simply as managers, taking on additional administrative and management roles as the law firm becomes more businesslike.

Law school librarians are moving into new roles as well. IT support is based out of the law library in a growing number of law schools, and academic law librarians are also teaching more courses on legal research, particularly advanced legal research courses. In a number of law schools, law librarians with law degrees are also teaching a wide range of substantive law courses and serving on law school committees. Some academic law librarians are even tapped for interim appointments as assistant and associate deans and even as deans.

Publicly funded state, court, and county law libraries increasingly promote their services to citizens and to key decision makers who have become convinced that such libraries may not be necessary because "it is all on the Web." As more legal information becomes available for free from websites, law librarians find that they must remind key administrators as well as the general public that the vast majority of key legal materials are only available in print, microform, or subscription-based electronic sources. Law librarians also promote their services in making available and helping researchers use the vast array of secondary sources and annotated primary resources that are only available by purchase.

In all settings, the law reference librarian is monitoring the needs of users and the opportunities to shift and expand information management services.

INTERLIBRARY LOAN AND OTHER COOPERATIVE AGREEMENTS

Interlibrary Loan and Document Retrieval

Interlibrary loan (ILL) is sometimes linked to circulation and sometimes to reference. It is a service based on the kindness of other libraries. Many law libraries have agreements with other libraries to share materials with or without fees for the service. When a library does not own a title that one of its users wants to use, that library sends a request to other libraries to borrow the material to meet the local user's needs. ILL developed during a time when libraries were based on books, journals, microform, and other physical types of collections. In recent years, electronic resources replaced some of these materials, and ILL adjusted. The ILL staff now check not only the library catalog to make sure requested material is not in the collection, they also check the library's electronic journal indexes and search the library's databases for the requested material. This initial search of the local resources prevents the library from using ILL except when the library does not have access or when the material is already in use by another library user.

Licenses

As law libraries replace print materials with electronic options, ILL can become difficult. While copyright law allows for legally owned copies of copyrighted material to be shared through limited ILL photocopy services, publishers generally avoid copyright law by selling access to electronic databases that require libraries to agree to license contracts governing the use of these materials. Often, interlibrary lending is not permitted under the publisher's license agreement. As another chapter ("Collection Development, Licensing, and Acquisitions") outlines, librarians should anticipate this restriction on use and negotiate for ILL use consistent with copyright law.

Universities, Consortia, and Informal Sharing

Law libraries may participate in a variety of collaborative efforts that include ILL agreements. These groups may agree to share resources and may even agree to share without a fee. In the academic law library, the most common sharing is among libraries on the same campus, where sharing may include the electronic catalog and borrowing privileges for all law school and other university library users. In some academic law libraries, the law professors are provided a document retrieval service that delivers campus library materials to the faculty member. Regional law library consortia provide varying levels of collaborative support, including ILL, to their members. Chapter 10, "The World of Library Consortia," provides an in-depth view of these arrangements.

Other types of cooperation that affect ILL may be formal or informal. Law firm librarians geographically or institutionally linked may simply telephone each other to borrow needed materials, and these services may draw on institutional traditions or on a collegial relationship between the librarians at each firm.

From ILL to Document Retrieval to Collection Development

ILL is a library service that can support and draw on several other library services, such as collection development, circulation, and reference. In a small library, it is easier to make the connection between an ILL request, a missing item, and collection development, because only a few staff members or even only one staff member is involved. In a larger law library, communication among staff and even departments may be required to make these connections. The ILL staff should consider forwarding selected or all ILL requests to the librarian who selects materials for purchase, particularly if the material is new and can be obtained quickly. Similarly, if the material is supposed to be in the library but is missing from the collection, the ILL staff member should alert other librarians who might search for the missing item, adjust the catalog record, and/or purchase a replacement. Ideally, when a library user says, "The library is missing *Wood on Fire Insurance*; can you get it for me?" the ILL staff member will initiate a missing book search, consider purchase of a replacement copy, and conduct an ILL search for a lender.

Some ILL requests may trigger the purchase of specialized material that should be obtained through ILL or purchased just for the interested library user rather than for the library collection. Such materials might be documents held by a government agency but not published or posted electronically. If the library has a large and specialized staff, the task of locating this material might be forwarded to a reference librarian.

LIBRARY HOURS/ACCESS

For many law libraries, the circulation department is the area responsible for opening and closing the library, and reflects the sense that the circulation function is the most basic and most essential function of a library. Some libraries, however, allow particular users or categories of users to gain access to the library after hours. This arrangement serves attorneys working late in the law firm or professors or law students working late in the law school. Such a practice may be full time or only in response to limited-time requests. After-hours access presents an added challenge to the circulation staff charged with keeping order and control over the library inventory. Unless systems are available for users to check out materials themselves, the library may lose track of items that after-hours users take from the library. Nevertheless, libraries may find that this loss is worth the expense to meet users' needs and to serve the institution properly. So, when the law review student facing a deadline asks, "Is the library open Friday after Thanksgiving? Can I come in when the library is closed?" a supervising librarian in the law school library might provide a key to this student to use during the holiday.

Of course, electronic resources are generally available around the clock and do not require a physical library to be open to provide access. If the library space itself is limited, library hours become less defining, and public services in general shift away from circulation services.

POLICIES

Policies used for circulation and reserve support guidelines that benefit library users and library staff alike. Length of circulation periods, renewal options, and overdue and replacement fines forewarn library users of their obligations and support library staff who interact with users. Consistency in applying the policy provides predictability and fairness and helps the circulation staff depersonalize any frustrations or complaints of users. On the other hand, having some flexibility can be important in serving the larger library goals. A law firm librarian who attempts to penalize a productive partner for losing a volume of a treatise will discover that the library policies have unwritten gaps to accommodate such lapses.

Like circulation, reference benefits from having clear written policies with the ability to make exceptions to serve the greater good of the institution. Policies in reference may include levels of service, limitations on service, and hours of service. Other policies may address expectations of library users to help maintain an environment conducive to research and preservation of library materials. Many libraries, either on their own or in conjunction with an IT person or department, have policies outlining permissible and sometimes impermissible uses of the computers and of the Internet. Law libraries are also likely to include in their policies the confidentiality of library research. In law firms and court libraries, the policy may be a component of protecting the attorney-client confidentiality, an important obligation of the attorney to the client. In law school libraries and in public libraries, state laws require the library to maintain the confidentiality of circulation records and other information about users' research.

ILL also benefits greatly from written policies. The lending function is very like circulation, so loan periods, as well as fines or fees for late or missing items, should be incorporated into posted policies for the library. In addition, the cost for the service should be outlined, and any stratification of user groups, such as consortia members, public libraries, law firms, and so forth, should be detailed. Having a policy, of course, does not mean exceptions are unwise. When a borrowing library reports that its library user has lost an ILL-loaned book, the lending library should consider the past behavior of the borrowing library before applying a lost book fee. Libraries that do each other favors express goodwill with a flexible approach to policy enforcement. Additionally, strict adherence to circulation, reserve, and ILL policies is more common in larger libraries because it is difficult to train a large staff to make such judgments while ensuring fairness. Training programs and manuals cannot substitute for experience and a broader perspective on the library's goals. In larger settings, an appeals process to the access services librarian or some other supervisor can be the best solution to a problem at circulation, reserve, or ILL.

SHAPING THE PHYSICAL ENVIRONMENT

The law library's physical environment can both shape and reflect library use. Those served by the library may be inside the library facility or may be remote, using electronic resources at any time of day or asking for print materials to be delivered. Many law libraries struggle to retain their space given the shift toward electronic materials. The popular misconception that legal information is all on the free Internet puts the law library on the defensive as administrators in the firm, court, or law school eye library space to meet other space needs. The best offense is to maintain an attractive, comfortable space that provides amenities appropriate for most of the users. Wireless Internet access, small rooms for group study or for conferences, and even areas for coffee and food are approaches used in a variety of law libraries. Safety, too, is an important component of the library as place. Law libraries work toward safety with policies about appropriate user behavior, staff emergency procedures and training, and physical approaches ranging from architectural openness to the installation of emergency phones to the hiring of security personnel.

The physical environment should also accommodate disabled library users and disabled library employees to the extent that the budget can reasonably support. A variety of enabling designs and adaptive technologies can improve access to the library space and to library collections. In the spirit of service and in response to the Americans with Disabilities Act, many libraries develop accommodations both in anticipation of the need and in response to specific requests.

WHEN PEOPLE AND MACHINES BEHAVE BADLY

"What do you mean, I can't have my pizza delivered here in the library?"
"I just spent five dollars at the photocopier, and the copies are blurred."
"How does the scanner work?"
"Why don't you ever have staplers available?"

The details and logistics of maintaining an environment supportive of research can be as important as the intellectual challenges of providing public services in the law library. Sometimes people behave badly, and sometimes machines malfunction. In these situations, the public services library staff must respond.

The problem patron has inspired a number of articles on how to manage the situation. Just as the reference interview requires both strategies and finesse, dealing with difficult people can be a matter of training and natural interpersonal skills. Written policies, active listening, and, ultimately, referral to a supervisor are useful approaches. In some extreme cases, calling the police is in order. Machines, too, can misbehave, and the public services staff may be called upon to teach the user how to coax the machine into productivity, to attempt a minor repair, or to call in experts. A reference librarian may shift from patent research instruction to locating paper misfeeds in a matter of minutes. And the most pleasant discovery of a key resource for a researcher can be followed by asking a library user to take the pizza outside the library. The reality is that work in public services is unpredictable, and those in this area must have some sense of adventure to embrace the full gamut of possibilities.

AMERICAN ASSOCIATION OF LAW LIBRARIES CORE COMPETENCIES, SPECIALIZED COMPETENCIES

Many law librarians are members of the American Association of Law Libraries (AALL), which has a set of core competencies as well as specialized competencies, including a list for reference, and research and client services. These two sections are reproduced below. A separate section addresses competencies for teaching, an activity closely aligned with public services. The full document is available at the association's website at www.aallnet.org.

Competencies of Law Librarianship
Approved by the Executive Board March 2001, Tab34A
The AALL seeks to define the profession of law librarianship and its value to the legal field, today and in the future, by identifying, verifying, and actively promoting competencies of law librarianship. Competencies are the knowledge, skills, abilities, and personal characteristics that help distinguish superior performance. (1) These competencies may be acquired through higher education such as library and information science programs, (2) through continuing education, and through experience.

The first section, "Core Competencies," includes those that apply to all law librarians, and will be acquired early in one's career. The subsequent sections are related to specific areas of practice. Some law librarians (for example, solo librarians or librarians in smaller institutions) may have multiple responsibilities and need to be proficient in more than one of the "Specialized Competencies." Other law librarians may specialize in just one area or in a subset of one area.

Individual librarians may use the AALL Competencies for coordinating their continuing education as they identify areas for professional growth. Employers may use the Competencies to make hiring, evaluation, and promotion decisions, and to make recommendations for professional development. The American Association of Law Libraries uses the Competencies as a framework within which to structure professional development programs. This framework provides guidance to ensure that the programs offered will assist law librarians in attaining and maintaining the skills or knowledge necessary for their current and future work.

1. Core Competencies
Core Competencies apply to all law librarians and will be acquired early in one's career.
    1.1 Demonstrates a strong commitment to excellent client service
    1.2 Recognizes and addresses the diverse nature of the library's clients and community
    1.3 Understands and supports the culture and context of the library and its parent institution
    1.4 Demonstrates knowledge of the legal system and the legal profession

1.5 Understands the social, political, and economic context in which the legal system exists

1.6 Demonstrates knowledge of library and information science theory, information creation, organization, and delivery

1.7 Adheres to the Ethical Principles of the American Association of Law Libraries and supports the shared values of librarianship [3]

1.8 Exhibits leadership skills including critical thinking, risk taking, and creativity, regardless of position within the management structure

1.9 Demonstrates commitment to working with others to achieve common goals

1.10 Acts within the organization to implement the principles of knowledge management

1.11 Exhibits an understanding of the importance of a multidisciplinary and cross-functional approach to programs and projects within the organization

1.12 Shares knowledge and expertise with clients and colleagues

1.13 Displays excellent communication skills and is able to promote the library and advocate for its needs

1.14 Communicates effectively with publishers and other information providers to advance the interests of the library

1.15 Recognizes the value of professional networking and actively participates in professional associations

1.16 Actively pursues personal and professional growth through continuing education

2. Specialized Competencies

Specialized Competencies relate to specific areas of practice. Some law librarians may have multiple responsibilities and need to be proficient in more than one of the Specialized Competencies. Other law librarians may specialize in just one area or subset of one area.

3. Reference, Research, and Client Services

3.1 Provides skilled and customized reference services on legal and relevant nonlegal topics

3.2 Evaluates the quality, authenticity, accuracy, and cost of traditional and electronic sources, and conveys the importance of these to the client

3.3 Assists clients with legal research using both print and electronic resources

3.4 Assists non-lawyers in accessing the law, within the guidelines provided by the American Bar Association's Model Code of Professional Conduct and other applicable codes

3.5 Aggregates content from a variety of sources and synthesizes information to create customized products for clients

3.6 Creates research and bibliographic tools (handouts, aids, pathfinders, bibliographies) on legal and related topics

3.7 Monitors trends in specific areas of the law

Notes:
1. Kenneth H. Pritchaerd, CCP. Society for Human Resource Management White Paper, August 1997, reviewed April 1999.
2. See "AALL Guidelines for Graduate Programs," November 1988; AALL Professional Development Policy, July 1996.
3. American Association of Law Libraries Ethical Principles, 1999.

NOTE

1. The phrase "public services" is a common one in law libraries, particularly academic law libraries. It is used to describe services that normally involve interaction with the persons using the library. Other services such as technical services, IT services, and administration are distinguished as usually being behind-the-scenes activities. Terms such as "user services" or even "reader services" are similar to "public services." Sometimes the distinction is a matter of fashion; sometimes it is a matter of environment. Those whom the library serves are addressed with a variety of names, including "the public," "library users," "the readers," "library patrons," "library customers," and "library clients or clientele." Each of these has its own nuances. In this chapter, the terms "public services," "researchers," and "library user" predominate.

Chapter 5

Collection Development, Licensing, and Acquisitions

James S. Heller

MISSION, GOALS, AND RESPONSIBILITY

The first rule of collection development: There are no rules. Every law library is different, and the policy should fit the library. There are clear differences between, say, a state or county law library that is open to (indeed, welcomes) the public, and a private law firm library. But even libraries of the same type are different from each other. Law schools range from fewer than 300 students to more than 2,000, and although most are part of a university, others are free-standing, with no larger affiliation. A boutique law firm may have ten or twenty attorneys doing very specialized work, while some firms have a thousand or more lawyers working in dozens of different practice areas in offices throughout the world.

There is only one guideline to follow when determining what a library's collection should look like: it must meet the needs of its users. A library's mission statement is a good place to begin. A law school library might have as its mission statement the following:

> The fundamental mission of the Lincoln Law School Library is to serve the educational and research needs of the Law School community.

A county law library that is open to the public might use the following mission statement:

> The mission of the Lincoln County Law Library is to provide current, practice-oriented law and law-related information to attorneys, judges, other county officials, and members of the public.

The mission statement of a law firm library will be much narrower, such as:

> The library serves the information needs of the law firm, including its attorneys and paralegals, other staff members, and its clients.

From the mission statement will flow the library's goals, and from that, its collection development policies, priorities, and practices. A law school library's goal statement might look like this:

> The goal of the law library's collection development program is to maintain and provide access to a collection of information resources that support law school programs, research, the curriculum, and the needs of library users. The primary objective of the law library is to select, organize, preserve, and make available to members of the law school community information resources that will aid them in these pursuits. The collection shall support the law school curriculum and faculty and student research, and meet the standards set forth by the American Bar Association (ABA) and the Association of American Law Schools (AALS). As a secondary objective, the law library will select materials for use by the College community, the Lincoln bench and bar, and other library users, in that order of priority.

And for a county law library, the following:

> The law library's primary goal is to select, organize, and make legal information available to the county bench and bar, to other members of the local legal community, and to citizens of Lincoln County. As a secondary goal, the library serves other members of the State bench and bar and citizens of the State who do not reside in Lincoln County.

The collection development policy should acknowledge that the acquisitions budget cannot support in-depth collection development in every subject area. It should state clearly, however, that the library *will* acquire what its primary users need. The key words are "primary users" and "acquire." The latter includes purchase, access to electronic information via licenses, or by using interlibrary loan (ILL) and document delivery. Libraries open to the public cannot meet every need of every person who walks through their doors. Most libraries will establish priorities among their patrons, such as a law school library, which will focus its collection development on the needs of law faculty and students. A law firm library, which is not open to the public, probably need not identify primary users; the attorneys and paralegals are all primary. However, if the library participates in ILL and document delivery activities with other libraries, it should acknowledge that fact—and also that the firm's lawyers benefit by the library's participation.

The policy should identify those who are responsible for implementing it. Although the director is responsible for all library activities, he or she may delegate to another librarian primary responsibility for the development and maintenance of the collection. In some libraries, several staff members may participate in collection development activities. Although these individuals usually will be librarians, that needn't be the case. For example, a staff member who is a cinemaphile may select films for a library's collection.

The policy also should encourage core library users—faculty and students in a law school, judges and their law clerks in a court, or attorneys and paralegals in a firm—to make recommendations. You should expect two things: first, that the person who made the recommendation will not have looked at your online catalog to see if the library already has the item, and second, that in most cases the library already has it, or it's on order.

COLLECTION INTENSITY, SCOPE, GUIDELINES, AND CRITERIA

The library's selection policy may specify levels of collection intensity, with levels from "minimal" to "research." In a law school library, the levels may look like this:

Current and projected courses, individual research projects, and other law school activities will be identified to help establish the degree of acquisitions intensity in specific areas. Depending on the area, the law library collects on the following levels:

- *Minimal Level:* An extremely selective collection that is very limited in both scope and depth.
- *Basic Level:* A selective collection that provides the user a basic introduction to and outline of the subject. This collection includes introductory books such as hornbooks and nutshells, a few selected treatises, and only the most widely used specialized periodicals. Collection at this level will support only general research into the subject area.
- *Instructional Level:* A collection that adequately supports JD course work and somewhat broader research into the subject area than is provided at the basic level. Collection at this level will contain the most authoritative multijurisdictional treatises, the most important treatises, several widely used specialized periodicals, and access to specialized computer information services and databases.
- *Research Level:* A collection that includes major published source materials required for independent scholarly research by law school faculty and students. Included are all significant multijurisdictional treatises, loose-leaf services whose contents are not duplicated—in other print

sources or electronic databases—in substantial part, the best historical and current treatises, all widely used specialized periodicals, the major reference works in the area, significant nonlegal treatises that will aid in the understanding of the subject area, and access to specialized computer information services and databases.

- *Comprehensive Level:* At this level the library attempts to collect, as far as possible, all major works on a given subject, both current and retrospective. This collection will support the most rigorous, in-depth research.

In a "typical" law school library—if one exists—most collection development likely will take place at the instructional or research levels. If the school or its faculty is known for a particular expertise—First Amendment law, for example—the library may collect materials on that topic at the comprehensive level. Conversely, the library may collect at either the basic or introductory level on topics rarely taught at the school, and where there is no ongoing faculty research.

The same is true for a law firm; expect the library in a firm that specializes in telecommunications law to have a strong collection on that topic. By contrast, state, court, and county law libraries are unlikely to have collections that are inordinately strong in particular subjects. They will, however, have a very strong collection on the law of their state, including both primary and secondary materials. (There always are exceptions, of course: The library for the U.S. Court of Federal Claims will have a great government contract law collection, and federal bankruptcy court libraries will have strong bankruptcy and debtor-creditor collections.)

Having the collection development policy address the general scope of the collection, as well as particular types of materials, will prove helpful. Such statements serve as a guide to what the library does—and does not—collect. A law school library's scope of collection statement may look like this:

Most treatise acquisitions are in the area of American law. New treatises are selected in accordance with the priorities outlined in this policy. As a general matter, the library attempts to collect one copy of each multijurisdictional or federal legal treatise by reputable publishers that support the curriculum, or faculty or student research. The library will acquire all materials from the Commonwealth of Lincoln CLE. Other materials designed exclusively for practitioners will, however, be acquired very selectively.

Acquiring current materials—titles published within the past three years—is a much higher priority than acquiring retrospective materials. Generally, little attempt is made to purchase retrospectively except for specific subject areas in which there is a demonstrable need for historical materials, or areas in which there is special funding.

Serials involve a commitment to ongoing costs, binding, and storage. The large number of law and law-related serials makes it impossible to purchase every title, and they are acquired selectively. The library will consider the availability of a journal title on Lexis, Westlaw, and HeinOnline in making a decision whether to enter a subscription.

The collection scope statement in a law firm may appear as follows:

The collection consists of a variety of formats, including a balance of print, electronic, and online resources. It includes both current materials and, more selectively, historical materials as needed. Information resources are provided within the budgetary, space, and technological constraints outlined by the Library Committee and the firm's CEO. In all cases, acquisition of resources will take into account the research skills of and amount of use by attorneys and paralegals. The library will use interlibrary loan as a substitute for purchase for infrequently used titles.

And for a state law library, the following:

Generally, the library will collect primary legal materials from the federal government, U.S. territories, and the states. We will acquire secondary materials on a wide variety of legal subjects, especially practical materials that will be used by attorneys and citizens of the state. The library will maintain a comprehensive collection of this state's legal materials, both current and historical. The library will not collect international law materials, foreign law materials, nor materials in a language other than English. The State Law Library relies heavily on interlibrary loan and document delivery for materials not within the scope of this policy.

The policy should include guidelines that address issues such as cost, currency, language, format, and institutional priorities. If others must approve the policy—for example, the library committee in a law school or law firm, trustees in a county law library, or the chief judge and clerk of court in a court library—the guidelines will both explain and justify collection development decisions. Guidelines that you may find in a law school library's collection development policy may include the following:

- Current publications of lasting and scholarly value are given priority over retrospective materials.
- With minor exceptions, foreign language publications are not collected.
- Availability of materials online (e.g., Lexis, Westlaw, or the Internet) or in other libraries through cooperative acquisition programs will be considered for infrequently used material, in particular, for the laws of foreign countries.
- Duplicate copies are purchased for heavily used materials, or for items likely to be checked out indefinitely to a faculty member's office.
- In-depth materials for specific student research projects, or for short-term faculty research projects, are not purchased unless the library's

acquisition policy specifies collection development at the "Research" or "Comprehensive" level in that area. Such materials will be borrowed from other libraries as needed.

- Materials in support of the instructional and research needs of Lincoln Law School faculty and students are favored over those for use by the rest of the university community, by the bench and bar, or by the general public.

Selection criteria also help those who are responsible for collection development. Always remember that a decision not to acquire an item *is* a collection development decision. Selection criteria for any type of law library—not necessarily in order of importance—may include

- Reputation of the author and publisher
- Significance of the subject matter
- Accuracy and timeliness of the material
- Usefulness of the title with respect to other materials already in the collection in print or electronic format
- Appearance of the title in important bibliographies, lists, and other reviewing sources
- Current and/or permanent value of the material
- Cost, including upkeep
- Format
- If electronic, the terms of the license
- Availability of the material in other libraries

UPKEEP, DUPLICATION, AND GIFTS

In most law libraries, the majority of the collection development budget is not used for collection development, but rather for collection maintenance and currency. Most print legal materials—codes, reporters, treatises, journals, loose-leaf services, and finding aids—are updated with pocket parts and other supplements, replacement volumes, new issues, and the like. You will find that most law libraries spend 80 percent or more of their budget to update materials already owned.

When deciding whether to acquire an item, consider both the initial cost and future supplementation. In some cases, the upkeep may be a relatively small percentage of the initial cost, such as $150 for a new title, and $40–$50 for subsequent annual supplementation. In other cases, annual upkeep may cost nearly as much as the initial purchase. (In the summer of 2005 you could buy *Moore's Federal Practice* from LexisNexis/Matthew Bender for $3,999; annual upkeep for 2005–2006 will cost about $3,200.)

Most libraries try to get by with one copy of an item. Today, even the largest law libraries may have only one copy of print court reporters due to the availability of decisions on Lexis, Westlaw, or some other electronic source. But there will be some duplication. You will find that a faculty member, an attorney, or a judge will check out a new treatise as soon as he or she sees it on the library's "New Books List." Chances are good that the book will never see the light of the stacks again. The duplication section of a law school library's collection development policy may look like this:

Generally the library acquires only one copy of a work unless there is a demonstrable need for additional copies based on faculty or student use. Two copies of a monograph generally will be acquired, however, when the library anticipates that one or more faculty members will want to check out the book on a long-term basis.

Multiple copies of the following types of materials are acquired as a matter of course:

- Commonwealth of Liberty primary materials
- Reserve materials, specifically hornbooks and nutshells or other similar texts directly related to the curriculum
- Self-help books (one copy for the self-help collection, one for the stacks).

Duplicate copies of other books and subscriptions to journals will be acquired in accordance with the following guidelines:

- Additional copies may be purchased for the reserve collection at the request of the instructor if such copies will be of long-term value.
- Duplicate materials received as gifts will be subject to the same considerations for addition to the collection as materials suggested for purchase.
- Past policies and historical circumstances alone will not justify new and continued duplication.

Beware of retired lawyers bearing gifts. Gifts are great—if you want them. A retired attorney may want to donate her books, thinking not only that she can get a tax deduction for a charitable contribution, but also that she is doing the library a great favor. In other cases, the spouse of a long-deceased lawyer finally cleans out the attic. Although there may indeed be some treasures, more often than not there will be little wheat and a lot of chaff. State codes, regional reporters, legal encyclopedias, and treatises that haven't been updated are, for the most part, worthless.

The library probably will want to reject many, if not most, gifts. You will, however, have to accept some—not for the gift's value, but because the donor is a VIP. (Wealthy retired alumni definitely fit into this category.) The collection development policy should state that gift materials will be accepted if they conform to the selection guidelines, and also make clear that once a gift is made, the library—not the donor—decides on retention and location. A statement such as "The director retains the right to determine the disposition of donated materials at any time and in any manner deemed appropriate" will suffice. The library should not appraise the value of gifts for tax purposes, although it may help donors obtain prices in catalogs of secondhand dealers, or procure services from an appraiser.

MULTIPLE FORMATS

Print versus Digital

There is no magic answer to the question "How should I balance my collection between print and electronic information?" The answer depends on what *your* users need. During the 1990s, most law firm libraries downsized their print collections, often dramatically. Libraries lost floor and shelf space, and often their outside windows. Law school libraries also are migrating from print to electronic. A library that had three or four copies of print court reporters in 1990 is likely to have one copy in 2005. Similarly, many law school libraries have migrated from Commerce Clearing House's (CCH) and Bureau of National Affairs (BNA) loose-leaf services to their electronic counterparts.

The ability to rely extensively on digital information is more difficult—if not impossible—in a library whose mission is to serve the public, such as a county or state law library. First, the general public will have more problems using legal databases than those who use legal information every day, such as lawyers, law students, law faculty, and court personnel. Second, the library may be unable to secure licenses for electronic products that adequately serve the public, including *pro se* patrons. Licenses will be addressed later in this chapter.

The collection development policy should address both print and digital information—and their relationship to one another—throughout. It also may include a separate section on Internet resources in the policy, such as fee-based digital subscriptions (LexisNexis and Westlaw), digital consortia (such as the Virtual Library of Virginia [VIVA] or the Ohio Library and Information Network [OhioLINK]), and information that is free on the Internet (GPO Access). A law school library may address these issues thusly:

> The Law Library participates in the Lincoln Virtual Library (LVL) consortium. Through LVL we have access to hundreds of electronic publications,

probably the most important of which are LexisNexis Congressional, Dissertation Abstracts, Dow Jones, Encyclopedia Brittanica, JSTOR, New England Journal of Medicine, Social Science Abstracts, Statistical Universe, and WorldCat. The Law Library itself subscribes to several online CCH and BNA services, and to typical indices and legal databases found in most law libraries, such as Current Law Index, LexisNexis, and Westlaw. The law library also subscribes to HeinOnline, and is a member of LLMC Digital.

Access to law-related information on the Internet—including LexisNexis, Westlaw, HeinOnline, LLMC Digital, and governmental sites—have led to the cancellation of many print resources, including nearly all Shepard's Citators and West digests. In other cases, electronic access may justify cancellation of multiple copies of sets, such as case reporters.

The library has an interest in maintaining continuing access to Web-based information. License agreements should, whenever possible, include provisions for the permanent right to access and use information that has been paid for in the event that a licensed product is subsequently canceled or removed, including the right to make or obtain electronic or print copies for archiving and for patron use.

A county law library might have the following statement:

The Liberty County Library subscribes to information in both print and digital format. In most cases, electronic information complements the print collection, although there may be duplication for core materials. In making decisions to acquire digital resources, the library will consider the following: patron need, the extent to which the digital information is unique (and if not, whether it can effectively substitute for print materials), cost, ease of use, and our ability to provide technical support.

Most libraries will consider the availability of materials online commercially (e.g., LexisNexis, Westlaw, Loislaw, BNA, CCH, and HeinOnline) or otherwise as a possible alternative to print, especially in deciding whether to purchase or continue to maintain infrequently used materials. In all cases, decisions to acquire digital products should be made in accordance with the entire collection development policy, not independent of it. Whether a library considers materials available online as a substitute for print materials depends on several factors, including:

- How often the materials are used
- The content and quality of the product
- Ease of use
- Usage restrictions (especially the ability to download and print)
- Availability of the same information in other formats
- Cost
- Continued access to the content after the subscription expires

Multiple formats raise many questions about collection development and retention. For example, a library may subscribe to a microform version of the *Federal Register*, yet also be able to access the *Register* in PDF on HeinOnline (from the first issue), on GPO Access (also in PDF, since 1994), and on Lexis and Westlaw (since 1980, but not in PDF). If you feel comfortable that the online versions will remain available and can serve as an archival copy, cancel the microform subscription. If this makes you uncomfortable, don't.

More and more government information is available on the Internet, but librarians have encountered many speed bumps on the information superhighway. The federal governmental printing program has been in flux for many years. In the 1980s the superintendent of documents issued many titles—often sporadically—in microform. In the 1990s we saw a migration to electronic format. Today, one can access federal government materials from all branches of government via GPO Access or directly from the governmental unit, such as an agency, a congressional committee, or a court website. But understand that there is no hammer forcing governmental entities to publish their materials on the Internet.

This is pretty much the case for state publications. State statutes, regulations, and cases—as well as documents from state agencies—generally can be found on a state's official website. Unfortunately, even the government officials responsible for putting materials on the Web do not know if these materials will remain online forever, or even a year or two from now.

The same is true for local government materials. Beginning in the 1990s, counties, cities, and towns began putting gobs of information on the Internet, from local ordinances to property ownership and valuation information. Because ordinances from thousands of jurisdictions throughout the United States are available on the Internet for free, today most libraries get only those ordinances from their immediate or neighboring localities in print. It would be wise to hold onto all print editions of your local codes; governmental websites are likely to include only the most recent version.

Case law is no different. Most state court websites include both recent and past decisions, usually going back to the mid 1990s. Some states—Oklahoma is a notable example—have *all* of their decisions (both territorial and state) available online. Whether a library believes it needs to acquire—or retain—court reports from states other than its home state may depend, in part, on the citation bible, *The Bluebook: A Universal System of Citation.*

The *Bluebook*'s longstanding preference for print format confounds and frustrates many librarians—especially law school librarians who deal with law-review cite checkers—but its rules do give law libraries some flexibility regarding state court reporters. *The Bluebook* does not require a case citation to an official state reporter—if one exists at all, for the majority of states use a West regional reporter as their "official" reporter—unless the case is cited in a document submitted to courts of the state that originally decided them. Consequently, a law library need only subscribe to the official reports for the state in which it resides, and may rely on the regional reporters for other state court decisions.

Although every state appellate court decision cannot be found in regional reporters, there *is* significant overlap between official state court reports and West's National Reporter System. If a library is short on shelf space and needs to weed its collection, withdrawing some state court reporter volumes may be an obvious choice. To begin, the library must identify the overlap. The West Publishing Company began publishing regional reporters at different dates between 1879 and 1887. Use the *National Reporter Bluebook* (NRB) to determine the date when state court decisions from the "official" state court reporters first appear in the regional reporters. The NRB tells you, for example, that the *South Western Reporter* includes cases from *Missouri Appeal Reports* beginning with volume 94, and that the *North Eastern Reporter* includes cases from *Illinois Appellate Court Reports* beginning with volume 284. A library that wants to keep one print copy of state court decisions—but not *duplicate* copies—can withdraw the state reporter volumes that overlap with the regional reporters. For helpful information on the publication of court decisions, consult a legal research text such as Mersky and Dunn's *Fundamentals of Legal Research*.

Although many law libraries want to rely heavily on electronic sources for court decisions, the *Bluebook* still favors citation to a print version. The increasing amount of PDF images on the Web, such as Westlaw, including PDFs of decisions published in West reporters from at least 1920 to date, give libraries more flexibility in deciding how to balance their collections between print and electronic formats.

Digests are another matter. During the last few years, many law libraries—even large law school libraries—have canceled subscriptions to print digests, such as West's *General* and *Decennial Digests*, the *Federal Digest*, regional and state digests, and specialty digests such as *Education* or *Social Security*.

Today, most researchers find it easier to locate relevant case law by doing a full-text search, by using Lexis' Search Advisor or Westlaw's Keysearch, or by using the digests online in Westlaw. In fact, Westlaw's online digest covers more cases than the print version. West has added to its Westlaw database headnotes and key numbers to thousands of court decisions from the nineteenth century that were published in official state reporters, even though those decisions never appeared in a West reporter. Although a researcher cannot find these cases using one of the *American*

Digest Century Editions or an early decennial digest, you *can* if you use the online digest on Westlaw.

LexisNexis and Westlaw are not viable alternatives for every library, as they can be very expensive. Most law firm libraries probably sign annual or biennial contracts that give them unlimited use for a set dollar amount. The rate will be adjusted at the end of the contract term if use rises, of course. In law schools, the cost for LexisNexis and Westlaw is reduced tremendously so as to encourage use by law students. Although Lexis-Nexis's and Westlaw's law school licenses allow only law school faculty, students, and staff access to their respective databases, LexisNexis Academic and Westlaw for Patrons give others access to portions of these databases.

Collection development—especially balancing print versus online sources—is not simply a matter of dollars and cents; a library always must consider how its users do research. Shepard's Citators probably are the best example of print resources being supplanted by superior electronic products, and elimination of print citators from library collections. A case in point: In 1990, several dozen Shepard's titles occupied more than 120 linear feet of shelving at the William & Mary Law Library, and also were very expensive to maintain. In 2005, print Shepard's take up six inches of space; the law library has only its state citator (*Virginia Citations*) in print. Using Shepard's on Lexis, or KeyCite on Westlaw, are far superior to "Shepardizing" in print. That Lexis and Westlaw offer public-access subscriptions to Shepard's online and KeyCite, respectively, makes it easier for libraries to get rid of the books, saving both space and money.

Foreign legal materials are another area where we have seen a significant migration to electronic access. Print legal materials from foreign countries usually are very expensive. U.S. law libraries—especially large law school and state law libraries—historically maintained print primary source materials for Canada and Great Britain, and in many cases materials from the United Nations and the European Union, including laws, treaties, and court reports. Some libraries long ago decided to build and maintain very strong collections in the law of specific countries. Today, more and more materials from foreign nations, as well as entities such as the United Nations, the European Union, and the World Trade Organization, are available on the Internet, usually for free. When deciding whether to acquire foreign and international law materials in print—or to *continue* to subscribe to them—consider their cost, how often the materials are used, and whether the Web is an adequate substitute. Many libraries have concluded that Internet access suits their researchers just fine, and that they can save lots of shelf space and dollars by forgoing the books.

All types of legal literature—including treatises—should be in play when considering electronic versus print. Lexis, West, Aspen, and other publishers offer online versions of many of their treatises. Although Lexis and West have an increasing number of their treatises on their online databases, the same cannot necessarily be said for other publishers. Some Aspen titles are available on Loislaw or CCH Online (which, like Aspen, are part of the Wolters Kluwer publishing empire), while others may be available through a separate subscription. Like all other situations involving digital information, the terrain can be bumpy, and there may be dead ends and unexpected jogs in the road.

Regardless, most researchers still prefer treatises in book form, and a library must answer several questions in deciding whether to substitute electronic for print: (1) Does the library have the space to shelve the print versions? (2) Can it afford the updates? (3) Does it have staff to file the updates? (4) Are the electronic versions easy to use, download, and print? and (5) How confident is it that the materials will remain online? Because the vendor may only have the current edition of a title online, you also need to know whether your patrons need older editions. (And if the answer is "yes," will ILL satisfy patron needs?)

Microforms

Microforms were invented in the 1830s and became popular for archival preservation and mass storage a century later. If shelf space is at a premium and a library does not feel comfortable relying on electronic information, microform is an alternative. Like most other mediums, microforms have their plusses and minuses. The upside: microforms take up very little space, are a stable medium, and you own what you buy. The downside: many people don't like using microforms, you need equipment to read it, and a misfiled fiche is probably gone forever. As for preservation, silver halide film and the current generation of films that meet certain ISO/ANSI standards can have a life expectancy of 500 years.

Microforms may make up a significant part of a law library collection. (In many larger libraries, microforms may make up 40 percent or more of the total volume count.) However, the availability of so many materials on the Internet—especially when a title is in PDF—have led many libraries to reconsider long-held policies regarding their microform collections. A library's collection development policy might address microforms as follows:

The library collects materials in microformat primarily when:

- The materials are infrequently used, and
- The materials would take up a great deal of shelf space were they in paper format, or

- The materials are not available in paper format, or
- Preservation in microformat is superior to hard copy, or
- The cost of the materials in microformat is significantly less than the cost of the materials in paper format.

In all cases, the library will consider the availability of the material digitally—especially when in PDF—as an alternative to microforms. Digital information may be a cost-effective alternative to microform when the library is confident that the digital materials will be available indefinitely.

Same Content, Different Wrapper

There is significant duplication in the world of legal materials, but not much competition. LexisNexis (owned by Anglo-Dutch publishing behemoth Reed Elsevier) and Thomson-West (Canadian publishing giant Thomson) dominate the world of American legal publishing. The Dutch company Wolters Kluwer is a distant third. Both Thomson-West and LexisNexis publish annotated federal codes (West's *United States Code Annotated* (*USCA*) and LexisNexis's *United States Code Service* (*USCS*), as well as parallel codes in several states (California, New York, and Virginia, to name a few).

As for the *USCA* and *USCS*, larger law libraries probably will want both; firms and smaller libraries generally choose one or the other. Even though one publisher will brag that its version is superior to the competitor's, it makes little difference which a library chooses. The same is true for state codes. A law library in Virginia probably will subscribe to both the long-standing *Code of Virginia* (LexisNexis) and to *West's Annotated Code of Virginia.* Conversely, a Virginia law library need only subscribe to *West's Annotated California Code* or to *Deering's Annotated California Code* (LexisNexis), but not to both.

Form and practice materials are an example of duplication *between* titles. Larger law libraries historically collected most general and federal form and practice materials from reputable publishers, such as West, Lawyer's Cooperative, Matthew Bender, and Callaghan. These materials—today nearly all of which are published by Thomson-West—are not only expensive to maintain, but may be duplicative. A library that subscribes to *AmJur Legal Forms, AmJur Pleading and Practice Forms, Federal Procedure Forms (Lawyer's Edition)*, *West's Federal Forms*, and *West's Legal Forms* may find, on close examination, that it really does not need them all. Furthermore, many form and practice materials are available on Westlaw or LexisNexis, and many forms are available for free on the Internet, often on governmental websites.

You can expect to find overlap among titles from competing publishers, but probably less today than existed before the consolidation of the legal publishing industry. Some overlap—as in the form books mentioned above—will be pretty obvious. Another example is *American Jurisprudence* (*AmJur*) and *Corpus Juris Secundum* (*CJS*). Both are published by Thomson-West, and they cover the same territory. Annual pocket parts, along with numerous volumes being replaced each year, make them expensive to keep current. Although law school libraries probably will have both *AmJur* and *CJS*—perhaps more out of habit than need—other libraries probably will do quite well with only one of these titles. And you may not even need the books; *AmJur* is available on both Lexis and Westlaw; *CJS* can be found on Westlaw.

As noted above, treatises can be very expensive to maintain. Whether a library needs several different titles on a particular topic depends on the needs of its users. To determine whether titles on your shelves are being used, blow on the top to see if they are collecting dust, and look at the circulation records. Plumes of dust usually mean that the book isn't being used; it may be expendable. You will find that titles cited in journal articles and court decisions are more likely to be in demand. Search for the book's author and title in Lexis's and Westlaw's law review and/or court decision databases to see how often it has been cited, especially during the past five years. And if you want to find out if a title may be obtained via ILL, log onto OCLC's FirstSearch to see which libraries own it.

PARTICULAR SELECTION ISSUES

Newsletters

Newsletters can eat you alive, if you let them. They often are expensive, and usually have a limited shelf life. Many libraries subscribe only to newsletters that are routed to someone—an attorney in the firm, a judge, or a faculty member, for example—and renew a subscription only after verifying that it still is needed. Electronic alternatives, such as CCH's Internet Research Network and BNA Online, and also Westlaw's WestClip and Lexis's Eclipse services, are increasingly popular. A law firm's policy on newsletters might look like this:

> The library only subscribes to newsletters that are being used by attorneys, paralegals, or staff. Every newsletter is reviewed annually to assess current use. In all cases, e-newsletters are considered as an alternative to print. BNA and CCH offer summaries of daily and weekly reports sent via e-mail with links to full-text subscriptions. Even though more costly than print alone, the electronic subscriptions allow individual access without the risk of violating copyright laws, and provide immediate access to current awareness information. LexisNexis and Westlaw also can be used to keep current.

The Law Firm has subscriptions to several BNA and CCH titles. Depending on the practice area and the needs of individual attorneys, an electronic subscription might include only e-mails of highlights and summaries, or it could include e-mails plus access to the full text of each issue.

Indexes

Periodical indexes should be treated in the same manner: Get what you need, but no more. There are two major legal periodical indexes, *Index to Legal Periodicals* (*ILP*) and *Current Law Index* (*CLI*). *CLI* indexes more titles, and utilizes the same Library of Congress subject headings that staff and patrons probably use to find other materials. *ILP* indexes fewer titles, and uses its own less descriptive subject headings. In deciding which to acquire, you may want to answer this question: If our library already subscribed to *CLI*, and a publisher just introduced a new periodical index that covers fewer titles and uses less helpful subject headings, would we acquire it?

CLI and *ILP* are available in print and online. The print versions are published monthly and compiled annually. The online versions cover more than a quarter century, and searching the database is much more efficient than doing a year-by-year search through print volumes. An online index may be available directly from its publisher, and perhaps also through Lexis or Westlaw. Because some publishers "bundle" their print and online versions, you may find that you cannot access the index on Lexis or Westlaw unless you already have either a print or separate electronic subscription with the publisher.

Superseded Materials and Earlier Editions

Holding on to superseded materials can be both a benefit and a bother. For some titles, the benefits are clear. For example, because the official *United States Code* is published every six years and is updated with new volumes annually, someone doing historical research can quickly see what the law looked like at a certain date. In contrast, the privately published annotated codes, *USCA* and *USCS*, are updated with annual pocket parts, and the publishers replace volumes on no particular schedule. Even if a library holds on to superseded pocket parts and volumes—something done only in larger law libraries—a researcher cannot quickly locate earlier versions of the law. If you have the space, keep older editions of the *United States Code*.

As for treatises, most larger libraries—especially academic and state, court, and county law libraries—will keep every edition. A law firm library that serves attorneys who do little historical research may choose to keep only the most recent edition. Indeed, many firm librarians do *not* keep older materials because they know they can get them through ILL from another library. A library that retains prior editions may want to label the volumes "Newer Edition Available" to avoid possible confusion.

Loose-Leaf Services

Loose-leaf services are the print materials most likely to become extinct within the next decade. The development of the administrative state created the need for lawyers to find, in one place, statutory, administrative, and judicial materials. Thus the birth of Commerce Clearing House (CCH) in 1913, and the Bureau of National Affairs (BNA) in 1929. Today's lawyers and legal researchers can access these primary source materials— and more—from a computer.

Whether a library chooses to continue to subscribe to the loose leafs, to BNA's or CCH's online versions, or to both, will depend on its resources—subscription costs, shelf space, and staff to file the services—and also how its patrons research. As much sense as it makes for a library to cancel print loose leafs and migrate to the CCH Online Research Network or to BNA Online, it may find it hard to do so if the lawyers in your firm, judges in your court, or faculty in your school insist on using the print. Old habits sometimes die hard. To help ensure that you don't join the unemployment line, get input before converting.

Bibliographies

Print subject bibliographies arguably were more important in the twentieth century than in the twenty-first. Online bibliographic databases, catalogs, and indexes are so common, and in most cases easy to search, that many librarians see little need for published bibliographies. (One exception may be annotated bibliographies that cover subjects particularly important to the institution or its researchers.) A library that very selectively acquires annotated bibliographies might have the following policy statement:

> Current annotated subject bibliographies are rarely acquired, but may be done so based on the needs of the reference staff and library users, the subject matter covered, the quality of the work, and the availability or unavailability of other materials on the subject. The library will acquire historical bibliographies (such as Cohen's *Bibliography of Early American Law* and Vaughan's *Early American Indian Documents: Treaties and Laws, 1607–1709*) as such titles support staff and user needs. Brief nonannotated bibliographies are not purchased.

Popular Reading

Most libraries have a casual reading area that includes newspapers and magazines. Typically, a library will have the local papers, and also national publications such as the *New York Times, Wall Street Journal, Washington Post*, and *USA Today*. The same is true for legal newspapers; the library will subscribe to its local and state legal newspaper, and probably also to *American Lawyer, Legal Times*, and the *National Law Journal*.

The magazines to which you subscribe should be those your patrons want to read. They usually will include the popular news weeklies (*Newsweek, Time, U.S. News and World Report*), business, entertainment, and sports magazines (*Business Week, People, Sports Illustrated*), and policy-related magazines (*New Republic* and *The Nation*). Magazines are inexpensive, and they give the library a lot of bang for very few bucks.

Many law libraries have popular book collections that are . . . well . . . popular. They include fiction (John Grisham and Scott Turow), current events, biography and history (David McCullouch and Bob Woodward), and humor (Al Franken and Jon Stewart). Keep the book jackets; they attract readers like honey attracts bears. Like popular magazines, these inexpensive additions to your collection (hardcover editions usually cost less than $40) are a great value, and are guaranteed not to collect dust.

Reserve

Many libraries—especially law school libraries—have a reserve collection that remains under the control of library staff. A law school library's reserve collection usually has materials requested by faculty or which are heavily used in conjunction with a course, and also items that are high risk (i.e., likely to be stolen). The collection may include practice and CLE titles from the home state, hornbooks, nutshells, and audiovisual materials. Some libraries have current (unbound) law review issues on reserve. This collection is dynamic; materials no longer needed on reserve should be moved to open stacks.

Reference Collection

Most libraries' reference collections have shrunk in size—often significantly—due to the Internet. Much information that used to be available only in a print directory may now be freely available on a website. The collection policy should recognize that reference materials include information in both print and digital format, and that the "reference collection" provides users current, useful, and authoritative resources for frequently researched issues. Some libraries will include every reference source in a discreet reference collection that usually is located near the reference desk. Others will spread reference books throughout the library. A library that takes the latter approach may have a policy that looks like this:

This policy offers guidelines on which works should and should not be included in the Library's reference collection.

I. Works shelved in the Reference Collection. These include those used frequently by librarians and by a wide variety of patrons, and also works covering diverse subjects that are difficult to shelve in one category in the stacks. The Reference Collection will include:

  A. Authoritative general reference works, including
    1. Well-regarded, general-purpose nonlegal works such as general dictionaries (Oxford, Webster, etc.), encyclopedias (the Britannica), and biographical dictionaries and encyclopedias, and
    2. General-purpose legal works, such as Black's Law Dictionary, West's Encyclopedia of American Law, and the Almanac of the Federal Judiciary.
  B. General reference works dealing with the State of Liberty
    1. Materials such as dictionaries of Liberty biography and guides to important moments or places in Liberty history, and
    2. Frequently used works specifically relating to the court system and/or political science.
  C. Current statistical resources
    Whether general-purpose or subject-specific, the current edition of statistical resources are shelved in the Reference section.
  D. Current bibliographies for the law in general
    These include items such as Hein's State Report Checklist and the Union List of Legislative Histories.
  E. Directories
    Both subject-specific (e.g., directories of environmental organizations) and general-purpose (e.g., Mar-Hub) directories.

II. Reference-type works shelved in the stacks. These include works that are easy to shelve in a specific category, and those that are normally accessed and used with other works on that subject. Patrons would not ordinarily think to look in the reference collection for these items. Reference-type materials shelved in the stacks under the Library of Congress classification system include:

  A. Subject-specific works, including subject-specific dictionaries and encyclopedias (e.g., Dictionary of Environmental Law), and
  B. Subject-specific bibliographies.

III. Prior editions. The library will only keep the newest edition of a work in the Reference Collection. Prior editions are kept selectively, and always will be shelved in the stacks. Materials retained indefinitely in the stacks include:

  A. Publications with a significant change in coverage between editions,
  B. Selected biographical materials,
  C. State of Liberty materials, and
  D. Fact-based annual publications, such as almanacs.

Annex Collections

Some libraries maintain annex collections throughout the larger institution, such as a faculty library in a law school. Because so much is available in PDF today—law journals on HeinOnline and court decisions on Westlaw—many law schools have done away with or significantly reduced their faculty library. A library that provides materials for other locations—whether it be a law school's career services suite or a judge's chambers in a court—should maintain some control over them. Process the materials through the library: Use the library stamp, label them to indicate their location, and check them out to the unit or office where they are shelved.

Lost Materials

Books will disappear. Guaranteed. A library will declare an item "lost" when it has been off the shelf for a certain period of time, is not checked out, and cannot be located. Some libraries declare an item lost when it's been gone for three or four months, while others may wait as long as a year. Decisions on replacing lost materials should be made using the selection criteria set forth in the collection development policy: Don't automatically replace an item that was lost; instead, find out if you still need it. Because some lost items may be out of print, the library may need to contact both new and used book dealers when trying to replace them.

Cooperative Agreements

As has been noted above, cooperative agreements and ILL are alternatives to acquiring items that do not fit within the "need-to-buy" category for the library's collection. Many libraries are members of consortia whose members agree to provide ILL and document delivery services for each other at no cost. The collection development policy should recognize that the availability of materials from other libraries—particularly for costly or infrequently used titles—will be considered in making acquisitions decisions. Remember that ILL and document delivery are never free; there are indirect (staff time) and direct (supplies, postage, and perhaps lending fees) costs.

WEEDING, UPDATING, AND MONITORING

The collection development policy should include the library's practices regarding superseded materials and weeding. Judicious and systematic discarding of certain materials is important for the maintenance and usefulness of any collection. Items that law libraries typically weed include multiple copies of infrequently used materials, multiple copies of old editions, superseded replacement volumes of current editions, substantially incomplete runs of periodicals in peripheral subject areas, and loose-leaf services to which the library no longer subscribes (while keeping bound or transfer volumes).

As noted earlier, a library will likely keep superseded volumes of the *United States Code* and its own state code. Many larger libraries also will keep old pocket parts to its state code. To avoid confusion, superseded materials (such as superseded volumes of the state code) often are shelved in a secure area. In all cases, the volumes should be marked "Superseded" on the spine.

For a long, long time, legal publishers believed that the voice Ray Kinsella heard in *Field of Dreams*—"If you build it, they will come"—would apply to librarians: "If you sell it, they will buy." When updating costs began to spike in the late 1980s, however, some libraries decided not to acquire every update that was published. Whether a law library chooses to receive every update to a title depends on its budget, its philosophy on updating, and the update's content. Some librarians believe that the integrity of a publication is compromised when it does not include the most recent update; others willingly forgo updating certain titles, especially if the update does not include substantive changes to the text, but instead, only citations to recent court decisions.

In deciding whether to update a particular title, determine how useful the item will be if it is not updated, and whether researchers will be harmed if they do not have the current update. (During this process you may find that you do not need the title at all.) Some items are logical targets for nonregular updates (every third year, or so), such as Matthew Bender's *Art of Advocacy* series. The content changes very little for trial practice materials on topics such as opening statements, closing arguments, questioning witnesses, and the like. Always keep users informed; include a notice—where the supplement would normally be found—that the update in the book is not the most current that is available.

As faculty change in a law school, and practice areas in a firm, so too will the library's collection. That most legal publications have ongoing costs makes it imperative to continuously review your collection policy, and your subscriptions. The following law firm policy statement reflects the dynamic nature of collection development, and the need to regularly review the collection and seek input from library users:

> In order to provide attorneys and paralegals with the information they need, and to adhere to the library's budget, the library will:
>
> - Monitor changes in practice areas
>   - Add to the budget for titles in new practice areas
>   - Cancel subscriptions for titles no longer being used

- Continuously review subscriptions
  - Before renewal, ask attorneys in the practice area if they still need the item
  - As supplements are received, verify that the item still is needed
  - As attorneys are added to routing lists, add more subscriptions as needed
- Identify little used but still needed titles
  - If available via interlibrary loan or online, consider canceling
  - Review need for continuous supplementation; alternatives include occasional updates, or periodic purchase of replacement sets
- Review current awareness routing
  - Review number of copies requested
  - Change number of subscriptions as appropriate
  - Compare e-mail vs. print subscriptions

STANDARDS AND ACCREDITATION

There are no required collection standards for law libraries, except for law schools accredited by the American Bar Association (ABA) and/or the Association of American Law Schools (AALS). In the summer of 2005, the ABA adopted revisions to the library standards, recognizing the impact of technology on library collections. In the words of the ABA's Council on Legal Education and Admissions to the Bar, the proposed revisions recognize "the increasing importance of and reliance upon cooperative agreements in developing library resources. At the same time, the proposed revision continues to make it clear that cooperative agreements *alone* [their emphasis] are not sufficient to satisfy Standard 601." One can find the complete standards—and their interpretations—at the ABA website (www.abanet.org). In a nutshell, here is an abridged version of the most important standards and interpretations:

Standard 601 states that the library should be an active and responsive force in the educational life of the law school, with sufficient financial resources to support the law school's teaching, scholarship, research, and service programs.

The interpretation to Standard 601 states that cooperative agreements may be considered in determining if faculty and students have efficient and effective access to the resources necessary to meet the law school's educational needs. However, the standard cannot be met solely by access to other law libraries, or through electronic access to information.

Standard 606 addresses a library's collection more specifically, providing that:

(a) the law library shall provide a core collection of essential materials accessible from the law library;

(b) in addition to the core collection, the library shall provide a collection that, through ownership or reliable access, meets the research and educational needs of its students and the law school curriculum and supports faculty teaching, scholarship, research, and service and the objectives of the law school;

(c) a library must formulate and periodically update a written collection development plan; and

(d) a library must have suitable space and adequate equipment to access and use all its information.

The interpretations require that the collections be complete, current, and in sufficient quantity or with sufficient access to meet faculty and student needs (Interpretation 606-1); that the format mix depends on the needs of the library and its clientele (606-2); that agreements for sharing resources (except the core collection) meet Standard 606 if they are in writing and provide faculty and students with the ease of access and availability necessary to support the law school's programs (606-3); that it is permissible to store nonessential material off-site so long as the materials are organized and readily accessible (606-4); that the dean, faculty, and law library director should cooperate in formulating the collection development plan (606-6); and that the library must have the equipment necessary to use its microform, electronic, and audiovisual materials (606-7).

Interpretation 606-5 sheds more light on the core collection. It must include:

(1) all reported federal court decisions and reported decisions from the highest appellate court of each state;

(2) all federal codes and session laws, and at least one current annotated code for each state;

(3) all current published treaties and international agreements of the United States;

(4) all current published regulations of the United States and those of the state in which the school is located;

(5) federal and state administrative decisions appropriate to the law school's programs;

(6) U.S. Congressional materials appropriate to the school's programs;

(7) significant secondary works necessary to support the school's programs; and

(8) tools such as citators and indexes necessary to identify primary and secondary legal information and update primary legal information.

Although the standards certainly will not be met if the entire core collection is electronic—or perhaps even a significant amount of it—clearly a good many of these items may be in electronic format. It is especially important to note that many of the interpretations give a library flexibility to determine the materials it needs that support the law school's programs.

The AALS' bylaws speak very generally to the law library collection: It must be "adequate to support and encourage the instruction and research of its faculty and students" and "possess or have ready access to a physical collection and other information resources that substantially" meet the research needs of students, satisfy curricular demands, support individual faculty research interests, and serve any of the school's special research and educational objectives.

The bottom line for ABA and AALS standards is flexibility. Both accrediting organizations recognize the dramatic changes in the publication of law and law-related information, and also that a library's collection should be tailored to the needs of its institution.

In July 2005, the American Association of Law Libraries (AALL) State Court and County Special Interest Section (SCC-SIS) and the AALL Executive Board approved *Standards for Appellate Court Libraries and State Law Libraries*. The standards—which actually are collection of "guidelines"—address local (home state) and federal resources, and national publications. The SCC-SIS Standards Committee that drafted the policy writes that their recommendations constitute a "core of a strong appellate court library or state law library print collection," and that "when selecting materials from other states, emphasis should be given to those from surrounding states." They write that cooperative resource sharing with libraries "within a reasonable geographic area or providing electronic access to selected materials" satisfies the requirements if a library has staff who can help users access electronic or off-site resources.

Although conceding that online information will "anchor the research capabilities of future libraries," the committee writes that " the shape of that technology remains unknown, and issues concerning the digital preservation of materials are just beginning to be addressed." They conclude that print continues to be important, and "must be retained, in view of the many uncertainties of the electronic future." It is no surprise, then, that the guidelines are heavy on print. The complete standards can be found at www.aallnet.org.

LICENSING

As this author wrote in *The Librarian's Copyright Companion* (from which much of this section on licenses was adapted), here is the bottom line: read the license carefully, and then read it again. Because these agreements are drafted by the information vendors, they may not give the library—or the library's patrons—the rights they need. Feel free to amend the proposed agreement; write in the changes you want to make, and initial them. Send two signed copies to the vendor, with instructions that one be sent back to you with the vendor's signature. Because vendors sometimes will not send back the amended agreement, in your cover letter, and on the license itself, write that if the vendor provides the product, then it assents to your terms.

Without going into great detail (you can find information on licenses in a variety of places, including "Liblicense" from the Yale University Library, "licensingmodels.com," and any number of recent books on copyright and libraries), here are some issues to consider.

Most libraries want to be able to access the product using an IP address. By using a proxy server—a local computer that serves as an intermediary between off-site users and restricted online resources—authorized users can access the information from any computer, anywhere.

The library will want to provide for simultaneous access by as many users as is necessary, but no more; wider access usually costs more money. Although you may work in a 500-person law firm that has a labor practice with thirty attorneys, all 500 lawyers do not need simultaneous access to online labor databases, or even the thirty who practice labor law. A license that gives a handful of users simultaneous access may be all you need.

The license is likely to include definitions. These are vitally important: How terms are defined will delineate rights and responsibilities, and also determine how the license will be construed. For example, most licenses will define "Authorized Users." In *your* contract, "Authorized Users" should include all those whom you anticipate will use the product. In a law firm, this usually will be "the employees" of the firm, or the "revenue-generating employees." In a law school, authorized users certainly should include students, faculty, and staff affiliated with the law school, but could include all those affiliated with the university, as well as others who, although unaffiliated, use the library's computers (i.e., walk-in patrons).

Make sure users have the rights they need. You certainly want the license to permit downloading and printing. But don't stop there: The license should permit the making of copies by and for users to the extent allowed under U.S. copyright law.

Some licenses are rather general, while others will be very detailed. If you want specific rights in your license, you may have to write in those terms. For example, a law school library may want the content of the database to be available on its electronic reserve system, a firm library will want the right to make copies for its clients, and a public law library will want to make sure that its patrons—most of whom will not be affiliated with the library—can use the online product, and also print and download.

Most libraries will want the same ILL/document delivery rights for digital materials as it has for print. To do this, include a statement that "the library may distribute copies of individual items to other authorized users, including to other libraries for purposes such as ILL and document delivery." If you want to be more specific, the license could read "consistent with Section 108 of the Copyright Act, the licensee may provide to another library, in either print, fax, or digital format, a single copy of an individual document that is part of the licensed materials."

The license should make clear that neither the library nor its parent institution assumes responsibility for acts not under its control. In other words, unauthorized acts by users are not a breach of contract, and infringing acts by users will not be attributed to the library. (Remember that the library and its parent institution are the parties to the contract, not the library's patrons). The vendor should not be able to unilaterally suspend or terminate access without prior notice if it believes that the library or any users have violated any terms. Insist, instead, that the vendor notify the library in writing of suspected violations before it suspends or terminates access, and insist also on the right to respond to such accusations. The library may want to include in the agreement how disputes will be handled, including arbitration, and who will pay for dispute resolution.

If the vendor asks that the library take some action if it becomes aware that a user is violating the terms of the contract, the library should agree to take steps it—the library, not the vendor—believes reasonable. The library should not, however, agree to be an informer or a cop; it should *not* agree to inform the vendor when the library believes that a user might be violating terms of the agreement.

Include the term of the agreement, which usually will be one or two years. Because vendors sometimes want to change the terms while the contract is in force or ready for renewal, insist that proposed changes must be submitted to the library in writing. E-mail is not a substitute; your e-mail filter may consider messages from a publisher to be spam.

Librarians are justifiably concerned about the "now you have it, now you don't" dilemma of electronic information. Ideally, the license will permit some continued access to the content even if the contract is terminated. The best you can hope for is continued access to the materials that you once had access to. For example, if your digital subscription included access to fifty journal titles from 1990 through 2005, and the library cancels the agreement at the end of 2005, the best you can expect is access to those fifty titles through 2005.

The agreement should provide for technical assistance and support. Try not to settle only for e-mail support; hopefully you will find, when necessary, a human being to whom you can speak. Don't be surprised to read that the vendor does not guarantee uninterrupted service. It's fine to agree that "the vendor will not be responsible for minor or occasional interruptions in service" or for "minor or occasional errors in the data." By contrast, *major* interruptions (several days or longer) or *significant* data errors should be considered a breach of the contract, and cause for either termination by the library or a reduction in the contract price.

It is important to understand that many information providers are *not* information creators. LexisNexis is, for the most part, a middleman. It makes nearly all of the information on its database available to you only because it has licenses to do so. Consequently, LexisNexis cannot guarantee that all of its databases will be available perpetually. The license should provide that the vendor will notify the library of withdrawn material. And if the amount withdrawn is substantial, the library should have the option to get a refund, or if it chooses, to terminate the agreement.

Don't be surprised if the vendor tries to disclaim both express and implied warranties. Do not let the vendor negate the "warranty of merchantability" or the "warranty of fitness for a particular purpose." These two implied warranties give the library important protections in the event that the vendor or the product does not perform as promised or expected. If the database or some part of it cannot be used for the purpose for which it was acquired, the library may want to terminate the contract, or at least adjust the subscription cost.

Most contracts will have a "choice of law" provision stating that the validity and interpretation of the contract will be governed by the law of a particular jurisdiction. Usually that jurisdiction is the law of a state chosen by the vendor. Because the library may want the contract to be interpreted under the laws of *its* home state, this may put you at odds with the vendor. Indeed, if the library is publicly funded, your state may require that contracts be interpreted under its laws. If you and the vendor cannot agree, your best option may be to delete the "choice of law" provision.

Many licenses will include a section on prohibited users. You probably can live with some of these prohibitions, but not with others. If the license prohibits the removal of copyright management information (such as the author's name, the copyright notice, or other identification) do not object. You should never remove that information—indeed, U.S. law prohibits your doing so. If the contract prohibits systematic copying, don't be alarmed; systematic copying is not permitted under the Copyright Act. Similarly, do not panic if the contract prohibits the library or a user from distributing the licensed material on an electronic network—including the Internet—other than on a secure network. You should agree not to make the information available to the world at large. Using a secure network should make everyone feel, well, secure.

The license should include a "hold harmless clause" by which the vendor warrants that the content does not infringe copyright or any intellectual property rights of others. Hold harmless clauses protect the library if the product includes infringing content.

Finally, libraries often want data on how much—or how little—a licensed product is being used. This information will help you decide whether to renew the license at the end of its term. The license should permit the vendor to collect usage data, consistent with state and national privacy laws. Although you want usage information, you do *not* want to know who used what. The license must preserve the privacy and confidentiality of users.

Chapter 6

Technical Services

Sonia Luna-Lamas

In an academic law library, traditional technical services include the functions of acquiring, processing, classifying, and organizing information for retrieval. Acquisitions, cataloging, and serials/continuations almost always fall within the purview of this department. Occasionally stacks maintenance, circulation, and interlibrary loan (ILL) functions also fall under the umbrella of technical services. Technical services librarians often serve as systems librarians, interacting with the integrated library system (ILS) effectively and efficiently.

Historically, change came slowly to technical services departments. Technology brought the first changes. Many technical services functions, such as ordering, checking in, claiming, and processing materials were automated. This automation, coupled with the integration of these functions into integrated libraries systems, meant that technical services librarians were the first librarians within a library to experience, use, and embrace technology.

While technology has altered the workflow and processes in technical services, it has not eliminated the need for technical services librarians. Acquisitions librarians must now negotiate the number of simultaneous users with vendors while also acquiring IP ranges for EZ proxy servers. Catalogers routinely include URLs in the 856 field and include electronic resources within the catalog.

Changes in technical services departments include several common trends. Some of these trends are:

- the outsourcing of in-house processes such as cataloging, physical processing, authority control, and maintenance services;

- the development of digital collections, moving away from the emphasis upon print collections;
- the new reliance upon digital periodicals such as HeinOnline that mean traditional print periodicals are no longer bound; and
- switching from manual or online ordering to the use of EDI (electronic data interchange).

Some of these trends create questions. Are law libraries building online catalogs for the use of patrons or for the use of librarians? Are law libraries saving money by outsourcing technical service responsibilities? Will law libraries continue purchasing and binding periodicals or will digitization products such as HeinOnline be used instead? Should law libraries stop manual ordering and claiming, and rely on EDI (electronic data interchange)? Should law libraries provide links to electronic resources on Web pages, in catalogs, or in both places? Should law libraries purchase machine-readable cataloging (MARC) records to add individual titles to their online catalogs? What formats should be collected? Why? How should a law library's titles and volumes be counted? Should these items be counted? Should electronic resources be included in these counts? If so, how? What is the American Bar Association (ABA) annual report attempting to measure when it requires title/volume count?

Technical services will be involved in answering the above questions. Why? Because I believe that technical services is the "heart of the library." Without technical services, the library could not function. Without technical services, materials are not ordered, checked in, processed, classified, or organized. Thus information retrieved by public services librarians and patrons becomes impossible. In technical services, materials are purchased and paid for via acquisitions, initially bibliographically identified for correct accessibility via cataloging, and then placed on the shelves for use. Lastly, these tasks are all counted, creating statistics. In order for an academic law library to effectively function, the above tasks must transpire smoothly.

ACQUISITIONS

Some would say that libraries begin in the acquisitions department. This department is responsible for the ordering, purchasing, and receiving of new library materials. While a collection development team selects the materials for acquisitions, the acquisitions department actually orders, checks in, and pays for the materials selected.

After the material is chosen, the acquisitions department will engage in *preorder searching,* which weeds out duplicate orders and identifies any series or serials the library may already hold. The law library's online catalog is then searched to ensure that the materials are not currently held by the library. Finally, an online bibliographic utility is searched to verify once more that the title in question is not held by the law library.

Once it is determined that the law library does not hold the materials, vendor selection begins. There are publishers, vendors, and jobbers. What do these terms mean? Can they be used interchangeably? According to the *Serials Acquisitions Glossary*, revised in 2005 by the Association for Library Collections and Technical Services (ALCTS), these terms are defined as:

> *Publisher:* a company or service that prepares and distributes books, newspapers, journals, or music (usually for sale to the public).
>
> *Vendor:* individuals or companies, other than publishers, from whom library materials are purchased. There is a distinction made between book and serial vendors. *Book vendors* provide law libraries the convenience of buying the books of numerous publishers and receiving a consolidated invoice for their purchase. They may also provide the library with standing orders, electronic ordering, claiming, and shelf-ready book processing. *Serial vendors* place and renew a library's serial order and offer the benefits of consolidated billing and claiming. They will both provide customer service.
>
> *Jobber:* may be used synonymously with vendor. A jobber is also commonly referred to as purchasing agent, a middleman who will purchase the material for the library from the publisher, invoice the library, and take care of any customer service issues such as claims.

The decision may be made to go directly through the publisher, vendor, or jobber. It is much easier to deal with a few vendors and jobbers rather than with several hundred publishers. This decision is dependent upon the nature of the material, its subject matter, the country of publication, and whether a need exists to expedite the materials. Common law library publishers, vendors, and jobbers are ABA, Hein, BNA, CCH, West Group, LexisNexis, EBSCO, Puvill, Gaunt, Oceana, Coutts, and YBP (Yankee). Many others exist, and there are some that offer shelf-ready delivery of materials to a law library, such as YBP Library Services and Coutts Library Services.

After this process, the order is placed. A purchase order is commonly entered into the acquisitions module of the library system. The order is then placed with the chosen vendor. This may be done in a variety of ways. The order can be mailed in, phoned in, faxed in, sent via e-mail, placed online, or sent via electronic data interchange (EDI). EDI is a set of computer interchange standards for documents such as invoices, bills, and purchase orders that replaces traditional paper documents. Paper-work is eliminated, and time is saved with EDI. When a purchase order is entered into a law library's integrated library system's acquisitions mod-ule, an order is sent electronically to the vendor via EDI. This is the newest and most efficient way of placing an order, maximizing the use of staff and time. Most of the major integrated library systems and major vendors support this type of ordering.

At the time the purchase order is created, a bibliographic record may be selected in the bibliographic utility of choice and downloaded. It may also be manually keyed into the integrated library system's acquisitions mod-ule. Once the materials are received in the law library, the order record is compared to the item and verified for accuracy. After checking in the item, it is then sent to the cataloging department for cataloging, classification, and processing.

Finally, the acquisitions department is responsible for claiming materi-als not received by the library. It will claim materials that do not arrive in a timely manner. It will also compare the material with the order record and verify that the law library is correctly and accurately invoiced for ma-terials ordered and received. Invoices are then turned over for payment to the accounts payable department in the law library or university.

CATALOGING

The cataloging department is responsible for the cataloging, classification, authority control, and physical processing of library materials. With this process, print materials are made shelf ready for patrons. Will the library be *cataloging* or *classifying* these materials? Cataloging requires the de-scription of an item's physical appearance. It will be described using spe-cific rules that will allow the patron to retrieve it. To physically describe materials, cataloging departments follow the rules listed in the Anglo-American Cataloging Rules (AACR2). These rules are designed for the use and aid of the construction of library catalogs. They cover the de-scription of the material and provide access points for the material. These rules answer these questions:

- What does the material look like?
- Who published it? And
- What are the *access points*—title, author, subjects?

Classification attempts to define what materials will be shelved to-gether as well as what *call number* will be assigned. If the correct subject analysis is not done on the material, then the correct call number will not be assigned. If this happens, the material may not be found and could be lost on the law library shelves. If the physical location of the material was not decided in the acquisitions department, it is decided now. Again, this depends on the arrangement of the individual library collection and the type of material that was selected.

Authority control is another function of the cataloging department. Authority control is the consistent use and maintenance of the access points or forms of names, subjects, and uniform titles. These access points are usually revised against an online bibliographic utility such as the Online Computer Library Center (OCLC) for accuracy. The authority control can be done by the copy-cataloger or the cataloger at the time these staff are revising and editing the bibliographic record for addition to the library catalog. Authority control should be done regularly as part of database maintenance. Many integrated library systems run reports that advise the users of authority conflicts. If authority control has been outsourced, the cataloging department can periodically send copies of the most recent bibliographic records for authority control processing to vendors. Two vendors that offer this service are Marcive, Inc. and Library Technology, Inc. During this process, copies of bibliographic records are sent to the vendors. Corrections are then made to the bibliographic records. The corrected bibliographic records are then returned to the law library and they are replaced in the integrated library system.

When materials arrive from the acquisitions department, they may be divided into shelf-ready materials, copy-cataloging materials, or materials that need to be routed directly to a professional cataloger for review. The shelf-ready materials need minimal processing. Shelf-ready materials arrive at the law library with property stamps. Barcodes are attached and call number labels are placed on the spine. Barcodes must be entered into the law library's local catalogs for easy access; call numbers may be shelf-listed. In the process of shelf-listing, the call numbers that are on the spine will be revised against the law library's local catalogs for conflicts with other works, for multiple copies, and for other library-specific location changes. Many law libraries have copy-catalogers who may revise and review materials received before forwarding these materials to professional catalogers. These individuals usually catalog the materials—that is, physically describe them—but leave the subject analysis and the call number assignment to the professional catalogers.

Most law libraries are arranged according to the Library of Congress (LC) Classification System and LC subject headings. Currently, both the schedules and the subject headings are available in a variety of formats. For the benefit of space and accessibility, many law libraries opt to hold the schedules and subject headings electronically, usually either via LC Classification Web or Hein (Dershem's Classification Web). Both of these are paid subscription services that offer comprehensive integrated LC classification schedules and subject headings with hyperlinks. The benefit of the electronic format is that licensing for multiple users can be purchased, allowing usage by more than one cataloging staff member at a time. The downside is that browsing generally tends to be more difficult and network availability is essential for working with up-to-date schedules or subject headings.

Many law libraries are members of computer library services, such as OCLC or RLIN (Research Libraries Information Network). These services provide catalogers with bibliographic utilities and online union catalogs as well as support in the form of training and tutorials. Member catalogers may use these networks to assist them with bibliographic data information. Member libraries share in the input and editing of bibliographic records and holdings into this online union catalog, and these records are then exported and made available to the general public via their online catalogs. OCLC offers its members WorldCat, which is the world's largest online union catalog. WorldCat allows law libraries to process, manage, and share information resources. WorldCat makes its records available to Web users on popular Internet Web search sites, allows links to contents in library collections, and makes member library collections more visible.

Another function of the cataloging department is that of database maintenance. Database maintenance involves location changes of materials, removal from the catalog of titles withdrawn from the shelves, and addition of added copies. This process provides integrity assurance that the data loaded into the ILS database is correct. Due to the advent of online integrated library systems, an interrelated environment has been created where data placed in one module of the library system directly affects how other modules are able to utilize the data. For example, the library staff member in cataloging who handles these issues needs to work closely with the acquisitions department as well as the serials/continuations departments when there is a location change. The item's records—including bibliographic, item, and location holdings— not only need to be updated but if the item is a serial, the check-in record as well as the purchase order record also need to be updated. If this is not done, materials will not go to their proper location when they are updated again. If the library decides to cancel a title and withdraw it from the collection, the acquisitions and/or serials/continuations departments need to be notified to cancel their records as well; if not, they will be claiming materials from vendors for which they have canceled their subscriptions.

Some law libraries are outsourcing many technical services functions such as the cataloging and processing of materials as well as delegating authority control. Law libraries should realize that sometimes this out-sourcing may create more work and generate more problems that need to be resolved. The law library should fully understand what services it is getting when it is outsourcing. It should maintain open communication channels with the service provider in order to ensure a smooth and pro-ductive relationship. Profiles need to be carefully created and reviewed. Several trial runs should be conducted before any service agreements are entered into. When these services are successful, they greatly benefit the library. If the services become a burden, the law library should review the decision and relationship. If outsourcing is decided upon, it is essential that law library administration involve technical services personnel in the planned outsourced process. These staff members are a great asset during the profiling and trial period. Since they have experience doing the work, the staff can identify potential problems.

Another area that is usually handled within the technical services de-partment and specifically by the cataloger or bibliographic control li-brarian is that of integrated library system maintenance, implementa-tion, and migration. Since maintenance, implementation, and migration usually involves many decisions that are based on bibliographic data, the technical services librarian is the most qualified individual to assist and make suggestions. Data migration has specific parameters that need be decided before any data are loaded onto a current database for use. If the data are not correctly identified and transferred into the cor-rect fields or parameters, they will be useless for the library's staff and its patrons. In many law libraries, the cataloger is the one involved with technical software issues concerning the new integrated library system as well as training staff to use the various modules such as circulation, acquisitions, or serials.

The technical services professional is usually the one responsible for monitoring the availability of the integrated library system on a daily ba-sis. This individual puts together any information or training that may be needed after there is an upgrade or migration from one system to another. These are related to staffing issues and workflow reassignment within the specific library. This position may also coordinate the need for in-house training by the library vendor when deemed necessary. Few technical ser-vices professionals have any formal training in the systems operations but they are an invaluable source of information for the IT departments, which usually handle the hardware issues involving the integrated li-brary systems. Technical services staff have an understanding of how ma-terials are arranged in an online environment and how these items can best be searched. This, if coordinated and properly addressed in an online environment, will ensure the success of any integrated library system that is implemented.

SERIALS/CONTINUATIONS

The majority of the materials that law libraries acquire and collect fall into the following formats: monographs, serials/continuations, electronic resources, and microforms. For purposes of budgeting and statistics, they are divided into these categories as well. How are these different formats defined? AACR2 defines the terms as:

Serial: a continuing resource issued in a succession of discrete parts, usually bearing numbering, that has no predetermined conclusion. In other words, it is material that is uniquely identified with enumeration, chronology, and possibly a date that is usually issued in successive parts and is intended to be continued indefinitely. In law libraries, all materials seem to be serials.

Monograph: a bibliographic resource that is complete or is intended to be completed within a finite number of parts or within a fixed period of time—meaning, nonserial in nature. These works are either complete in one part, or intended to be completed in a finite number of separate parts, with no intention of updating or supplementing.

Electronic Resources: materials (date and/or programs) encoded for manipulation by a computerized device. These materials may require the use of a peripheral directly connected to a computerized device or a computer network. These materials may be in the form of CD-ROMs, databases, or websites.

Microform: any medium, transparent or opaque, bearing images. In this format we find microfilm and microfiche.

Since law is dynamic in nature, most of the materials will fall into the serials/continuations format. Serials subscriptions will be in the form of periodicals such as law reviews, newsletters, and journals, as well as annuals of different types. They are also pocket parts and supplements to law library monographs. Checking serials provides technical services with an endless amount of work. Checking materials into the integrated library system assists the librarian and the online catalog user to locate the most current issue, update, or supplement that has been received. The check-in process also assists the law library with invoicing. It helps to ensure that the law library is paying for materials that it has received and currently owns.

Law libraries spend a great deal of time keeping services up to date and subscriptions to periodicals current. Print reporters, loose-leaf services, and periodicals all require continuous updating and monitoring. Sometimes these services are also outsourced. In order to effectively outsource these services, law libraries should randomly monitor the services to ensure that they follow library procedures concerning discards, duplicates, or missing issues.

The serials/continuations department often handles binding. Traditionally law libraries have bound periodicals. With reduced budgets and the advent of online electronic periodicals, many law libraries no longer bind their periodicals. Should a law library decide to continue binding periodical issues, there are several commercial binderies available for their use.

ELECTRONIC RESOURCES

Futurists are positing that the library of the future is a *virtual library*. Virtual libraries provide patrons with electronic access to information. How is an electronic resource defined? The AACR2 defines an electronic resource as "materials (date and/or programs) encoded for manipulation by a computerized device. These materials may require the use of a peripheral directly connected to a computerized device or a computer network. These materials may be in the form of CD-ROMs, databases or websites."

While law libraries are still required to maintain collections in a variety of formats, most now offer access to print and electronic materials. How are technical services departments affected by electronic resources?

Electronic resources present significant issues for acquisitions, cataloging, and serials/continuations. In acquisitions, librarians are faced with licensing issues. In cataloging, decisions need to be made as to whether the item will be listed on the law library's Web page or also included in the library's catalog. If the individual title access within a catalog is decided, adding individual records to the library databases may be cumbersome and the linked sites must be regularly checked for new, deleted, and updated titles in order to keep the catalogs up to date. Who will be responsible for checking the accuracy of the links? Will this be the responsibility of the cataloging department? If so, they will need to engage the assistance of commercial link-checking software if the integrated library system does not supply one. In the serials/continuations department, check-in records can be created so that the law library can track annual renewals for electronic subscriptions so that there is no service interruption for the user.

STATISTICS

What are we counting? What should we be counting? How are we counting? For whom are we counting? To whom should we be reporting our counting?

What are we counting? In technical services, everything is counted. The workflow is methodical and concrete. Materials arrive, they are handled, and they are put out on the shelves. When the materials arrived, what categories did they correspond with? Were monographs or serials purchased? If it is an electronic resource, is it a database in nature? Does it provide access to full text or simply citations?

What should we be counting? Again, *everything!* The counts seem to be used to justify law library budgets, need for extra personnel, as well as describing what library staff spend their time doing. Law librarians have devised several methods of counting. Most law libraries are moving to keeping statistics using the aid of their online ILS. Usually the ILS will report statistics for usage; added bibliographic records; deleted item records; purchase orders entered; items ordered, received, or checked in; and titles cataloged in a certain classification.

The information reported by the online library systems is accurate. Do all online library systems count the same things the same way? The answer to this question depends upon the operator entering the original order or bibliographic record. If the codes used are not standardized, the output for statistics will be unreliable. Most law libraries have devised local statistics on spreadsheets that allow them to customize what and how they want things counted. Librarians count to justify that there is a need for an increase in law library budgets. They are also required to report annual statistics to the ABA as well as law library consortia memberships. Numbers are important, and we will probably have to keep counting forever. Innovative as we are, we will keep devising ingenious ways of keeping statistics in the future that will not involve having individuals keep manual counts of any type.

What should we be counting? While the ABA annual report requires volumes and titles, it is unclear as to whether electronic titles can be counted. Can they be counted if cataloged? At this time, there is no clear answer as to what we should be counting.

CONCLUSION

Technical service in law libraries has traditionally involved the acquisition, processing, and classification of materials. While technology has changed the workflow of the department as well as some of the job tasks, it has not eliminated the need for technical services librarians. Acquisitions, cataloging, and serials/continuation continue to require the presence of trained, professional librarians. Technology may be changing how these jobs are done, but it is not eradicating the need for these jobs to be done.

REFERENCES

Anglo-American Cataloging Rules, 2nd ed. Ottawa, ON: Canadian Library Association, 2002.

Cataloger's Web. www.catalogersweb.com (accessed November 15, 2005).

Chan, Lois Mai. *A Guide to the Library of Congress Classification*, 5th ed. Englewood, CO: Libraries Unlimited, 1999.

"Classification Web: World Wide Web Access to Library of Congress Classification and Library of Congress Subject Headings." *Library of Congress*, http:// classificationweb.net (accessed July 1, 2005).

"The Future of Law Libraries: A Symposium on the Impact of Technology on Law Libraries and Law Classrooms of the Future." Symposium held at Amelia Island Plantation in Jacksonville, FL, March 10–11, 2005.

Krieger, Tillie, ed. *Subject Headings for the Literature of Law and International Law, and Index to LC K Schedules: A Thesaurus on Law Subject Terms*. Littleton, CO: Rothman, 1996.

Lembke, Melody Busse, Rhonda K. Lawrence, and Peter Enyingi. *Cataloging Legal Literature: A Manual on AACR2R and Library of Congress Subject Headings for Legal Material* (Littleton, CO: Rothman, 1996).

Library of Congress Subject Headings for Legal Materials, 3rd ed. Littleton, CO: Rothman, 1996.

Library Technologies, Inc. www.librarytech.com (accessed August 6, 2005).

Marcive, Inc. www.marcive.com (accessed August 8, 2005).

"Serials Acquisitions Glossary." 3rd ed, rev. *American Library Association*. www .ala.org/ala/alctscontent/alctspubsbucket/webpublications/alctsserials/.

Chapter 7

Foreign, Comparative, and International Law Librarianship

Mary Rumsey

Foreign, comparative, and international law librarianship is a vibrant and growing field. Librarians who work in this area are often called "FCIL" librarians, or foreign, comparative, and international law librarianship librarians. These librarians have an interest or background in foreign cultures, languages, or international affairs.

WHAT IS FCIL LIBRARIANSHIP?

As mentioned above, the FCIL umbrella contains three areas of focus: foreign law, comparative law, and international law.

Foreign Law

Foreign law covers the national and subnational laws of other countries. "Subnational" means the law of political subdivisions such as Canadian provinces, Australian states and territories, or German *Länder*. People and businesses frequently cross national borders; this creates foreign law issues. For example, U.S. immigrants with family in their country of origin may be required to prove that a foreign adoption, marriage, or divorce satisfies U.S. requirements. Often FCIL librarians receive requests regarding information on Vietnamese adoption law, Moroccan divorces, or Eritrean marriages.

Businesses also face legal questions when they enter foreign markets, outsource work, or make contracts with foreign suppliers. Their legal issues may include:

- "Are there any legal hoops we have to jump through before we can sell our software in France?"
- "What is the best way to work with a Chinese company to distribute our product—a distributorship, a joint venture, an acquisition or merger, or something else?"
- "Are foreign companies allowed to buy land in Poland?"

Comparative Law

Comparative law, the second FCIL area, is a way of studying law. People who do comparative law study the similarities and differences between the legal systems of different countries. For example, a law professor might write an article comparing the U.S. law on products liability with the law in Japan. Practicing lawyers do not often engage in comparative law; usually law professors and law students actually make the scholarly comparisons between legal systems.

Comparative law issues are typically foreign law issues. When aiding a comparative law researcher, the FCIL librarian must identify and locate foreign law sources.

International Law

The third area of FCIL librarianship, international law, has increased its importance since World War II and the birth of the United Nations. According to the concepts of international law, countries must follow specific rules when dealing with each other, with people, and with companies or international organizations. After World War II and the Holocaust, countries agreed that international law affected the manner in which a country recognized the rights of its own citizens particularly in the extreme case of genocide.[1] In addition to human rights, international trade and the environment are among the new subjects of international law.

As recently as thirty years ago, foreign, comparative, and international law was a small area of interest. A handful of law professors taught, thought, and wrote about it, but few lawyers or law students focused their time or energy on the topic. The rise of international organizations such as the World Trade Organization (WTO), increased immigration, and increasing economic interdependence between countries have focused attention on this subject.

WHO ARE FCIL LIBRARIANS?

Frequently, law librarians receive foreign and international questions. Few law librarians specialize in FCIL work. In the United States, approximately seventy-five law librarians have job titles that reflect their FCIL responsibilities. Many more librarians, perhaps as many as 150, are the unofficial FCIL librarians at their workplace. Most work at law school libraries. Often large law firms have a librarian who handles most of the foreign and international law work. Large county law libraries, in Chicago and Los Angeles, have librarians with "foreign and international" in their job titles.

THE WORK OF FCIL LIBRARIANS

Duties vary widely, but generally fall under the headings of reference, teaching, collection development, or cataloging. Most FCIL librarians do some reference work.

Reference

Foreign law reference questions range from "Here's a citation to a foreign law. Can you find me a copy?" to "What is the law on doctor-patient confidentiality in Chad?" Some patrons may require help deciphering a foreign citation, such as "Loi fédérale du 19 décembre 1958 sur la circulation routière, SR 741.01." Other patrons may need to examine the inner workings of a foreign legal system. They need assistance with identifying the relevant sources of law, such as a civil code and regulations. Further help is then necessary to help the individual locate the necessary materials on a topic.

Foreign Legal Systems

Many foreign countries have different legal systems. While the United States and most countries settled by Great Britain have a common law system, most European countries have a civil law system. Civil law systems differ from the U.S. system in several ways. In civil law systems, the emphasis is on legislation rather than court opinions. In civil law systems, courts still decide criminal cases and do not have trials by jury. Courts resolve disputes between parties, but they rarely establish general legal rules.

FCIL librarians routinely explain foreign legal systems to researchers. If a researcher assumes that a foreign country has a legal system that matches the U.S. system, he or she may ask for information that is not available or is not useful. For example, American lawyers sometimes research jury instructions, which are summaries of the law that a judge reads to the jury before the jury makes its decision. An American lawyer who wanted German jury instructions would learn that no such materials exist.

For many foreign law questions, the librarian can use English-language books, articles, research guides, and databases to identify the relevant sources of law. One source that many FCIL librarians call the "bible" of foreign law research is by Thomas A. Reynolds and Arturo Flores, *Foreign Law Guide: Current Sources of Codes and Basic Legislation in Jurisdictions of the World (1989–)*. This title is available on CD-ROM, or as a series of eight loose-leaf volumes, or as an Internet database. The *Foreign Law Guide* is arranged by country. For each country, the authors provide a brief summary of the legal system and a list of basic legal publications. This list is followed by a longer list of legal subjects, from abortion to workers' compensation. For most subjects, the authors list the relevant law in the country.

The *Foreign Law Guide* helps librarians identify the material their patrons need. For example, suppose a U.S. lawyer asks a librarian to find the Austrian laws on data protection. The *Foreign Law Guide*'s chapter on Austria has the index entry "Information and Data Protection," which gives the following useful information: "Datenschutzgesetz 2000 in Bundesgesetzblatt 1999 no. 165." This is the name and citation of the law in German. Where the authors of the *Foreign Law Guide* have found no English translation, their entries usually stop. With this citation, the librarian could retrieve the German text from the Web, or at a minimum make an interlibrary loan (ILL) request for it.

In this case, the *Foreign Law Guide* entry continues: "In force 1 Jan 2000. Replaces the 1978 Data Protection Act." From this information, the librarian learns that the effective date of the law was January 1, 2000, and that the 1978 law is no longer in force. Knowing the effective date will help the researcher distinguish between discussions of Austria's old law and its new one. Too often, especially on the Web, legal commentary does not include citations to the law.

The entry continues: "Summarized in *Data Protection Laws of the World*. English translation at www.coe.int/T/E/Legal_affairs/Legal_co-operation/Data_protection/Documents/National_laws/." For most patrons, an English translation or summary is the most-desired object of their research. The *Foreign Law Guide* does a great service to foreign-law researchers by pointing to English-language translations and summaries wherever available.

Of course, the *Foreign Law Guide* does not provide citations to every foreign law. Its focus is on those laws most likely to be required by U.S. legal researchers. If the *Foreign Law Guide* does not provide a citation, the librarian embarks on a more difficult search. The librarian may need to search indexes or digests of foreign laws, Internet sources, article indexes, or other sources. For these searches, the librarian will probably need a working knowledge of other languages.

Many of the *Foreign Law Guide*'s references to translations point to "subject collections." These are large databases or loose-leaf sets on a particular topic, such as business law or copyright law, offering English translations of laws from a variety of countries. Good examples include the World Intellectual Property Organization's online "Collection of Laws for Electronic Access," which has copyright, patent, and trademark laws from over 100 countries. Another example is *Investment Laws of the World*, a large collection of loose-leaf volumes that covers basic investment laws from many countries.

The Internet has made foreign law research much easier. One useful tool is the country or regional research guide. These guides make great starting points. For example, a librarian confronted with a question about Caribbean law can refer to Yemisi Dina's *Guide to Caribbean Law Research*,[2] published at the GlobaLex site. Like most guides, Dina's guide gives an introduction to the legal system, lists major legal publications, and points to online sources where available. Websites such as LLRX.com and GlobaLex offer large collections of research guides.

International Law

International law questions have grabbed headlines in the twenty-first century. For example, has the United States violated international law against torture? Has Sudan committed genocide? Does child labor violate international human rights? More and more patrons are asking law librarians for help with international law research.

Most reference work in international law can be conducted using English sources. Nonetheless, international law research poses its own hazards. The variety of sources used in international law can overwhelm researchers. International law differs from national law because there is no real international government. In other words, there is no legislative body like the U.S. Congress, no executive like the U.S. president, and no executive agencies like the Environmental Protection Agency (EPA). The United Nations General Assembly and the secretary-general, which sound a bit like Congress and the president, lack the power to make laws. The International Court of Justice (ICJ), sometimes called the World Court, can decide cases between countries if they agree to go before it; however, its decisions are not binding on future disputes. Thus, the World Court is much less powerful than the U.S. Supreme Court.

The issue thus becomes: Who creates the rules of international law? Treaties, agreed to and signed by countries, form the clearest source of international law. For example, the Convention on International Trade in Endangered Species of Wild Flora and Fauna (CITES)[3] regulates the buying, selling, and shipping of endangered plants and animals.

Customary law is also a major source of international rules. Customary law refers to general practices of states (i.e., countries) and intergovernmental organizations that are legally binding and generally recognized by all states. An example of customary law is the practice of not executing juvenile offenders. Although a couple of nations still impose the death penalty on juveniles, the "general practice" of nearly every country forbids this punishment.

Other sources of international law include *general principles of law*, judicial decisions, and the teachings of the most highly qualified legal scholars, also known as publicists, of the various nations. General principles of law include concepts found in nearly all legal systems, such as the idea that a party can lose a right by repeatedly failing to assert it, that is, a waiver. Judicial decisions and scholarly writings can be used in international law to argue that states should follow a certain rule described in those decisions or writings.

International law lacks a clear ladder of authority. This makes international law research more confusing than U.S. law. When researching U.S. law, researchers understand that the Constitution supersedes statutes while statutes trump regulations. By contrast, an individual researching international law must often identify a hodgepodge of documents from which the lawyer infers a general principle of international law.

Even though treaties are the clearest source of international law, they are not a contract between the signatories. A state may add a *reservation* when it signs a treaty, saying that it refuses to be bound by certain parts of the treaty. More confusingly, a nonparty may find itself bound by rules in a treaty that it never signed. For example, even states that never signed the Genocide Treaty are considered bound by it.

Because international law is based, in part, on what states do, FCIL librarians must often track down examples of *state practice* in international law. State practice is found in treaties, decisions of national courts and international tribunals, national laws, diplomatic correspondence, opinions of national legal advisers, and the practice of international organizations. Identifying state practice can be so difficult that some distinguished FCIL librarians have published a loose-leaf set designed to simplify this research.[4]

The American Society of International Laws Electronic Information System for International Law (EISIL) project and its *Electronic Resources Guide* are two of the best starting points for international law research. The

EISIL database,[5] created by law librarians, organizes the field of law into numerous topics and identifies key resources in each area. As an example, a patron needing to research the international law of terrorism could start with the Terrorism category under International Criminal Law. EISIL summarizes and links to the most important treaties on this topic, and gives other useful information such as the date every treaty was signed, its citation, and links to related information.

The *Electronic Resource Guide*,[6] also prepared by law librarians, consists of a series of research guides on various international law topics, including human rights, environmental law, criminal law, and intellectual property law; for example, patents and copyrights. Like EISIL, the *Electronic Resource Guide* can help researchers sort out the important online resources from the flood of less useful Internet information.

Reference work in international law, like foreign law, has become easier with the advent of Internet sources. Many treaties, for example, can be found online. In addition to excellent online searching skills, however, an understanding of older, paper-based tools plays a part in most FCIL librarians' work.

Teaching

Some FCIL librarians teach formal classes on international and foreign legal research. Such teaching may consist of guest appearances in substantive law courses, such as a human rights or comparative constitutional law class. The librarian may teach a session on FCIL research as part of an Advanced Legal Research class. A few law schools offer a regular class or seminar focusing on FCIL research.[7] Other schools offer shorter courses on the topic. To support librarians who teach FCIL research, the Foreign, Comparative and International Law Special Interest Section of the American Association of Law Libraries (AALL) maintains a page of syllabi, presentations, handouts, exercises, and other class materials.

Collection Development

Another task for many FCIL librarians is collection development, which is the selection and acquisition of paper and electronic resources on foreign and international law. FCIL collection development has become increasingly expensive. With the upsurge in transnational and international law interest, publication of FCIL titles is booming. Also, the number of independent countries has increased threefold since World War II.[8] This increase means more countries from which law libraries might collect materials. In addition, new organizations and legal systems have sprung up, including the European Union (EU), the WTO, and the North American

Free Trade Agreement (NAFTA) system. These three organizations have created whole new areas of law to which FCIL collection development must respond. With new titles on EU law numbering in the hundreds each year, collection librarians must choose carefully.

Collection development librarians struggle with how to direct their foreign law budgets. Most of their patrons seek information about major Western European countries. Thus, libraries tend to duplicate one another's holdings. Partly because of this duplication, libraries have less money to buy materials from other jurisdictions. So while several libraries own the current German Civil Code, far fewer have codes from Latvia or Uganda. Occasional efforts to develop cooperative collecting arrangements have fallen prey to budget cuts, changes in library focus, and inattention.

Generally, everything that is difficult in collecting American law materials applies to FCIL work. Collections of foreign and international legal materials create enhanced difficulties. In addition to agonizing over whether to switch to electronic formats, librarians must cope with foreign currency transactions, overseas shipping costs, advertisements and catalogs in foreign languages, and vendors whose first language is something other than English.

Recently, the dollar's weakness against foreign currencies has made acquiring these materials even more expensive, increasing the budget limitations suffered by most law librarians. Also, libraries that collect from developing countries, such as most African jurisdictions, must deal with erratic publication schedules, unreliable vendors, and logistical obstacles such as poor communication and shipping infrastructures. Because of the wide scope and high cost of possible materials, few libraries can afford to collect them from every jurisdiction. Harvard and the Law Library of Congress have the most comprehensive global law libraries.[9]

Collection development may include extensive work in foreign languages at law libraries that acquire foreign monographs, but FCIL librarians in smaller libraries may look only at English-language publications. Most of the demand from U.S. patrons is for materials in English, making those materials the first priority for many collection librarians. After spending money on the first priority, little cash may remain for other choices.

Cataloging

Cataloging foreign titles often requires special skills and training. Fortunately, records for most titles are available through the Online Computer Library Center (OCLC) or the Research Libraries Information Network (RLIN), making copy-cataloging possible.

Many law libraries have a backlog of international and foreign materials to be reclassified. This backlog results from several factors. First, because the Library of Congress did not finish creating classification schedules for most foreign countries until the 1980s, most libraries that collected foreign law before invented their own systems for arranging materials. At the University of Minnesota Law Library, for example, many titles are still classed in the catchall section *Foreign Texts*. Patrons must search for items using the last name of the author. Other law libraries sort materials by homegrown abbreviations such as *Rus* for Russian and *Jap* for Japanese.

Second, changes to the Library of Congress classification system for international law have also made more work for FCIL catalogers. The JX class, established in 1910, originally covered both international relations and international law. As international organizations and international law grew in importance, works on these topics no longer fit neatly into the JX class. A drastic change was needed. In 1997, the Library of Congress split the class into Political Science (JZ) and Law (KZ).[10]

Islamic law and other religious law has been another challenge to FCIL catalogers. Until recently, the Library of Congress classification schedule had no place for it. Therefore, catalogers used a variety of approaches to works on Islamic law, scattering them among classes such as BP (Islam) or not classifying them at all.[11] The Library of Congress released the last piece of its religious law schedules in 2004. Reclassifying books on religious law will keep FCIL catalogers busy for at least a few years.

ATTRACTIONS OF FOREIGN AND INTERNATIONAL LIBRARIANSHIP

Variety

Most FCIL librarians cite its variety and challenge as the reasons they enjoy it.[12] While law librarianship itself is characterized by variety,[13] FCIL librarianship widens the scope of work dramatically. Foreign law questions can cover more than 190 countries while international law reaches from the deep seabed to outer space. FCIL research pulls librarians into foreign legal systems, calls on their foreign-language skills, exposes them to different cultures and different approaches to legal problems, and takes place in an ever-changing landscape of print and electronic resources.

Collegiality

Another benefit of FCIL work stems from the relatively small number of librarians in the field. New FCIL librarians often comment on the warmth of their seasoned colleagues when welcoming new FCIL librarians.[14] Because few libraries' foreign and international law collections come close to being complete, librarians tend to cooperate and share resources readily.

Employment Prospects

Generally, the market for FCIL librarians is strong.[15] American Association of Law Libraries salary surveys show FCIL librarians earn more money than law librarians in nearly all other positions, including reference, computer/automation librarians, and government documents librarians.[16] Probably much of this difference reflects the greater size and resources of libraries with large FCIL collections. The globalization of law practice will continue to increase demand for foreign and international legal information as well as the people who know how to find it. Lawyers whose practices never reached farther than the next state now find their clients doing business in foreign countries, inheriting property in other countries, or fighting child-custody battles with ex-spouses overseas.

QUALIFICATIONS OF FCIL LIBRARIANS

Education

Most FCIL librarians work in reference at law school libraries. For reference librarians, law libraries usually prefer to hire applicants with law degrees. However, not all academic FCIL librarians have them. Few of the law firm librarians who specialize in FCIL work have law degrees, although some do.

As with U.S. legal research, FCIL research may be easier for librarians with law degrees. Law school provides librarians a useful vocabulary, overviews of legislative and regulatory processes, and familiarity with dispute resolution mechanisms such as courts. Many law librarians have acquired an excellent understanding of lawmaking institutions and legal concepts without a legal education. The typical law school education does not include classes in foreign or international law,[17] though students may take them as electives.

Like most law librarians, most FCIL librarians have a master's degree in library and information science. Academic law libraries usually require this degree. Exceptions arise when talented paraprofessionals are promoted to jobs that ordinarily require the degree, or when law libraries hire a lawyer based on his or her research skills.

Languages

Foreign language skills are one of the "necessary strengths" for FCIL work.[18] Historically, French, German, Spanish, and Italian have been the most common languages used by FCIL librarians.[19] With increasing legal and financial interest in China, however, knowledge of Chinese might be even more marketable.

Librarians lacking strong foreign-language skills should not despair of their FCIL prospects. The most common use of foreign languages is the slow deciphering of written words, the easiest of the four basic skills of reading, writing, listening, and speaking. Generally, librarians do not translate material for patrons. Translating legal documents requires specialized training and a great deal of time. Willingness to wade through foreign language documents with a bilingual legal dictionary, however, is definitely required.

Online translators such as Babel Fish cannot substitute for translations by humans, but they can help librarians get the gist of a document or Web page. If an English translation of a foreign law is unavailable, the best a librarian can do is provide the law in its original language, and online translators can help find that. For example, foreign news stories about a recently passed law often contain a link to the law. By using a Web translator to help identify likely search terms, librarians can find these news stories, get the gist of them with a translator, and use the link to retrieve the full text.

Curiosity and Intelligence

Many FCIL librarians share an interest in foreign countries, international relations, or history. Librarians who like to grapple with new concepts, and who are willing to learn some background before jumping into search mode, flourish as FCIL librarians.

Training

Training in FCIL librarianship can be difficult to obtain. The best way to learn is by working with an experienced FCIL librarian. In large cities, it may be possible to have a foreign librarianship internship. More commonly, law librarians learn FCIL librarianship by combining on-the-job experience and attending educational programs.

In the mid-1990s, AALL and Oceana Publishing sponsored a series of workshops on foreign and international research. The papers from those workshops were published as several volumes that still offer invaluable guidance on FCIL librarianship. Unfortunately, they largely predate the Internet, making them an incomplete resource.

At its annual meeting, AALL usually has three to five programs concerned with international or foreign legal research. In addition, programs at other organizations offer some FCIL training. The International Association of Law Librarians (IALL)[20] has an annual meeting, usually held outside the United States, that features detailed, substantive legal topics. For the past several years, the Law Library of Congress has offered inexpensive, valuable, one-day workshops the day before the American Society of International Law meeting opens in Washington, D.C. Topics have ranged from Latin American legal systems to the new UN treaty on persons with disabilities. Finally, some AALL chapters occasionally hold programs on foreign or international topics.

One innovative approach to learning FCIL research takes the form of an online tutorial. Open to any user, the tutorial resides on Duke University's website.[21] The Center for Computer-Assisted Legal Instruction (CALI) has one tutorial on foreign law, and plans to add an entire library of lessons on FCIL research. Those lessons, however, are open only to students and staff at CALI-member law schools.

A DAY IN THE LIFE

The variety of FCIL work means that no day is typical. To give an idea of what my work is like, however, I kept track of the work I did one day as the University of Minnesota's foreign, comparative, and international law librarian. On another day, I might have taught a session of my class on FCIL research or spent a shift at the reference desk.

I started my day, like most of us do, by looking at my e-mail. In my personal e-mail, I found a request for help from a student. She is writing a paper on Islamic mortgages for a class on Islamic law and needs materials on the prohibition against paying interest. Fortunately, her professor has pointed her to some of the information she needs from Islamic religious sources. I can focus on more traditional legal resources. Like many law students, she doesn't know much about searching library catalogs or periodical indexes. In a few minutes, I retrieve some likely titles from our online catalog and the *Index to Legal Periodicals*. In the process, I learn that *murabaha* is one of the terms used for financing compatible with Islam. In my reply to the student, I explain my searches, list some useful results, and suggest that she try some Internet searching, using the term "murabaha."

The next e-mail is from a law librarian colleague at Georgetown University. She needs a copy of a Supreme Court case from India. The University of Minnesota has a large collection of Indian materials, most of which are stored in our basement. I take the e-mail downstairs, find the case, and ask our ILL librarian to scan it as a PDF file. Soon I'm replying to my colleague's e-mail with a copy of the case. I am returning her favor, as she faxed me an obscure German article last month.

One useful practice for FCIL librarians is to subscribe to various electronic discussion lists (listservs) and blogs. In my folder for listserv postings, I see a note from a South African law librarian who needs an old decision from the European Commission of Human Rights. I make a mental note to check back later to see if anyone has replied. If not, I'll try to locate it.

After dealing with the rest of my e-mail and skimming my blog feeds, I pick up a folder of publishers' advertisements and catalogs. Collection development never ends. Our library is responding to interest in China by acquiring more titles in this area, so I'm particularly interested in new offerings in Chinese law. I read through a description of a book containing English translations of Chinese business laws. It sounds a lot like a title we already have, *China Laws for Foreign Business*. In addition, we began a subscription last year to a database on Chinese law, isinolaw, that probably includes most of these laws. I decide to pass on this one. Before I can pick up the next flyer, the phone rings.

One of our professors, who teaches international intellectual property law, needs some statistics on patent application rates in various countries as well as information about the history of their patent laws. Fortunately, I remember that the World Intellectual Property Organization (WIPO) tracks patent applications for some countries. I check the WIPO site and pull off some of the requested information. For the rest, I'll have to spend some time in the stacks. We have several useful books on patent history, though they spend half their time in this professor's office. I'm skimming through a few chapters on early patent systems when a student knocks on the door.

He's writing a law review article comparing U.S. securities laws to Belgium's. I ask him if he can read French or Dutch; he says no. I check our *Foreign Law Guide* database, hoping to find an English translation. Once again, the *Foreign Law Guide* comes through, pointing to various laws that have been translated and published in large subject collections like *International Securities Regulations* and *Commercial Laws of the World*. I send him off with call numbers and a printout of the *Foreign Law Guide* page.

Checking my e-mail, I see that another professor needs information on a case before the European Court of Human Rights. In this case, the court decided that Turkey could prohibit an adult Muslim woman from wearing a *hijab*, a female headscarf, to graduate school.[22] The professor wasn't sure whether the court had issued a decision. If it had, he wants a copy. I know from reading an international law blog this morning that the case has been decided. I go back to the blog but the link provided for the case doesn't work. I go directly to the court's site and retrieve the case from HUDOC, its database of decisions.

Next the phone rings again; this time it's the reference librarian on duty. An immigration attorney needs help looking for Ethiopian law regarding the citizenship of children born to Ethiopian citizens who are not in Ethiopia. Yikes! My first best hope is a useful database from the United Nations High Commissioner for Refugees website. The research/evaluation page leads to a database of national laws on citizenship. I talk the reference librarian through getting to the database and retrieving the Ethiopian Nationality Law, which answers the attorney's question.

It wouldn't be a true FCIL day without striking out, however, and failure is never far away. A paralegal from the university's General Counsel Office calls to ask about owning a vehicle in Chile; apparently, a professor with a long-term research project in Chile needs to buy or lease a vehicle. He wants to do so in the University of Minnesota's name, but was told that the university has to be a legal entity in Chile for this to work. Not only does the paralegal want to know what a legal entity means in Chilean law, she needs the answer this afternoon. Tough question! First, I encourage her to ask the professor to go back to the international car leasing agency that told him about the legal entity requirement. Sometimes the person or organization with the most motivation finds the information fastest.

Meanwhile, I go through several sources in rapid succession, *Foreign Law Guide*, the Library of Congress's Global Legal Information Network (GLIN), a guide to the Chilean legal system at GlobaLex, Martindale-Hubbell's International Law Digest, and find nothing. From my experience as an attorney as well as a law librarian, I know that laws can define terms like "legal entity" differently depending on the context. I jump back and forth between searching for general definitions and for motor vehicle ownership and registration laws. Just as I am about to give up, the paralegal calls back and tells me that the professor has decided to buy the car in his own name and get reimbursed by the university. That's good news, because I wouldn't have found the answer.

While searching for the Chilean answer, I noticed a dead link in one of my research guides on the University of Minnesota Law Library's website. I take a few minutes to edit the guide, inserting the new link. I nag myself to check my guides systematically, making sure the links are working, but put it off for another day.

I finish skimming through various books on the history of foreign patent systems, and mark some sections for the professor to read. I take the selected books down to the circulation desk so they can be checked out and delivered to the professor.

For an hour, I work through publisher catalogs and advertisements. I grab one of the German-English legal dictionaries to help me review electronic slips from Otto Harrasowitz, a German distributor. After becoming Minnesota's FCIL librarian, I took a class in reading German, but I still need the dictionary to figure out some of the words in these descriptions.

Meanwhile, more e-mail questions have come in. A student needs help finding an international law topic for a law review article. I refer her to EISIL and a few of the international law blogs. Another professor wants a bibliography of articles on the rights of noncitizens. I search online periodicals indexes, including the *Index to Foreign Legal Periodicals*. This professor reads French and some Spanish, so I include articles in those languages. The index terms in the *Index to Foreign Legal Periodicals* are in English, and I know French and Spanish well enough to decide which citations to include. I also search full-text articles in Westlaw and Lexis-Nexis's database of law reviews. In addition to the most recent articles, I always find a few older articles that didn't show up in the periodical indexes. I finish by checking some more obscure indexes such as the *RAVE Index of International Law Periodicals, Public International Law: A Current Bibliography of Books and Articles on the Max Planck Institute*, the *Legal Journals Index*, and *PAIS*.

While I'm working, an LL.M. student stops by my office. The LL.M. is a master's degree in law. At the University of Minnesota and many other law schools, foreign lawyers study U.S. law for a year, earning an L.LM. degree. The student needs help finding European and U.S. sources for a paper comparing fair trial concepts. Like many LL.M. students, she can read several languages, including English, French, Italian, and Spanish, in this case. Fortunately, our library has an excellent human rights collection. Since one of our professors specializes in comparative criminal procedure, we buy a lot of books in that area, including books in French. I'm able to load the student down with useful material and show her how to navigate through some indexes and other databases. Before leaving, she also asks me about exams, so I show her the old exams that the law library puts on the intranet.

Our foreign language cataloger also stops by. She has finished reclassifying all the Russian materials from our Foreign Texts area, and wants to know what jurisdiction to tackle next. None of the remaining jurisdictions are in high demand, so I leave it up to her.

I'm just packing up for home when the phone rings. It's a law firm librarian who needs a sample joint venture agreement for China. Lawyers always feel more comfortable working from a model form, but forms for international and foreign transactions are hard to find. I get so many questions about them, however, that I drafted a research guide on the topic, to be published on the LLRX.com site. I pull up the draft guide. In addition to *International Joint Ventures*, a treatise with chapters discussing joint ventures in various countries, I can recommend *Transnational Joint Ventures* and a few of our new China books.

I started the day with Islamic law, touched on India, China, Belgium, Chile, patent law, human rights, and ended up with China again. Maybe tomorrow I'll check those guides for broken links.

CONCLUSION

FCIL work is never boring. Foreign and international law librarianship offers all the rewards of law librarianship, with an extra dose of challenge. Trends in the globalization of law practice make employment prospects attractive. To become an FCIL librarian, learn foreign languages, seek out educational opportunities, and find opportunities to develop FCIL reference, acquistion, or cataloging skills at your current or future job.

NOTES

1. Convention on the Prevention and Punishment of the Crime of Genocide, December 9, 1948, 78 U.N.T.S. 277.

2. Yemisi Dina, "Guide to Caribbean Law Research," *New York University* (June 2005), www.nyulawglobal.org/globalex/Caribbean.htm.

3. Convention on International Trade in Endangered Species of Wild Fauna and Flora, March 3, 1973, 27 UST. 1087, 993 U.N.T.S. 243.

4. Ralph Gaebler and Maria Smolka-Day, eds., *Sources of State Practice in International Law* (Ardsley, NY: Transnational, 2002).

5. See www.eisil.org.

6. See www.asil.org/resource/home.htm.

7. FCIL-SIS Syllabi and Course Materials, *American Association of Law Libraries*, www.aallnet.org/sis/fcilsis/syllabi.html (accessed October 12, 2005).

8. Harper's Index, *Harper's Magazine* (February 2001): 13.

9. Andrew Grossman, "Towards Cooperation in Access to Foreign Primary Law," *International Journal of Legal Information* 30, no. 1 (2002): 28 (table 2).

10. Katherina R. Lin and Erin Murphy, "Reflections on a JX Reclassification Project," *Law Library Journal* 92 (2000): 459.

11. M. Lesley Wilkins, "Harvard Law School Library Collections and Services Related to Law of the Islamic World," *International Journal of Legal Information* 31, no. 380 (2003): 383–84.

12. See, for example, Mary Rumsey, "Strangers in a Strange Land: How to Answer Foreign Law Research Questions," *American Association of Law Libraries Spectrum* (July 2004): 16–17.

13. Mary Whisner, "Choosing Law Librarianship: Thoughts for People Contemplating a Career Move" (1999), *Law Library Resource Xchange*, www.llrx.com.features/librarian.htm. Whisner's article serves as an excellent overview for anyone considering becoming a law librarian.

14. See, for example, "New Member Profile: Julie Horst," *FCIL-SIS Newsletter* (February 2005): 17.

15. In an informal 2005 e-mail survey of law library directors, twenty-one of the forty respondents said that their libraries had an FCIL position. Of those, seven, or 33 percent, were created in the last five years. (Laura N. Gasaway, director of the law library and professor of law, University of North Carolina, sent out the e-mail inquiry; results are summarized in an e-mail from Teresa Stanton, Reference/Foreign and International Law Librarian, University of North Carolina, to Mary Rumsey, Foreign, Comparative & International Law Librarian, University of Minnesota Law School [November 7, 2005, 5:05 p.m. CST; on file with author].) Similarly, the number of FCIL positions listed in the AALL directory and handbook grew from thirty-six in 1991 to sixty-one in 2004, an increase of almost 70 percent. The membership of the FCIL-SIS has increased from 134 in 1985 to 390 in 2005.

16. American Association of Law Libraries, AALL 2005 Annual Salary Survey, Summary—All Library Types (2005), available to members only at www.aall.org/members/pub_salary05/s-7.pdf; American Association of Law Libraries, AALL 2003 Annual Salary Survey, Summary—All Library Types (2003), available to members only at www.aall.org/members/pub_salary03/s-7-s-8.pdf.

17. The University of Michigan is one exception to this generalization, as it requires its law students to take a class on transnational law. Jeffrey Lehman, "International Law and the Legal Curriculum," *American Society for International Law*, Proc. 96 (2002): 54–55.

18. Marylin J. Raisch, "Book Review," Review of Toward a Cyberlegal Culture by Mirela Roznovschi, *International Journal of Legal Information* 30 (2002): 369–70.

19. David McFadden, "Survey of FCIL Membership: Results," *FCIL Newsletter* (February 1992): 14, 17.

20. Silke Sahl, "Introduction," *International Journal of Legal Information* 31 (2003): 151. ("The program offers countless learning opportunities, including scholarly lectures, visits to libraries and information centers, and meetings with publishers and vendors. Last but not least, it offers the chance to meet new colleagues as well as to renew friendships and contacts with law librarians from around the world.")

21. Marci Hoffman and Katherine Topulos, "International Legal Research Tutorial," *Duke University*, www.law.duke.edu/ilrt/index-2.html (accessed November 21, 2005).

22. Sahin v. Turkey, No. 44774/98, http://press.coe.int/cp/2005/608a(2005).htm.

Chapter 8

Technology Trends in Law Libraries

Roy Balleste

If we have learned one thing from the history of invention and discovery, it is that, in the long run—and often in the short one—the most daring prophecies seem laughably conservative.—Arthur C. Clarke[1]

Without a doubt, law libraries should be admired and protected as institutions dedicated to safeguard legal education. Since my childhood years, I felt an attraction and admiration for history. Ancient stories such as the lost Ark of the Covenant, the Punic Wars, and the War of 1812 connected me in one way or another to the world of books. Sometimes I would spend hours trying to understand what these books and distant places meant. Other stories were closer to home. As my daydreams carried me over to the early years of Puerto Rico, I wondered about the days of imperial Spain, and of fantastic places: La Fortaleza (Santa Catalina's Palace), Fort San Felipe del Morro, and Fort San Cristóbal. Then, I would dream about our heroes, brave men such as Captain Antonio Correa and his militia men, fighting gallantly in their efforts to repel a British invasion. It was with those dreams that I found history and the nobility of the world of books. History was just like another novel waiting to be read. Sometimes I could not see the difference between the stories of the American Revolution and perhaps a fictional story like C. S. Forrester's *Horatio Hornblower*. Later, stories such as the *Time Machine* by H. G. Wells and *From the Earth to the Moon* by Jules Verne instilled in me a desire to explore science and future possibilities. I grew up in a small town in the beautiful mountains of Puerto Rico. In those days there were no libraries accessible to me. My first experience with a library was at my junior high library several years later—a very small room with few resources. Computers were nonexistent and belonged only in science fiction movies (or perhaps in major universities). I was twelve years old. Four years later, my ideas and expectations of libraries changed my life forever. My distant dreams became a tangible representation of history with my visit to Washington, D.C. I was sixteen years old, full of illusions, and looking to quench my thirst for knowledge. I visited about ten museums in one week, including my favorite, the Air and Space Museum. However, none compared to my experience at the Library of Congress. Today, I believe that to understand our mission as members of society, it is important to understand our responsibilities to that society. Humans have always been inclined to seek and to discover. We are explorers of our own existence. The future is here and now. What then, is the role of the law librarian in this technological age? Let's consider this question.

WINDS OF CHANGE

> Observe constantly that all things take place by change, and accustom thyself to consider that the nature of the Universe loves nothing so much as to change the things which are, and to make new things like them.—Marcus Aurelius[2]

Information is the power of our civilization. Looking into the past we have learned that humanity managed to achieve great levels of technological sophistication. If we look at our history closely, we learn that entire civilizations have disappeared, and with them, their valuable knowledge. Information lost has always been tied to a reversal of civilization. Are we today less technologically sophisticated than our predecessors? Did our civilization's development suffer from the loss of information? It is unclear as to whether we should answer the first question with certainty. The second must be answered in the affirmative. Probably one of the most fascinating examples is the story of the Antikythera mechanism.[3] Technology, as a concept, is a legacy for humanity to be preserved for the future, not just an instrument used to develop the present. Our predecessors, thousands of years ago, lost the ability to share valuable technological information. Perhaps they considered technology a tool for the few, or it is possible that valuable information was destroyed by senseless wars. Today, librarianship reminds us that information is for the ages. This concept is by no means a lofty idea, but rather it is our responsibility. It does not belong in the world of the abstract but very much in our present physical world. How do we avoid the mistakes of the past? How do we avoid losing knowledge? During the Ptolemy dynasty in the third century B.C.E., the Library of Alexandria came into existence.[4] The value of this library was treasured for many centuries as the great minds of antiquity poured all their knowledge in its vast archives. A series of catastrophes slowly destroyed the library, until its final annihilation in the middle of the fifth century C.E.[5] This terrible end for the library was not caused by a hurricane, or volcano, or perhaps an earthquake. This horrific catastrophe was caused by the "wars of men." Ignorance, fanaticism, and disrespect for knowledge brought down the Library of Alexandria to ashes. Many of the great inventions preserved there were lost, some to be rediscovered hundreds of years later, while others were lost forever in time. What kind of knowledge did humanity lose? What types of technologies are now hidden from us? The library's final destruction was one more sign of the end of the Roman Empire. The period that followed, the Dark Ages, represented a setback or a reverse in civilization, at least in Europe. Other examples of loss of valuable information were found across the ocean in the fascinating civilizations now known by the ruins at Tiahuanako, Bolivia, the great city of Teotihuacán in Mexico, and the city of the high Andes, Machu Picchu in Peru. These cities, along with their civilizations, disappeared and with them, their great architectural and astrophysical secrets. The destruction of these civilizations also brought the loss of knowledge for posterity. Yet, this type of loss of information is not confined to the

Figure 8.1. An artist's conception of the Great Hall of Ancient Library of Alexandria. From Cosmos, by Carl Sagan. A courtesy of Carl Sagan Productions, Inc. Copyright 1980 Carl Sagan Productions, Inc.

past. China's destruction of the libraries of Tibet[6] during the 1960s is a modern example and a tragedy that serves as a reminder of how civilization should guard information.

Today's knowledge is our responsibility. What will our legacy be to future generations? Thirty years ago, our computing technology world was dominated by massive machines. In those days, the space rockets of the Mercury, Gemini, and Apollo missions dominated our imagination. In essence, computer technology was accessible to a few selected groups of scientists and academics. Times have changed, and today computer access is more widely available to many individuals on a worldwide scale. This is by no means equal, as many countries still remain behind in their access to technology. Yet, this accessibility has been enhanced, in no small part, by libraries. Consider that technology is forever tied to our progressive vision, and its development is inevitably tied to the landscape of our law libraries. Arguably many electronic services will be discovered in years to come, tapping into the imagination of our civilization.

Today our law libraries enjoy the convenience of online library catalogs, and computers continue to make a direct impact in their daily operations. The "age of computing" continues to develop as we face new challenges with the additional breakthroughs in wireless standards, artificial intelligence, and quantum computing. These are the technology trends that will influence our future libraries. This chapter, thus, will present technological innovations, its present influence in libraries, and what could be next for our libraries' future. It will discuss the technological landscape that we inhabit today and a future panorama not yet realized, but with the potential to change how we deliver our information.

It is obvious in today's law librarianship world to feel the pressure of change. How much of librarianship will be changed by technology in the years to come? There is a conflict brewing slowly as to the avenues of information delivery. Who will reign supreme? Will it be print or electronic? It is difficult to ignore the fact that electronic resources have become more prevalent, and with them another question has arisen: Will we own or just lease our access to information? This is a very serious question that will continue to be debated for quite some time. For now, it is safe to say that we need both sources, although I predict that electronic resources will become the predominant—but not the only—source of our information delivery in a not-too-distant future. Still, we must not underestimate the power of our print collections. A power outage can easily block your access to an electronic database. The book in your hand is forever. The efforts of archeologists and historians to understand the history of the Olmecs, the oldest Mesoamerican civilization, have been frustrated for lack of information. The Olmecs' history was preserved for many generations by the Aztecs. Unfortunately destroyed during the Spanish conquest, the Aztecs' historical records would have been priceless to historians five hundred years later.

WIRELESS: TODAY AND TOMORROW WITH WI-FI

The most beautiful experience we can have is the mysterious—the fundamental emotion which stands at the cradle of true art and true science.—Albert Einstein[7]

When I started working in law libraries, my understanding of the wireless world began with an introduction to a wireless standard: 802.11b. This designation represented a doorway to a world that operated in total cloak. Our computers were connected to the Internet, but no cable seemed to be connected to the wall, and thus, to the network. How did this fascinating technology work? Understanding wireless standards brought me to the realization that libraries go beyond their physical walls. The law library network was not constrained to the library. Students could access the library resources from the classrooms, lounges, and even other buildings on a university campus. Wireless technologies, in essence, had enhanced the reach of our law libraries. Consider that this technology has expanded our access to the Internet. Although a detailed knowledge of wireless technology is not necessary to be a law librarian, it is helpful to have some basic knowledge of its inner workings, especially if you are interested in upper-management positions. Just five years ago, 802.11b, a standard for wireless local area networks (WLANs), was being used by most libraries. The authority on wireless standards is the Institute of Electrical and Electronics Engineers (IEEE), which specifies the technical standards for wireless networking. As time has passed, the 802.11g standard has gained prominence due to its ability to provide higher data speeds. While the next generation of wireless applications surfaces in the horizon, possibly in the form of 802.11n, the possibility for even faster delivery of information could show up in the near future. How exactly does it work? A workable wireless network, for example, requires access points through the library, allowing computers to access the network. In essence, the access points located on the roof of the library communicate with the internal wireless cards in the computers of staff, faculty, and students. The *access points* are pieces of hardware connected to the wired network, which allow multiple computers to connect through them to access the network. You should also be familiar with the word *router*. A router, or junction, connects the law library network, for example, with the rest of the university network. The bottom line is that devices connected to the network expand our ability to access information. This architecture allows faculty and law students, for example, to enjoy the ability to connect with their wireless-enabled laptops from practically any location on campus.

Wireless technologies have revolutionized our present mobile society. Our patrons have learned the convenience of this service, whether in the library, classrooms, office, courthouse, law firm, or at home. Across the country, law libraries continue to provide wireless connectivity, while keeping a close watch on the development of this technology. The ability to access e-mail in practically any location provides wireless fidelity (Wi-Fi) with an increasing fan base. I must point out that—as with anything related to the Internet—there is a potential for security attacks and vulnerability issues. Nevertheless, most of these can be avoided if appropriate measures are in place. It is not uncommon to encounter Wi-Fi-enabled facilities in places such as bookstores, restaurants, and airports. Academic law librarians can gauge the state of technology by the mere observation of technology usage by patrons in their daily lives. It is amazing to consider that McDonald's offers Wi-Fi services in thousands of their restaurants around the world. I am not amazed that McDonald's offers this service; however, what I find amazing is that this company is not in the service of providing access to information. It is true that many law libraries now provide Wi-Fi, but accessibility varies as some have access limited to specific areas of the library. Yet the usage of personal digital assistants (PDAs) is on the rise. Our patrons are accustomed to having access to these services, just as we were attracted, not too long ago, to the convenience offered by the typewriter or the pay phone. This trend will continue in the future and will no doubt influence the way we do business at our law libraries. This brings another consideration: Will computer labs be necessary in the future? Probably not, but only time will tell.

EMERGING TECHNOLOGIES: CONSIDERING AI TECHNOLOGIES

> Success is to be measured not so much by the position that one has reached in life as by the obstacles which he has overcome.—Booker T. Washington[8]

Artificial intelligence (AI) is another frontier to be explored.[9] AI has been for many years a topic considered by science fiction writers. Today AI technologies seem to be at a developing stage that allows librarians to begin considering their incorporation in libraries. The 27th annual clinic on Library Applications of Data Processing, held March 25–27, 1990, at the University of Illinois at Urbana-Champaign, contemplated the potential capabilities of artificial intelligence.[10] Surprisingly enough, issues such as cataloging, technical services, collection development, and reference services, among others, were analyzed at the conference from the point of view of AI technologies. To those terms, today we will add knowledge representation, neural networks, and agents,[11] terms related to artificial intelligence that could likely become conventional terminology among law librarians as AI technologies begin to be implemented in our libraries. As an example, let's consider AI agents.

Utilizing an artificial intelligence agent (AI agent) in the law library website would be a good example of applying a cutting-edge technology. An AI agent is intended to work as a virtual assistant that offers services in addition to the human services already provided. Consider that agents have the potential to enhance the distribution and management of information. What is an AI agent? AI agents or "chatterbots" as many in the AI design field like to call them, are virtual persons powered by artificial intelligence with the capability to communicate with patrons from the magic of their virtual environments. An agent is divided in three main components: face, voice, and brain. An agent should not be confused with a similar invention, usually called "stand-in." Stand-ins function with only a face and voice within their virtual person design. If the desired effect is to have a virtual person that only greets patrons when visiting the library website, then this solution is the right one. The "stand-in" only speaks once with a preset greeting. Once it finishes greeting a patron, there is no further communication. In other words, there will be only one-way communication. This solution is *not* an agent. An agent is much more advanced and provides patrons with a two-way communication experience. What makes the agent interesting is its brain, since this is the key for a successful two-way communication.

The design of an agent, as mentioned above, requires a *face*, a *voice*, and a *brain*. The agent's face provides a much more interesting and quite engaging session to the patron. To have a three-dimensional representation of a virtual person that smiles, moves, talks, and just pays attention to a patron's request enhances the utility of the library's website. This will be beneficial since the agent's "personality" attracts human curiosity, and by default, human learning. The face could be designed, for example, with the software provided by Oddcast Video Technologies. Oddcast provides a design engine that allows users to pick and customize their agents. The engine helps you select, among others, the gender, hair, eye color, facial features, wardrobe, and accessories.

The company's VHost product family provides a robust, easy-to-learn, end-to-end solution that enables organizations to sign up, design and program interactivity into existing e-marketing and e-learning platforms, all within a single interface. All of Oddcast's products are Web-based and ASP-hosted and can be delivered to any device even in low-bandwidth environments—PCs, CD-ROMs, and mobile devices.[12]

So now imagine a three-dimensional face hovering above a text chat box. Now you have a face to go with the words. The *voice* component is a "text-to-speech" or TTS engine. This is the engine that allows the AI agent to be able to respond via voice chat. The main advantage of TTS, as hosted by Oddcast, is the ability it gives the designer—in our case, the law librarian—to enable a "real" person's voice. Again, this is a much more attractive option for our patrons. The voice brings that personable component to an otherwise mechanic interaction with a computer. Yet, combining all three elements, face, voice, and brain, into one package brings about the creation of an AI agent.

The agent's *brain* is powered by a natural language engine. AIML, or Artificial Intelligence Markup Language, is one good example of an "engine" powering that brain. AIML is based on XML. The software is a design from the A.L.I.C.E. AI Foundation.[13] This is not the only solution, but this is a free solution provided by Dr. Richard Wallace and the A.L.I.C.E. AI Foundation. It is, in essence, an open-source AI "brain" language. Just as you could design a Web page using Dreamweaver, the A.L.I.C.E. AI Foundation provides Pandorabots, a free AI agent's design and hosting service. Better yet, Pandorabots is compatible with the software provided by Oddcast. In Pandorabots, your interaction with AIML is seamless and you need no knowledge of XML or AIML. When you first log in and enter into Pandorabots, you are faced with a powerful application and many possibilities. This application, as provided by the A.L.I.C.E. AI Foundation, is designed to help you create "an artificial intelligence natural language chat robot . . . [that] utilizes AIML . . . for creating stimulus-response chat robots."[14] Dr. Richard Wallace explains that

> The model of learning in A.L.I.C.E. is called supervised learning because a person, the botmaster [designer], plays a crucial role. The botmaster monitors the robot's conversations and creates new AIML content to make the responses more appropriate, accurate, believable, or "human," or whatever the botmaster intends. We have developed algorithms for automatic detection of patterns in the dialog data. This process, called "Targeting," provides the botmaster with new input patterns that do not already have specific replies, permitting a process of almost continuous supervised refinement of the bot.[15]

VIRTUAL REFERENCE OR VIRTUAL WORLDS

Study the past if you would define the future.—Confucius[16]

Virtual Reference Desk (VRD) services continue to hold great future potential. As the librarian role continues to be redefined, so will be the faith in this technology. Virtual reference services became an important subject for librarians around 2001. It seemed that between the year 2001 and 2004 there was an explosion of discovery and application of virtual technologies for reference desks. This trend continues today. Virtual Reference Desk (VRD) technology has been considered as an option to communicate with distant students, as an instrument to attract law students to the library resources, and as a marketing tool. Marketing the resources of the library to a new generation of patrons growing up with the Internet has proven a challenge and, to a degree, problematic. Yet VRD services could serve as the bridge that connects the law library to those users. Let's face it, these days the majority of our patrons turn to the Internet for information.

The adoption of Convey Systems' virtual reference software by the Online Computer Library Center (OCLC) into what we know as Question-Point, and its subsequent merger with 24/7 reference services, was a significant step that recognizes the power of virtual applications. This reminds me of how certain technologies have captured quite efficiently the attention of the general public. It is difficult not to notice that the AOL Instant Messenger is quite popular among students. The way AOL gains and retains our students' interest has become of some concern, especially as a potential distracter in classrooms. Now, handheld devices are starting to replace cell phones. It is in this technological age that we must continue to educate our patrons about the usefulness of VRD services.

On the other hand, VRD is not limited to this medium, since there is a complete graphical world where imagination and technology come together. Our present era is the gaming era. The advent of advanced computer graphics has brought to our civilization very complex gaming universes. This could turn to the advantage of law libraries. Consider that technology exists for the design of tridimensional law library in a virtual environment. Now consider Active Worlds,[17] a virtual-environment service that offers this fantastic graphical world to educational service institutions.

CASE MANAGEMENT SOFTWARE

Far better it is to dare mighty things, to win glorious triumphs even though checkered by failure, than to rank with those poor spirits who neither enjoy nor suffer much because they live in the gray twilight that knows neither victory nor defeat.—Theodore Roosevelt[18]

Case management software takes the law librarian beyond the traditional and into the information technology (IT) field. It is not too difficult to notice how the role of law librarians has changed in the past ten years. Our roles have evolved beyond mere information retrieval and delivery, and into the IT architect arena. Now we design websites, troubleshoot computers, and even participate in the assessment of our wireless networks. We have become semi-IT technicians in our own right. Some law librarians even have a particular degree or formal training in computer science. This knowledge, acquired by education or on the job, gives librarians the opportunity to extend their influence and visibility. Now another opportunity is available: participating in the world of case management software.

Case management software, as a tool, is utilized with great success in law firms. Programs such as Amicus Attorney, Time Matters, Abacus Law, and ProLaw, among others, are utilized worldwide. Law students, for example, will potentially encounter this tool at some point in their careers. It is to their advantage to know at least one of these tools. Some law schools utilize case management software in their clinics. This gives the law library an additional opportunity to get involved. The librarian could get involved in providing training, helping the IT department with installation and troubleshooting, or both. The law library, in essence, would provide training and technical support to faculty, staff, and students. As a law librarian, you may be involved in the deployment of similar software in your law school clinic. What is case management software?

Taking a closer look you discover that this software enhances and expedites the inner workings of a law firm. It is in essence an electronic communications and storage center. For example, the software would allow the user to search quickly in the "Contacts" section. Rather than browsing a Rolodex, the user conveniently looks through the contacts from within the program. This feature could be used along with an easy-to-search "Files" section. Now law firms are digitizing their documents and keeping them handy through an interface with the software program. In addition, the program allows the user to track e-mails and phone calls, check for conflicts of interest (a crucial feature for attorneys), create appointment reminders, allow the entire staff to view "to dos" and deadlines, and record billable time. These are just some of the many features within this kind of program. Now a link to the power of PDAs has been added so that this kind of software may communicate with them. As you may infer, the software is utilized by attorneys to manage and extend the boundaries of the information available to them. In essence, practice management software brings about the concept of the "virtual law firm."

LAW LIBRARIES 3.0: QUANTUM COMPUTERS

I have always imagined that Paradise will be a kind of library.—Jorge Luis Borges[19]

Computer science continues to evolve, and with it, the way we envision information delivery. Our era of computing soon will become the age of quantum computers. The modern computing world began to be developed during the early 1800s with the mechanical devices of the English mathematician Charles Babbage. On the other hand, the story of the Antikythera mechanism and Archimedes would put computer history hundreds of years further into the past. In any case, it is fascinating to consider the technological transition of computers over the past one hundred years.

Today our computers are capable of millions of calculations per second. What will their capabilities be in ten years? What about twenty years? The modern era of computer evolution began with the design of gears and wheels, then vacuum tubes redefined computers, later transistors revolutionized computing, and to our surprise, integrated circuits were even better. Now, in the twenty-first century, quantum particles will take computers to a higher level of performance. This is the quantum world that librarians will learn to embrace. It will be the era of quantum computers. The science of quantum computing emanates from quantum mechanics and the laws of physics. Since quantum particles exist at the atomic level, working with them will allow new computers to process calculations at speeds only found today in our imagination.[20] Your computer, for example, transfers information or bits. This information is transferred based on the binary code, which in turn is based on a value in relation to another, as in the case of a 1 or a 0.[21] This is the limited existence of today's computers. On the other hand, quantum computers are not limited to two states since information transfer is powered by quantum bits, or *qubits*. In quantum computers, information transfer is based on a 1 or a 0, or it can be a superposition that is simultaneously both 1 and 0.[22] Keep in mind that superposition is somewhat of a tricky concept to visualize. Recent developments in quantum mechanics have opened the door to the world of teleportation. Consider that in quantum computers, the existence of information may exist at the same time in two destinations, coexisting around that qubit. Now further consider that a *qubit* may be represented as a photon (a beam of light). In our universe an object exists in one place at a time—yet that is an assumption of conventional wisdom. A photon may exist in two places at once, allowing for the transmission of information at a speed faster than light. That is so because the *qubit* holds a relationship with its counterpart in another place of existence. This is called entanglement.[23] When two particles are entangled, they behave as one—regardless of how far apart they are. This is also the same principle being studied by scientists to develop further the science of teleportation. In essence, "teleportation could transfer quantum information between quantum processors in a quantum computer."[24]

To visualize further the inner workings of a quantum computer, consider for a moment this concept of teleportation. This idea, known as quantum teleportation, is a field of study that also belongs to quantum mechanics. As I explained, quantum mechanics, furthermore, is a field of study that belongs to physics. If you think that this is too fantastic, consider the theories presented by the German physicist Werner Heisenberg.[25] For any science fiction fan, teleportation is common lingo. The ability to be transported or being "beamed up" via a particle stream to another location in a matter of seconds is certainly science fiction reserved to shows such as the *Star Trek* series, correct? Heisenberg believed that it would be difficult to calibrate the position of an object (or person) as it traveled in the stream. In the *Star Trek* series, a device called the Heisenberg compensator is utilized to avoid the drawbacks presented by Heisenberg's principle. In the show, the transporters are equipped with a "compensator" to protect the integrity of the object while traveling in the stream, thus making teleportation a reality. Times have changed, and today progress has been made in the field of physics. The concept is now beyond science fiction. Quantum teleportation began its early stages of successful development in 1993 when a group of scientists from around the world managed to beam particles of light from one location to another thanks to the principle of entanglement, which helps to compensate for the shortcomings presented by Heisenberg.[26] Physicists found that a "fundamental feature of quantum mechanics, entanglement, could be used to circumvent the limitations imposed by Heisenberg's uncertainty principle without violating it."[27] Consider this illustration: On a direct flight from Miami to London, your trip would take about twelve hours. The same trip on a transporter would take about ten seconds. Just as with teleportation, quantum computers utilize entanglement to transfer information at super-fast speeds. Since quantum computers operate in more that one state at the same time, they provide information billions of times faster than today's computers. Dr. Seth Lloyd, professor of mechanical engineering at MIT, has said that "a quantum computer is to a computer what a laser is to a light bulb. The ability to store, retrieve, and manipulate data on atoms and subatomic particles instead of on silicon, plus the ability to have a bit of information be in more than one position at the same time, gives us a closer insight into this advanced technology."[28] He also explained that as computer chips get smaller, they also get faster. "Computer power doubles every few years (according to Moore's law) and we will soon reach a limit of manufacturing in which transistors will not be able to be produced. Why? Because by making bits smaller, we reach the atomic world, that is, the quantum world. In essence, we will be storing bits (information) on an atom."[29]

Dr. Anton Zeilinger adds power to the concept of quantum computing.

> I would argue that we can understand quantum mechanics if we realize that science does not describe how nature is but rather articulates what we can say about nature. Expressed in modern language, this means that quantum mechanics is a science of knowledge, of information. This is where the current value of fundamental experiments such as teleportation lies: in helping us to reach a deeper understanding of our mysterious quantum world.[30]

This technology is no doubt exciting. Our information universe, and thus our libraries, is at the verge of another major technological evolution. Imagine for a moment that you happen to dismantle your computer so that you may look inside. What would you see? You would see silicon-based circuits, cables, and screws. That is the nature of your digital computer. What would you see if you opened up and looked inside a quantum computer? Although there are proposals for the use of radio waves or magnetic fields to power quantum computers, the one option that seems very fascinating is the one that utilizes lasers and crystals. What would you see if you could open up and look inside a quantum computer? You would see crystals designed to catch information from photons delivered by laser beams.

Dr. Matthew Sellars of the Laser Physics Centre at the Australian National University in Canberra has illustrated in great detail this concept.

> What we've done here is create a quantum memory. Slowing down light allows scientists to map information onto it. The information is then transferred from the light to the crystal. Then when the scientists release the light, the information is transferred back onto the beam. Digital information can be expressed with pulses of light. If we can store the light pulses for a very long time, we have a memory that operates on a quantum scale.

How far are we from this technology? The technology is here! Mathematically, quantum computers are a possibility. Preliminary laboratory trials around the world have produced interesting and positive results. Consider that around 2015, the first quantum computers could appear in some university campuses. A practical quantum computer for consumers is not expected in stores until sometime around 2030—not too far in the future.

THE ELECTRONIC SERVICES LIBRARIAN

> We succeed only as we identify in life, or in war, or in anything else, a single overriding objective, and make all other considerations bend to that one objective.—Dwight D. Eisenhower[31]

In today's law library world, library users expect interactivity with Web resources. Our libraries' Web pages provide numerous personalized services to students, faculty, staff, judges, attorneys, and members of the public. In this digital world, electronic services librarians have become a high commodity. Their skills have proven very effective in connecting the library's technological world with our users. Librarians have always worked with library technology from the most rudimentary to the most complex that we see today. Yet, the electronic services librarian is, to a degree, a product of the computing age. What do they do? They spend a significant amount of time keeping patrons informed through Web page design efforts, involved with their IT departments, and acquiring knowledge of hardware and software. Their days are filled with projects that may involve designing, maintaining, and updating library websites. They may also work on the online catalog, in the management of Westlaw and Lexis passwords, tracking the installation of software versions, and attending conferences that discuss technology topics. They are also primarily librarians, and thus, they would have the traditional duties of reference, legal research, and evaluation of print resources with recommendations for future acquisitions. This position also allows the opportunity to teach faculty, students, and/or attorneys the electronics sources acquired by the library.

Yet this job is not limited to those duties. The electronic services librarian's strength comes from the knowledge of technology. This can be tricky since our technological world continues to change at a very fast pace. Knowledge of HTML is inescapable and, in some cases, you will have to work with JavaScript and XML. It is clear that traditional collection development procedures no longer reflect a complete picture of the acquisition activity within a library. Libraries are actively seeking new means to integrate electronic resources, while patrons are using online databases and the Internet for an increasing amount of research. Financial allocations directed toward collection development have increased to acquire additional digital formats. The presence of librarians, more than ever, must be emphasized as the current generation of students relies on more electronic resources for information.

Similar to the role of professional futurists, we must take a holistic approach to the future, considering the interrelationships between technology, our patrons, legal education, and the future of our collections. That is the nature of the electronic age. Librarians must stay informed about new trends in technology development while anticipating potential new trends. Librarians have become the bridge between technology and law school administration. They are the sentry that considers, analyzes, reviews, and scouts for new technologies that will be beneficial to the law library, and ultimately to the patrons they serve. It is worth noting that within the American Association of Law Libraries (AALL), the Computing Services Special Interest Section (CS-SIS) recognizes the importance of new technologies in law libraries and many electronic services librarians are members of the CS-SIS. Since technology continues to be such an important topic for our future libraries, it is recommended that all librarians join the CS-SIS. Consider its mission:

> The mission of CS-SIS has evolved in response to the increasing integration of computing in law libraries. Initially created to serve as a watchdog to the automation industry as it relates to law libraries, the SIS later focused on surveying the development of software designed for law libraries and conveying information on automation developments to law librarians. In recent years the opportunities and challenges of automation have had enormous impact on the field of legal information. Today the purposes of CS-SIS are to promote the communication of ideas, interests and activities concerning technological advances in law librarianship and the practice of law, and to meet the professional needs of all law librarians active in integrating computing technology to serve their users.[32]

I could not leave this section without sharing with you the importance of the Center for Computer-Assisted Legal Instruction (CALI) and the CALI conference. This group of legal academics, professors, and law librarians has worked together for many years while finding ways to apply technology to legal education. CALI is "a U.S. 501(c)(3) non-profit consortium of law schools that researches and develops computer-mediated legal instruction and supports institutions and individuals using technology and distance learning in legal education. CALI was incorporated in 1982 and welcomes membership from law schools, paralegal programs, law firms and individuals wishing to learn more about the law."[33] CALI is famous for its creative design and distribution of a CD containing CALI lessons (computer-based tutorials) very useful to all law students. CALI also promotes the creation of these lessons. The CALI conference has become the place to discuss, analyze, and project the use of technology in law schools.[34]

CONCLUSION

I shall be telling this with a sigh
Somewhere ages and ages hence:
Two roads diverged in a wood, and I,
I took the one less traveled by,
And that has made all the difference.

—Robert Frost[35]

This chapter has sought to present you with an innovative way of seeing technology in libraries. Our goal as information professionals is to maximize research, teaching, and learning via the application of educational technologies. To support this effort, we continue to utilize technology as the avenue of delivery that uniquely combines to distribute a superior learning experience. The ultimate purpose continues to be our efforts to gain a better understanding of technology as we seek to develop the effectiveness of our libraries. Long distances are no longer a barrier to information delivery and accessibility. Much work has been done over the past ten years to make information more accessible to law students. As educational technologies continue to become incorporated into higher education, it is important to understand how to maximize their utility. New software programs have appeared on the market that promise to enhance our ability to help our patrons. Now the very existence and multiusability of these software programs presents us with an opportunity to challenge ourselves as we seek to design new educational interfaces. These interfaces, in turn, allow us to provide better service to our patrons, as the law library becomes the nerve center of the legal world: the place where all roads to information connect. As we consider this new technological realm, think for a moment about Roy Tennant's Truths:[36]

1. You don't want to be the first or last in any technology.
2. Everything you do should be geared toward the user.
3. Don't expect users to know what they want until they see it.
4. Never underestimate the power of a prototype.
5. Always make a backup.
6. Buy hardware at the last possible moment.
7. Don't buy software with a zero at the end of the release number.
8. Never bother with Silo systems (they don't interact with anything else).
9. If you can't be with the operating system you love, love the one you're with.

There is no doubt that law librarians and computer science have both intermingled and forever are connected in library operations. This chapter, therefore, has brought to your attention the world of wireless technologies, artificial intelligence, virtual reference, case management software, quantum computing, and finally, the role of the librarian in technology implementation. Consider that, as a profession, law librarianship is in transition. Our profession is rapidly developing and will require that librarians become familiar with some computing matters. More importantly, it will require of librarians the desire to learn and adapt to these new changes. The survival of law librarians in the future will depend on just that, adaptability. I will humbly leave you with Roy Balleste's five postulates of the future. In a hundred years . . .

1. Law libraries will continue to be centers of learning.
2. Law librarians will not be called librarians.
3. The power of print will not be underestimated.
4. Library science will merge with computer science.
5. There will be a futurist in all of us.

To you, the student of library science, I say, join us in our understanding of present and future technologies. Your findings might surprise you, or at the very least enlighten you. We have an opportunity here and now to gain both a grasp of the different factors and dimensions that technology offers us and a chance to explore the ways in which these technologies take us into the ambit of the law library of tomorrow. It has been said that "teleportation [will] help us to reach a deeper understanding of our mysterious quantum world."[37] I believe that new trends in technology will help us reach a deeper understanding of our future library world.

NOTES

1. Arthur C. Clarke (1917–) is a physicist and science fiction author.
2. Marcus Aurelius was emperor of Rome from 161 to 180 C.E.
3. Whether the age of computing began in the eighteenth century remains to be seen. Derek J. de Solla Price, "An Ancient Greek Computer," *Scientific American* 200, no. 6 (June 1959): 60–67.
4. Luciano Canfora, *The Vanished Library* (Los Angeles: University of California Press, 1987), 119–22.
5. Canfora, *The Vanished Library*, 190.
6. Rebecca J. Knutt, "China's Destruction of the Libraries of Tibet," in *Lost Libraries: The Destruction of Great Book Collections since Antiquity*, ed. James Raven (New York: Palgrave Macmillan, 2004), 247–59.
7. Albert Einstein (1879–1955) was a physicist and one of the greatest scientists of the twentieth century. He proposed the famous theory of relativity.
8. Booker T. Washington (1856–1915) was an African American educator and author.
9. This section of the chapter is based on Roy Balleste's winning entry in the new member division of the 2004 AALL/LexisNexis Call for Papers Competition.
10. F. W. Lancaster and Linda C. Smith, eds., *Artificial Intelligence and Expert Systems: Will They Change the Library: Proceedings of the 1990 Clinic on Library Applications of Data Processing* (Champaign: University of Illinois, Graduate School of Library and Information Science, 1992).
11. Stuart J. Russell and Peter Norvig, *Artificial Intelligence: A Modern Approach* (Upper Saddle River, NJ: Prentice Hall, 2003), 16.
12. See the Oddcast website, available at http://vhost.oddcast.com/vhost_minisite/ (accessed November 7, 2005).

13. See the A.L.I.C.E. AI Foundation website, www.alicebot.org (accessed November 7, 2005).

14. Richard Wallace, *The Anatomy of A.L.I.C.E.*, www.alicebot.org/anatomy.html (accessed November 7, 2005).

15. Richard Wallace, *The Anatomy of A.L.I.C.E.*

16. Confucius (551 B.C.E.–479 B.C.E.) was a Chinese social philosopher.

17. See the Active Worlds website, www.activeworlds.com/edu/index.asp (accessed November 7, 2005).

18. Theodore Roosevelt (1858–1919) was the twenty-sixth president of the United States.

19. Jorge Luis Borges (1899–1986) was an Argentinian novelist and poet.

20. George Johnson, *A Shortcut through Time: The Path to the Quantum Computer* (New York: Alfred A. Knopf, 2003), 5–8.

21. Johnson, *A Shortcut through Time*, 6–8.

22. Johnson, *A Shortcut through Time*, 6–8.

23. Johnson, *A Shortcut through Time*, 41–44.

24. Anton Zeilinger, "Quantum Teleportation," *Scientific America*, special edition 13, no. 1 (May 2003): 34–43.

25. Zeilinger, "Quantum Teleportation," 39.

26. Zeilinger, "Quantum Teleportation," 40. For more information on entanglement, see Dirk Bouwmeester, Artur Ekert, and Anton Zeilinger, *The Physics of Quantum Information* (New York: Springer-Verlag, 2000).

27. Zeilinger, "Quantum Teleportation," 40.

28. See Dr. Seth Lloyd's discussion in "Closer to the Truth: Will Computers Take a Quantum Leap?" PBS, www.pbs.org/kcet/closertotruth/explore/show_08.html (accessed May 25, 2006).

29. Lloyd, "Closer to the Truth."

30. Zeilinger, "Quantum Teleportation," 43.

31. Dwight D. Eisenhower (1890–1969) was supreme commander of the Allied forces in Europe during World War II and the thirty-fourth president of the United States.

32. See the AALL Computing Services Special Interest Section (CS-SIS) website, www.aallnet.org/sis/cssis/about.asp (accessed November 7, 2005).

33. See the Center for Computer-Assisted Legal Instruction (CALI) website, www2.cali.org/ (accessed November 7, 2005).

34. See the Center for Computer-Assisted Legal Instruction (CALI) website, "Teaching the Law," www.cali.org/teaching.html (accessed November 7, 2005).

35. Robert L. Frost (1874–1963) was an American poet.

36. See Roy Tennant's professional website, http://roytennant.com/professional.html (accessed May 30, 2006).

37. Zeilinger, "Quantum Teleportation," 43.

Chapter 9

The Evolution of Government Documents

Jennifer Bryan Morgan

FEDERAL DOCUMENTS: A BRIEF HISTORICAL OVERVIEW

Foundations and the Nineteenth Century

The evolution of government documents is intertwined with the history of government printing. In the formative era of the United States, government printing was handled by private printers and newspaper publishers.[1] Following the American Revolution, public printing was first mentioned in a House recommendation in 1789; proposals were invited for "printing the acts and other proceedings of Congress."[2] Private printers were hired, and in turn, followed Congress from New York to Philadelphia in 1790 and then to Washington in 1800. The first inkling of a Federal Depository Library Program (FDLP) became evident in 1813 when Congress authorized legislation to ensure the distribution of congressional documents. The Resolution of 1813 provided that the journals of Congress would be furnished to certain universities, colleges, historical societies, and state libraries.[3] Thus, today's U.S. Government Printing Office (GPO) dates its core mission ("Keeping America Informed") back to 1813, when Congress determined the need to make information regarding the work of the three branches of government available to all Americans.[4]

The *United States Congressional Serial Set* (the earliest continuous and long-lived publication compiled under directive of the Congress) began publication in 1817 with the fifteenth Congress.[5] Today's Serial Set contains the House and Senate Documents and the House and Senate Reports and is bound by session of Congress. Historically, congressional material in the Serial Set included the committee reports, journals, manuals, and

administrative reports of both chambers in addition to a variety of directories, orations, and special publications (such as illustrated descriptions
of the Capitol). During the late nineteenth and early twentieth centuries,
executive-branch materials were also published in the Serial Set, including messages of the president of the United States, annual administrative
reports of departments and agencies, series publications (such as the *Geological Survey Bulletins*), and periodicals (such as the *Monthly Summary of
Foreign Commerce* and *Monthly Consular Reports*). Other types of serialized
executive documents published in the Serial Set included Bureau of Labor
and the Bureau of Labor Statistics bulletins, Census Bureau Statistical Abstracts, Smithsonian Institutions Bureau of Ethnology reports and bulletins, and Department of State commercial relations, commercial policy,
and foreign relations series.[6]

In 1818, concerned that its proceedings be accurately and promptly
recorded, Congress appointed a joint committee to consider whether a
statutory requirement was "necessary to ensure despatch [*sic*], accuracy,
and neatness, in the printing done by order of the two Houses [of Con-
gress]."[7] And in 1819 the committee's report recommended that Congress
establish

> a National Printing Office (with a bindery and stationery annexed,) which
> should execute the work of Congress while in session, and that of the vari-
> ous Departments of Government during the recess; and should do all the
> binding, and furnish the stationery, for the Departments, as well as for Con-
> gress. . . . The committee are of opinion that such an establishment under the
> superintendence of a man of activity, integrity, and discretion, would be
> likely to produce promptitude, uniformity, accuracy, and elegance, in the ex-
> ecution of public printing.[8]

The advice of the committee was not heeded and a resolution of March
3, 1819, directed the House and the Senate to elect their own printers, in-
struct their work, and establish what price to pay for the presswork.[9]

In the years that followed, numerous printers petitioned for employment by the Congress, bidding wars followed, a failed contract system of
printing was operated, appropriations continued to be made for "printing, stationery, and fuel," and various committees were appointed to investigate the subject of public printing.[10] These investigations into printing activities uncovered corruption, profiteering, excessive and useless
printing, and exorbitant political contributions paid by printers.[11] Records
describe how members of Congress contentiously debated the election of
printers. "In 1827 . . . the debates show that the public printing was regarded as patronage used by the party in power to aid in supporting its
'organ.' The abuse of this patronage, however, became so flagrant that the
House in 1828 ordered an investigation upon the subject of public print-

ing. This investigation exposed a most extraordinary condition of things and led to wholesome reforms."[12] Yet, future investigations continued to expose further corruptions and the committees continued to recommend the establishment of a Public Printing Office. Finally, in 1852, an act of Congress provided for the appointment of a superintendent of public printing and directed that he supervise the work done by the elected printers.[13] The superintendent position, however, became a political plum, as "politicians who had no practical knowledge of printing succeeded in securing the place of printer, and farmed out the work to practical printers at a percentage of the receipts. The dominant party elected the printer with a positive understanding that he would devote specified sums out of his own profits for partisan purposes."[14] The act also appointed a Joint Committee on the Public Printing, and empowered it to mediate disputes between the superintendent and printers, and to use any measures deemed necessary to remedy any neglect or delay in the execution of the public printing.[15]

By 1860, several House and Senate committees were investigating all phases of public printing and binding[16] and thus provoked the proposal of a reform bill calling for the establishment of a government printing office. The *Joint Resolution in Relation to the Public Printing* (No. 25) was signed into law by President James Buchanan on June 23, 1860, and provided that the superintendent of public printing be "authorized and directed to have executed the printing and binding authorized by the Senate and House of Representatives, the executive and judicial departments, and the Court of Claims. And to enable him to carry out the provisions of this act, he is authorized and directed to contract for the erection or purchase of the necessary buildings, machinery, and materials for that purpose."[17] The government purchased a private printing plant near the Capitol and the GPO opened for business on March 4, 1861, the same day that Abraham Lincoln was inaugurated president. The first GPO presses were steam powered and ink was made from a mixture of oil and lampblack. In the composing room, where gas fixtures illuminated the night, composers hand-set type and women were employed in the bindery to fold printed sheets by hand.[18]

During the nineteenth century, a succession of public printers oversaw the GPO through important events, such as the Civil War, Reconstruction, presidential assassinations, the installation of an electrical power plant, World War I, the Spanish American War, advances in printing technology, building additions and construction, and innovations in personnel management and accounting systems.[19] During the Reconstruction years, the GPO acquired the responsibility for printing the *Congressional Record*,[20] taking over the reporting of the debate and proceedings of Congress from the newspaper trade. GPO produced its first issue of the *Record* on March

5, 1873. However, the most significant event to occur during the nineteenth century was perhaps the passage of the Printing Act of 1895.[21] The act codified all of the laws relating to the GPO and to public printing in general. (Today, Title 44 of the U.S. Code includes chapters that define the activities of GPO and form the foundation for government printing and public dissemination). The Printing Act of 1895 centralized government printing in the GPO of the printing and binding required by the three branches of government and attempted to prevent printing at private plants. At that time, GPO truly became the federal government's primary centralized resource for gathering, cataloging, producing, providing, and preserving published information in all its forms. The Printing Act of 1895 also created the office of the superintendent of documents in the Government Printing Office. Prior to 1895, the secretary of the interior was responsible for the general distribution of government printed materials[22] until the act of 1869[23] created the office of the superintendent of public documents in the Department of the Interior. In 1895, "the new officer succeeded to the duty of distributing publications to depository libraries, was given authority to sell government publications, and was charged with the duty of preparing monthly, annual, and biennial indexes."[24]

In May 1895, Adelaide Hasse became the first documents librarian at the GPO. Her duties included caring for the documents in the GPO library, as well as pulling together collections that were stored around the Capitol. Within six weeks of her arrival at the GPO, she organized and classified nearly 300,000 documents, including duplicates.[25] But her most significant accomplishment was that during her employment at the GPO, Hasse developed the Superintendent of Documents (SuDocs) classification system.[26] The SuDocs system is still used by libraries today to classify and organize federal government publications.

The Twentieth Century

In 1912, the public printer replaced GPO's horses and wagons with electric trucks. Throughout the twentieth century, the public printers initiated many more modern transitions and oversaw important activities, such as instating hot-metal technology, constructing skylights, providing better ventilation and a new cafeteria in the GPO building, installing a five-color offset press, collective bargaining, traveling overseas, and becoming active in the international community of printers.[27] World War I resulted in the largest production in GPO's history as a rush was made for government printing from 1911 to 1918. Important changes were also in store for the Depository Library Program (DLP). Since 1895, all publications had been distributed to all designated depository libraries. Language in an appropriations bill for fiscal year 1923 allowed depositories to select particular publications by providing that "no part of [the appropriation for the Office of the Superintendent of Documents] shall be used to supply to depository libraries any documents, books, or other printed matter not requested by such libraries."[28] The superintendent of documents then sent to depositories a classified list of documents, from which they could select the materials that best suited the needs of their patrons.[29] During the Great Depression, the public printer, under the Economy Act of June 30, 1932, adopted a five-day (forty-hour) workweek and instituted a reduction in pay for GPO employees.[30]

A new public printer (Augustus E. Giegengack), at last, was able to convince Congress that the existing GPO buildings were hazardous firetraps. Construction was completed on the new eight-story GPO building in February 1940. Giegengack's other significant accomplishments during his tenure included modernizing and improving the appearance of publications by creating a Typography and Design Division and obtaining a reduction in costs through changes in makeup and typographic detail.[31] World War II brought increased production as the GPO began to receive war-related orders and Public Printer Giegengack conferred with leaders in the printing industry to arrange partnerships to secure supplemental commercial production. After the war, printing press technology evolved and the GPO shifted from hot-metal to offset printing.[32]

During the second half of the twentieth century, the public printers shepherded the GPO through the Korean War, civil defense concerns, modern improvements in lighting systems, the addition of new presses, McCarthyism, modernization of printing equipment and procedures, the installation of a new page photocomposition system, internal reorganizations, the assassination of President Kennedy, studies on the commercial procurement of printing, new technologies (such as microforms), and the "computer age."[33] The FDLP continued to grow, from 555 designated depositories in 1945 to 1,200 depositories in 1977.[34] In the early 1970s, concerns arose involving the lack of modernization in the DLP and the Document Sales Service.[35] Problems were addressed by boosting appropriations; increasing the number of full-time employees; automating the *Monthly Catalog*, mail lists, and order processing; and creating the online Publications Reference File. At this time, the Depository Library Council (DLC) to the Public Printer was formalized.[36] The council consists of fifteen documents librarians who are appointed by the public printer.

The purpose of the DLC to the Public Printer is to provide advice on policy matters dealing with the DLP as provided in Title 44 U.S.C. The primary focus of council's work will be to advise the Public Printer, the Superintendent of Documents, and appropriate members of GPO staff on practical options for the efficient management and operation of the DLP.[37]

In 1977, advances in technology allowed for the production of the *Federal Register* to shift from hot metal to photocomposition, and for the conversion of the entire text of the *Code of Federal Regulations* to an electronic database.[38] Technology also allowed the public printer to effect cost-saving measures, such as the use of microforms in sales and in the DLP. The DLC undertook the "Microform Project Initiatives" and in March 1977, the Joint Committee on Printing authorized the GPO to produce microfilm publications "to determine if there could be cost savings and/or better service provided to the library distribution program through the use of microfilm."[39] Coopers and Lybrand, the consulting firm that performed the study on GPO operations in 1978, observed that micrographics was the subject of intense debate at the time, and argued that microform distribution would increase the number of documents distributed and would save money (first-year savings estimated to be in excess of $1 million).[40] Coopers and Lybrand concluded "that GPO should be allowed to expand its use of microfilm technology to include sales by the Superintendent of Documents and allow micropublishing to be offered as a general GPO service."[41] In 1979, as a cost-reduction strategy, GPO offered depository libraries the choice of receiving the Serial Set in paper or as a microfilmed edition.[42]

During the 1980s, more of the congressional print work shifted to electronic processing and GPO facilities were converted to accommodate the ongoing computerization of the trade.[43] Public printers, throughout the history of the U.S. Government Printing Office, have set their goals on reducing the cost of printing, applying new technologies, and increasing productivity. However, during the last two decades of the twentieth century, GPO's production of printed documents decreased. The reasons were twofold—federal budgetary constraints and the electronic transformation of government information.[44] Actions to reduce the amount of paperwork[45] and to lower government expenditures curtailed funds for printing and publishing. In the 1980s and 1990s, as federal agencies were expected to justify their printing needs in an era of rising inflation, the number of publications that were available declined—titles were terminated, consolidated, or made available only on the Internet or on electronic bulletin boards; and, as a result, GPO's revenues dropped.[46] It became evident that GPO was facing serious challenges in "keeping America informed" as desktop publishing and electronic formats contributed to the deterioration of GPO's centralization and control of printing.[47] Focusing on the challenges posed by the developing electronic information phenomenon, Congress held hearings in 1985 to examine the status of federal information collection and dissemination technology and the surrounding policy issues, and in 1986, produced an assessment with their findings and recommendations.[48] "These findings revealed a relatively new technology of growing use and application, one conveying considerable discretionary capability to federal agencies concerning government information management, while simultaneously outstripping the existing practical limitations and legal structures governing many aspects of the government information life cycle."[49] Then in 1988 the Office of Technology Assessment published a report addressing the opportunities for improving the dissemination of federal information and highlighted two major problems: "maintaining equity in public access to Federal information in electronic formats, and defining the respective roles of Federal agencies and the private sector in the electronic dissemination process."[50] Focusing on the current and future roles of GPO and Superintendent of Documents and the DLP, the

> OTA concluded that the government needs to set in motion a comprehensive planning process for creatively exploring the long-term future (e.g., 10 to 20 years from now) when the information infrastructure of the public and private sectors could be quite different. At the same time, the government needs to provide short-term direction to existing agencies and institutions with respect to electronic information dissemination. A central challenge is setting future directions for the governmentwide information dissemination institutions.[51]

Congress mandated GPO's official transition into electronic publishing by enacting the Government Printing Office Electronic Information Access Enhancement Act of 1993.[52] The act amended Title 44 to require GPO to disseminate government information products online, to maintain an online directory or locator of federal information sources in electronic format, and to address permanent public access by establishing a storage facility for electronic information files. GPO launched its Internet information service site one year later, in June 1994, and, in addition to providing online versions of the *Federal Register* and *Congressional Record*, GPO created a legislative database that would contain all published versions of House and Senate bills starting with the 103rd Congress. Today, GPO Access provides free online access to more than 300,000 federal government document titles and the information published at GPO Access is considered the official, published version.[53] Developments concerning the challenges and opportunities of increased federal government use of the Internet continued to arise in the 1990s, and further studies examined issues such as preserving electronic material, ensuring public access, and "the erosion of the Public Printer's authority to supervise the public printing system."[54] GPO had become as much a procurement agency as a printer, with the majority of noncongressional production being obtained under standing contracts negotiated by GPO with the private sector.[55]

During the era of government downsizing and economizing in the mid-1990s, Congress, working with the staff of the Joint Committee on Printing, held hearings to examine issues affecting the reform of Title 44, whose provisions were seen as arcane and not accommodating of changing technology and policy developments.[56] In the 104th Congress, proposals were made to downsize GPO, reduce its resources, privatize public printing, and abolish the Joint Committee on Printing.[57] Printing reform was revisited by the 105th Congress and a legislative working group was formed, consisting of staff from the Joint Committee on Printing, the Office of Management and Budget, and the Senate Committee on Rules and Administration. The three main goals for reform of Title 44 were to:

- Resolve constitutional issues regarding the appropriate roles of the legislative, judicial, and executive branches in the production of government publications and other printing;
- Improve efficiency and economy in the production of government publications and the printing of government materials, including relying increasingly on private sector procurement; and
- Enhance public access to government publications in the electronic era, while ensuring that a safety net exists for those without computer technology.[58]

Subsequently, a consensus reform bill, the Wendell H. Ford Government Publications Reform Act of 1998,[59] was introduced on July 10, 1998. The bill initially enjoyed broad support, including support from the library community, which was "united in the belief that [the Act] must be passed . . . to strengthen the current FDLP and to enhance public access to both tangible publications and those created or transmitted through an electronic communications system or network."[60] However, the proposed legislation was not enacted before the close of the 105th Congress, and due to leadership changes in the 106th Congress, efforts were not made to renew the reform effort.

During this same period, librarians began to discuss their vision of a reinvented FDLP. In 1993 two documents were reported out of these discussions, which articulated the tenets of a model federal information program:

- The FDLP would be characterized by timely, equitable, and no-fee provision of government information to the public with a cooperative network of information-producing agencies, geographically dispersed participating libraries, and a central coordinating government authority.

- The information would be made available in formats most appropriate to content, use, and audience, and defining legislation would be broadly inclusive of all types of information in all formats and media.
- Agency participation would be ensured and the program should facilitate partnerships between its constituents.[61]

In 1995, Congress directed the public printer to initiate a cooperative study to help redefine a new and strengthened federal information dissemination policy and program. The study involved representatives from the legislative, executive, and judicial branches of the government, as well as the depository library community, the national library associations, the information industry, and other appropriate government and public entities.[62] A draft report was issued after the study concluded in March 1996. The basic principles for federal government information, developed as part of the study, are as follows:

- Principle 1: The public has the right of access to government information.
- Principle 2: The government has an obligation to disseminate and provide broad public access to its information.
- Principle 3: The government has an obligation to guarantee the authenticity and integrity of its information.
- Principle 4: The government has an obligation to preserve its information.
- Principle 5: Government information created or compiled by government employees or at government expense should remain in the public domain.[63]

Public comment was invited in response to the document, and the public printer issued the strategic transition plan for completing the move from print to electronic format in his final report in June 1996. The implementation timetable initially projected a two-and-one-half-year conversion schedule, but after receiving input from publishing agencies and depository libraries, the public printer extended the time frame to a more realistic and cost-effective five- to seven-year transition schedule.[64] The transition plan resulted in an aggressive program of conversion to electronic formats both at the production level and at the distribution level. GPO's transformation became swiftly evident. For example, within two years of the final report's issuance, the percentage of paper products distributed to depository libraries dropped from 45 percent to 30 percent, and microfiche dropped from 50 percent to 20 percent—while electronic products increased from 5 percent to 50 percent.[65] At the present time, more than 92 percent of new titles that are made available through the FDLP are electronic, whether or not they are also available in tangible form.[66] In fiscal year 2005, GPO distributed a total of 5,285,169 tangible copies of 10,301 titles to depository libraries (7,714 of these titles were in paper).[67]

GOVERNMENT DOCUMENTS IN THE TWENTY-FIRST CENTURY

At the beginning of the twentieth century the activities of the Government Printing Office fell into three classes: public printing and binding; the furnishing of blank paper; and the distribution of printed publications.[68] By 1978, GPO distributed publications in microfiche; CD-ROM products followed in 1988; the GPO Access website for online publications was developed in 1994; and other initiatives to harness government information on the Internet soon followed. While the *Congressional Record* and *Federal Register* continue today to be produced at its main plant, GPO has transformed into a twenty-first-century digital information processing facility.[69] At the end of 2004, GPO released a document, *Strategic Vision for the 21st Century*, which provided a framework for how it would carry out and fund its transformation goals—to develop a future digital system to anchor all future operations, to reorganize the agency into new product- and service-oriented business lines along with investment in the necessary technologies, to adopt management best practices agencywide, including retraining to provide needed skills, and to relocate the GPO to facilities that are sized and equipped to meet future needs.[70] So, in an attempt to cope with economic realities, GPO concentrated on disseminating information rather than on printing it, and made plans to bring revenues in the door. Law librarians expressed concerns with some of the policies proposed in *Strategic Vision*—that the policies didn't ensure GPO's commitment to no-fee public access, that changes in the distribution of print materials would have a negative impact on authentic government information, and primarily, that, "the important issues of version control, authenticity, and permanent public access [would] not [be] addressed."[71]

The information environment has changed rapidly in the last ten to fifteen years. The federal government continued to develop its Internet presence and offer emergent electronic services to the public, and as the twenty-first century dawned, depository librarians and libraries again considered redefining their roles. In 2001, Shuler argued that "a national system of depository libraries [was] no longer needed"[72] to distribute government information because "the Internet has redefined and displaced the concepts of 'ownership' and accessibility."[73] Meanwhile, Jacobs, Jacobs, and Yeo asserted, in 2005, that in the digital age, the traditional roles of FDLP libraries in selecting, acquiring, organizing, preserving, and providing access to and services for government information are more important than ever.[74] Over the last few years, the DLC worked to draft a discussion paper that would envision the future of the provision of government information and the federal depository libraries' role in it.[75] The DLC held conversations with GPO staff and solicited input from librarians at meetings of the DLC in the fall of 2005. At the fall meeting, the DLC presented the major points of the discussion paper to the public printer, GPO staff, and attending librarians. The DLC identified the following four issues for strategic planning: roles of federal depository libraries in the nonexclusive environment of the Internet, managing collections and delivering content, deploying expertise, and adding value.[76] The next steps for the depository library community would be to continue the discussion on the DLC Vision Future Scenarios Blog,[77] encourage community participation in the discussion, and formulate goals and action items for the next meeting of the DLC in April 2006.

CURRENT GPO INITIATIVES

At the present time, GPO is working on multiple enterprises to continue its transformation from a nineteenth-century printing-press operation to a twenty-first-century electronic information agency, including the following:[78]

- An integrated library system (ILS) to modernize GPO's older legacy systems. One component of the ILS, the new *Catalog of Government Publications (CGP)*, is part of the *National Bibliography of U.S. Publications* (a comprehensive index of public documents from all three branches of the federal government).
- An authentication initiative to procure the necessary tools and capabilities for GPO to automate the application of digital signatures on Adobe Acrobat PDF files. This will assure users that the information made available by GPO is official and authentic.
- A future digital system that will manage, preserve, version, provide access to, and disseminate authentic digital content.
- A digital legacy collection, in which GPO will partner with the Library of Congress and the National Archives and Records Administration to implement a plan to digitize tangible collections of historical

documents in federal depository libraries. GPO has developed a registry that will be a locator tool for publicly accessible collections of digitized U.S. government publications (located at www.gpo access.gov/legacy/registry/index.html).

- A revision of the list of *Essential Titles for Public Use in Paper Format* and a next generation *Federal Depository Library Manual* and *Instructions to Depository Libraries*.
- The GPO LOCKSS pilot project, which currently makes five government e-journals available to participating pilot libraries. LOCKSS (Lots of Copies Keep Stuff Safe) is open-source software that provides institutions with a way to collect, store, and preserve access to their own local copies of e-journal content.
- A pilot project for Web discovery and harvesting, in which efforts are being made to discover and retrieve publications from federal agency websites that fall within the scope of the FDLP and the National Bibliography Program.
- A review and proposed model for revision of the item number system used by libraries in the FDLP to select tangible and electronic titles.[79]

As depository librarians continue to consider the future of the FDLP and reinvent themselves to accommodate the transformation of government information products, we can only be certain of one thing: "The 19th century is not coming back. . . . The times have changed and the GPO must change with them if it is to continue carrying out its core mission to keep America informed."[80]

CHRONOLOGY OF SIGNIFICANT EVENTS AND PUBLIC LAWS RELATING TO GOVERNMENT PRINTING

1777 In October, the Continental Congress adopts a resolution authorizing the Committee of Intelligence to take measures for getting a printing press erected in Yorktown.

1789 The subject of printing the acts and proceedings of Congress is referred to a special joint committee. A report is adopted by both houses, in which it is left for the secretary of the Senate and the clerk of the House to contract for printing and binding.

1789 From 1789 to 1872 Congress orders that laws be printed in newspapers.

1801 The District of Columbia becomes the seat of the national government. A committee is appointed to expedite the printing of the House. The committee's report directs that a printer for the House be appointed, but is not carried through.

1803 Departing tradition, President Jefferson sends a message in writing to Congress with accompanying documents, spurring violent debate over the proposal to have it printed. Five hundred copies of the "Message and Documents" are printed.

1804 Congress empowers the secretary of the Senate and clerk of the House to advertise for proposals for printing. Until 1819 government printing is done under contracts made with the lowest bidder.

1813 On December 27, the first act to specifically authorize the distribution of government publications to libraries in the United States (3 Stat. 140) provides that one copy of the journals and documents of the Senate and House of Representatives be sent to each university and college and to each historical society incorporated in each state. The secretary of state is responsible for distributing publications.

1818 A joint committee is appointed in December to consider the need for further printing laws, and recommends the establishment of a national printing office.

1819 The passage of a joint resolution (3 Stat. 538) provides for each house to elect its own printer. Gales & Seaton, of the *National Intelligencer,* is elected printer by both houses.

1828 The House orders an investigation into public printing, exposing political corruption, excessive and useless printing, and exorbitant profits obtained by trickery.

1845 The government contracts with Little, Brown & Co. to produce a collection of all public and private laws, foreign treaties and Indian treaties chronologically arranged by session of Congress, a series known as *Statutes at Large.*

1846 In hopes of preventing fraud, a joint resolution is passed to establish the contract system of printing.

1852 The Printing Act of 1852 (10 Stat. 30) provides for the appointment of a superintendent of public printing (within the Department of the Interior) to oversee the work done by the printers selected by the Senate and House.

1857 The secretary of the interior is authorized (11 Stat. 253) to distribute government publications and to designate the libraries that receive publications.

1858 A joint resolution (11 Stat. 368) provides that the representative from each district and the delegate from each territory may designate a depository library.

1859 An act (11 Stat. 379) provides that each senator may designate one library to receive government publications. The secretary of the interior is charged with the distribution of all books printed or purchased for the government, with some exceptions (11 Stat. 379). Distribution includes the shipping of documents to depository libraries.

1860 An investigative committee (Select Committee on Public Printing) reports to Congress that the contract system of public printing is a corrupt failure. The Government Printing Office is established by the 1860 Printing Act (12 Stat 118). The act authorizes the superintendent of public printing to purchase the buildings, machinery, and materials needed to execute the public printing.

1861 The Government Printing Office opens for business on March 4. Abraham Lincoln is inaugurated sixteenth president of the United States on the same day.

1869 On March 3, the Office of the Superintendent of Public Documents is created at the Department of the Interior (15 Stat. 292) and is charged with the general distribution of certain government publications.

1873 GPO takes over compiling and printing the *Statutes at Large*. The first GPO-produced issue of the *Congressional Record* appears on March 5.

1874 Dr. John G. Ames becomes superintendent of public documents and retains the post until it is abolished in 1895. "The three great contributions of Dr. Ames were his checklists, with serial numbers assigned to all Congressional Documents from the First to the Fifty-third Congresses, the comprehensive index of government publications covering the years 1881 to 1893, and his work in developing sentiment in Congress for the creation of the office of superintendent of documents in the Government Printing Office."[81]

1876 An act changes the title of the "superintendent of public printing" to "public printer" and makes the position a presidential appointment.

1882 An electrical lighting plant is installed at the GPO.

1895 The Printing Act of 1895 (28 Stat 601–624) codifies the laws relating to the Government Printing Office and public printing in general. The act abolishes the office of superintendent of public documents in the Department of the Interior and creates the office of superintendent of documents in the Government Printing Office. In addition to distributing publications to depository libraries, the superintendent is now authorized to sell government publications and is ordered to prepare monthly, annual, and biennial indexes. The act provides for executive department publications to be distributed to depository libraries and designates as depositories the state and territorial libraries, the libraries of the existing (in 1895) executive departments, the Naval Academy, and the Military Academy. There are 420 depository libraries in 1895. The *Monthly Catalog* first appears in 1895. The first depository shipment, containing eleven congressional publications, is shipped on July 17. Congress authorizes the GPO to distribute the *Statutes at Large* to depository libraries. The superintendent of documents (SuDoc) classification system is developed by Adelaide Hasse (in the library of the GPO) between 1895 and 1903.

1896 With the implementation of a new electrical lighting plant, the GPO shifts from steam-powered presses to direct electrical-powered machinery.

1904 The superintendent of documents is given authority (33 Stat. 584) to reprint publications other than congressional.

1907 The library of the Philippine government is designated a depository (34 Stat. 850). The libraries of the land grant colleges are designated depositories (34 Stat. 1014).

1910 The Printing Investigation Commission of Congress issues a preliminary report (61 Cong. 2 Sess, S. Doc. 652) on the subject of branch printing establishments and recommends that all public printing be centralized at the GPO. The printing office of the Weather Bureau is abolished by authorization of the Joint Committee on Printing.

1912 Additional responsibilities charged to the superintendent (37 Stat. 414) include the storing and mailing of executive department publications. The public printer replaces the majority of horses and wagons at the GPO with electric trucks.

1913 An act (38 Stat. 75) provides that the depository designation of a library shall remain permanent.

1917 The legislative, executive, and judicial appropriation act of March 3 (39 Stat. 1083) directs the abolishing of state, war, and navy branch printing offices.

1919 Because printing is still being operated outside the GPO, the legislative, executive, and judicial appropriation act of 1920 (approved March 1, 40 Stat. 1270) includes a clause to order the centralization of printing at the GPO, with a few exceptions.

1920 The Joint Committee on Printing (JCP) conducts a thorough investigation of the cost of work done at the GPO versus the cost of commercial printing (or private contractors). The JCP concludes (66 Cong. 2 Sess., S. Doc. 265) that "printing and binding can be done at the [GPO] at less cost to the government than printing of similar quality . . . obtained from commercial printers."

1922 An act (42 Stat. 436) provides that depository libraries can select the classes of publications that they wish to receive, instead of receiving every publication issued. For the first time, the superintendent of documents sends to depositories a "Classified list of United States public documents for selection by depository libraries, July 1, 1922." A joint resolution (42 Stat. 541) gives the superintendent of documents the authority to reprint congressional publications.

1923 There are 418 depositories in 1923.

1924 The GPO is charged (4 Stat. 592) with the new activity of supplying blank paper and envelopes to all government establishments in the District of Columbia. The geological and patent gazette depositories are discontinued.

1938 On June 27 the original building where GPO first opened for business on March 4, 1861, begins to be demolished. In its place is erected an eight-story building, composed of 481,975 square feet, completed in February 1940.

1943 The bullet and item number are added to the *Monthly Catalog* to indicate shipment of publications to depositories.

1945 There are 555 depositories. Research and development at the GPO during the postwar years leads to the shift from hot-metal to offset printing.

1947 The first Biennial Survey of Depository Libraries is conducted.

1950 The first modern GPO shipping list begins around 1950.

1962 There are 594 depositories. The Depository Library Act of 1962 (PL 87-579) discontinues the payment of postage by depositories and allows depositories to discard materials after a five-year retention period. The act adds libraries of independent federal agencies and authorizes the designation of not more than two libraries in each state and in the commonwealth of Puerto Rico to be regional depositories.

1966 Freedom of Information Act (FOIA), 80 Stat. 250; 5 USC 552. Amended in 1974, 1976, 1986, and 1996.

1967 Modernization of printing at the GPO continues as the Linotron system is installed in October. The Linotron system utilizes computer-generated magnetic tape to produce page photocomposition.

1968 An act provides that a depository designation can be removed by the superintendent of documents for failure to abide by the laws governing the depository program.

1970 GPO proposes studying the feasibility of making government publications available in microfiche.

1972 An act (86 Stat. 507) adds the highest appellate courts of the states to the depository program. The DLC to the Public Printer (consisting of fifteen documents librarians) is formalized. At GPO, proposals are studied for the automation of a new order processing system, production of the *Monthly Catalog*, mailing lists, and the creation of a Publications Reference File online.

1973 *Public Documents Highlights,* an irregular GPO newsletter for the depository community, begins in May. The publication is discontinued in September 1983.

1974 Privacy Act of 1974, 88 Stat. 1896; 5 USC 552a. Amended in 1986.

1977 There are over 1,200 depositories. GPO receives approval from the Joint Committee on Printing and begins to distribute microfiche to libraries. Production of the *Federal Register* converts from hot metal to photocomposition.

1978 An act (92 Stat. 199) adds law libraries to the depository program. GPO installs an interactive page makeup system, which facilitates computerization as page formatting shifts from metal-type to photocomposition and electronic processing. The entire text of the *Code of Federal Regulations* converts to an electronic database.

1979 U.S. House of Representatives begins televising its proceedings on the Cable Satellite Public Affairs Network (C-SPAN) on March 19.

1980 Paperwork Reduction Act (PRA) of 1980, 94 Stat. 2812; 44 USC 3501 *et seq. Administrative Notes,* a GPO newsletter, begins in September to increase communications with the depository community.

1986 U.S. Senate begins televising its proceedings on C-SPAN on June 2.

1993 On June 8, the Government Printing Office Electronic Information Access Enhancement Act of 1993 (PL 103–40; 107 Stat. 112; 44 USC § 4101 *et seq.*) requires the GPO to disseminate government information products online. In June, *Administrative Notes* makes its electronic debut on the listserv GOVDOC-L.

1994 The *Administrative Notes Technical Supplement* is first published in January. In March, GPO LPS adopts GOVDOC-L as a method of e-mail communication. GPO Access is launched in June—providing Internet access to information from all three branches of the government (www.gpoaccess.gov/).

1995 PRA of 1995, 109 Stat. 165–66.

1996 Electronic Freedom of Information Amendments (E-FOIA), 110 Stat. 3048; 5 USC 552.

1996 Report to Congress—*Study to Identify Measures Necessary for a Successful Transition to a More Electronic Federal Depository Library Program* (Washington: Government Printing Office, June 1996).

1998 Government Paperwork Elimination Act (GPEA), 112 Stat. 2681–749, Title XVII.

2000 FirstGov is launched on September 22—the single federal portal to all national government websites (www.firstgov.gov).

2004 GPO publishes *Strategic Vision for the 21st Century* on December 1.

2005 In March, 794 depositories participate in a survey to identify "essential titles" that should continue to be distributed in a tangible format (http://gpoaccess.gov/essential/statistics.html). GPO launches LOCKSS pilot project in June (www.access.gpo.gov/su_docs/fdlp/lockss/index.html).

2006 GPO discontinues paper distribution of *Administrative Notes.* GPO-FDLP-L becomes GPO's primary vehicle for communicating with depository library staff. February 1, GPOExpress, based on a contractual agreement between GPO and FedEx Kinko's, begins supplying printing services to federal agencies. February 14, GPO posts revised versions of the briefing papers (www.access.gpo.gov/su_docs/fdlp/selection/index.html) outlining proposed changes to the system used by federal depository libraries to select tangible and online titles.[82] On March 9, GPO launches the enhanced version of the *Catalog of U.S. Government Publications* (CGP) at http://catalog.gpo.gov/. This version of the CGP is the online public access catalog (OPAC) module of the GPO's new integrated library system. With the availability of the new CGP, Phase 1 of a larger modernization plan to replace older legacy systems is complete.[83]

U.S. GOVERNMENT DOCUMENTS: A SELECTIVE LIST OF FINDING AIDS AND RESOURCES

Bibliographic Tools (Catalogs, Indexes, and Checklists)

Catalog[ue] of the Public Documents of the [Fifty-third–Seventy-sixth] Congress and of All Departments of the Government of the United States . . . (generally known as the *Document Catalog[ue]*, 1893–1940). A comprehensive index of public documents, the *Document Catalog* lists all publications issued in two-year periods. One volume contains the congressional publications of an entire Congress and the executive branch publications covering two fiscal years. Indexes proclamations and executive orders. Arrangement is alphabetical by personal and government author, subject, publishing office, and title. Includes cross-references to related topics. "The Ames comprehensive index of the documents of the Fifty-first and Fifty-second Congress is recognized as the most successful predecessor of the present volume" (Preface, v. 1, p. 3).

Checklist of United States Public Documents, 1789–1909 . . . Vol. I, List of Congressional and Department Publications. Arranged by publishing offices, classes of publications, and series, of all publications issued by the government during the period covered. Useful to research the breadth of an agency's publishing from 1789 to 1909.

CIS Indexes and Abstracts. "The CIS Index, now a CIS collection from LexisNexis, makes a comprehensive effort to collect all the publications of Congress (except the *Congressional Record*), including publications of the Congressional Budget Office, and to provide full access to them promptly." (From the User Guide for the CIS Index and Related Services.) Historical indexes include:

- CIS Index to Presidential Executive Orders and Proclamations (1789–1980)
- CIS Index to Unpublished U.S. House of Representatives Committee Hearings . . . (1833–1972)
- CIS Index to Unpublished U.S. Senate Committee Hearings . . . (1823–1980)
- CIS Index to U.S. Senate Executive Documents and Reports: Covering Documents and Reports Not Printed in the U.S. Serial Set (1817–1969)
- CIS U.S. Congressional Committee Hearings Index (1833–1969)
- CIS U.S. Congressional Committee Prints Index (1830–1969)
- CIS U.S. Serial Set Index (1789–1969)

From 1970, indexing of congressional materials is provided by *CIS/Index to Publications of the United States Congress* (CIS/Index), 1970 forward. *LexisNexis Congressional* is a Web-based service that provides access to the CIS/Index, with hypertext links to the full text of related congressional documents, 1789 forward. It is the most comprehensive online resource available for congressional publications and legislative research. You can search *LexisNexis Congressional* collections from 1789 to the present. Collections are indexed by committee, author, publication number, public law numbers, bill numbers, SuDoc numbers, and subject terms. Use a basic, advanced, or "search by number" form.

Clarke, Edith. Bibliography [of government publications] (In her *Guide to the Use of United States Government Publications*, Boston: Boston Book Co., 1918, pp. 241–88.)

Guide to U.S. Government Publications. Detroit: Thomson Gale, published annually since 1959. (Generally known as *Andriot*.) Arranged in SuDocs class number order, provides a brief history of the creation of agencies and a listing of current series issued by each agency. The "Agency Class Chronology" traces the history of all agencies current or defunct. Indexed by both agency and title. Updated annually.

Index to the Reports and Documents of the —— Congress, with Numerical Lists and Schedule of Volumes (generally known as the *Document Index*). Washington, D.C.: G.P.O., annual 1908–1933. Contains only the documents and reports of Congress. Entries are arranged alphabetically by subject, names of publishing offices, committees, and in the case of reports, by the name of the senator or representative submitting that report. The documents and reports are also listed in numerical order.

Internet Archives. *CyberCemetery*, at the University of North Texas Libraries (http://govinfo.library.unt.edu/default.htm), provides permanent online access to electronic publications of selected federal government agencies that have ceased operation. The *Internet Archive* (www.archive.org/) is also useful for locating government Web pages that have disappeared. It contains multiple copies of the entire publicly available Web and has an index (the *Wayback Machine*) that allows surfing archived Web pages over multiple time periods back to 1996 (www.archive.org/web/web.php).

Internet Search Engines. Useful for locating federal (and state) agency documents. Use *Google's Uncle Sam* (www.google.com/unclesam) to search all .gov and .mil sites. *FirstGov's* search engine (advanced search option at www.firstgov.gov/) allows users to search only federal government websites, eliminating results from state and local governments if desired. *Vivisimo's* FirstGov cluster search identifies groups of relevant results. Using the main Vivisimo search page, type a search and select "FirstGov" from the drop-down list to the immediate right of the search box. Use general search engines to find collections of archived digital documents hosted by academic institutions or FDLP content partners, such as the "Historical Publications of the United States Commission on Civil Rights" at Thurgood Marshall Law Library or U.S. Census Bureau Data at Case Western Reserve Library.

Monthly Catalog (1895–). *Catalogue of United States Public Documents.* Washington, D.C.: GPO, 1895–1907. Continued by *Monthly Catalogue, United States Public Documents.* Washington, D.C.: GPO, 1907–1933. Continued by *Monthly Catalog of United States Public Documents.* Washington, D.C.: GPO, 1933–1939. Continued by *United States Government Publications Monthly Catalog,* Washington, D.C.: GPO, 1940–1951. Continued by *Monthly Catalog of United States Government Publications,* Washington, D.C.: GPO, 1951– . (generally known as MoCat). Monthly, with semiannual and annual indexes. The most comprehensive ongoing source for federal publications. Lists every new publication of all offices of the government. Publications are listed according to publishing offices. Each publication is listed by title and serial number. Available online as *Catalog of U.S. Government Publications* (CGP), 1976– , (http://catalog.gpo.gov/ or http://purl .access.gpo.gov/GPO/LPS844). This version of the CGP is the OPAC module of GPO's new integrated library system and offers more than 500,000 records to both historical and current government publications. These records have been created or updated since July 1976. Plans are under way to include records for publications dating back to the late 1800s.

Tables of and Annotated Index to the Congressional Series of United States Public Documents [15th to 52nd Congress] Washington, D.C., Government Printing Office, 1902. "Contains a list of, and an index to the documents of the Fifteenth to the Fifty-second Congress, both inclusive." Contents include: preface; congressional series tables; congressional series index; appendixes—(I) table showing number of documents, (II) list of title-pages and imprints, and (III) reference tables (duration of sessions, etc.).

For information on additional finding aids, consult Morehead, Introduction to United States Government Information Sources, 6th edition.

Electronic Databases

CQ.com—a full-service legislative tracking website from Congressional Quarterly Inc. Databases include full text of bills, committee reports, the *Congressional Record*, committee testimony, congressional transcripts, *Federal Register*. Services include bill analysis and tracking, floor votes, *CQ News*, *CQ Today*, and *CQ Weekly*. Topical databases include the CQ Budget Tracker, Green Sheets, HealthBeat, House Action Reports, SenateWatch, and more. Databases are generally searchable by congress number, word or phrase, bill numbers, member names, date, subject, stage in legislative process. This commercial database is available at www.cq.com/.

GPO Access—a service of the U.S. Government Printing Office that provides free electronic access to information and full-text documents produced by the three branches of the federal government. GPO Access's resources are arranged topically and by branch. Site searching as well as an A–Z resource list are available. When viewing resources by branch, the database offers both search and browse functionality. For example, you can conduct a keyword search of Senate reports across multiple Congresses (1995 forward) or you can browse a catalog list of Senate hearings available in electronic format from the 108th Congress. Full-text documents are available in both PDF and text formats. GPO Access is available at www.gpoaccess.gov/.

HeinOnline—generally known for its law journal library, HeinOnline has digitized an impressive collection of government documents. The "Federal Register Library" contains a full run of the *Federal Register* and its indexes, FR *List of Sections Affected*, *Weekly Compilation of Presidential Documents* (a historical CFR library and *Public Papers of the Presidents* are forthcoming). The "U.S. Federal Legislative History Library" contains bibliographies and compiled full-text legislative histories on historically significant legislation. HeinOnline also contains a full run of the *U.S. Statutes at Large*, *U.S. Reports* (bound volumes preliminary prints and slip opinions), U.S. Attorney General Opinions and the Opinions of the Office of Legal Counsel of the United

States Department of Justice. The "Treaties and Agreements Library" contains official and unofficial treaty publications, treaty guides and indexes, and other texts. A forthcoming "U.S. Federal Agency Library" will contain Administrative Decisions, *FCC Record, Tax Court Reports,* and a number of other notable U.S. federal agency publications. All documents are available in PDF format and are retrievable by citation and metadata search. This commercial database is available at http://heinonline.org/.

LLSDC's *Legislative Source Book*—maintained by the Law Librarians' Society of Washington, D.C., the source book provides a wide variety of resources and links to federal and state legislation and information pertaining to federal and state legislation (www.llsdc.org/source book/index.html).

LexisNexis Congressional—a Web-based service that provides access to indexing, abstracts, and full texts of congressional documents from 1789 forward. Indispensable to legislative research, *Congressional* is the most comprehensive online resource available for locating congressional publications. Collections are indexed by committee, author, publication number, public law numbers, bill numbers, SuDoc numbers, and subject terms. Use the basic, advanced, or "search by number" form to retrieve indexing, abstracts, or full-text documents in PDF or text formats. This commercial database is available at http://web.lexis-nexis.com/congcomp.

Thomas—a free service of the Library of Congress that provides summary and full texts of congressional publications (bills, hearings, reports, debates, and statutes). Thomas also contains committee information and information on the legislative process. Search a single Congress or across multiple Congresses, by keyword, bill number, law number, report number, committee or sponsor name. Coverage extends back to 1967 for treaties, 1973 for bills and laws, 1995 for reports, 1989 for the *Congressional Record.* Thomas is available at http://thomas.loc.gov.

Additional online resources for government documents at the Library of Congress include:

American Memory—a digital record of American history that provides free online access to written and spoken words, sound recordings, still and moving images, prints, maps, and so forth. To access the legal documents, go to "Browse Collections by Topic," choose "Government, Law" then select: "Documents from the Continental Congress and the Constitutional Convention, 1774–1789" or "A Century of Lawmaking for a New Nation: U.S. Congressional Documents and Debates, 1774–1875." These documents include the early journals and debates of Congress, bills and statutes, the U.S. Serial Set, and more. The collections are searchable by number or word, and are available as full text in image (TIFF) or text format. American Memory is available at http://memory.loc.gov/ammem/index.html.

Tools for Depository Management and Information

FDLP Desktop—news, information, and communication for and about the FDLP. Categories include News and Updates, About the FDLP, Depository Management, Electronic Collection, Locator Tools and Services, Processing Tools, Publications, Q&A (www.access.gpo .gov/su_docs/fdlp/index.html).

Finding Aids—provides links to finding aids to assist in searching or browsing for government information (www.access.gpo.gov/ su_docs/tools.html).

Catalog of U.S. Government Publications (CGP)—a search-and-retrieval service that provides bibliographic records of U.S. government information products. Use it to link to federal agency online resources or identify materials distributed to federal depository libraries. Coverage begins with 1976 and new records are added daily (http://catalog.gpo.gov/f).

New Electronic Titles—a finding aid used to locate, by month, online federal government publications that were acquired for the Federal Depository Library Program Electronic Collection. Full bibliographic information for the titles in these lists can be found in the *Catalog of U.S. Government Publications*. The weekly lists may be found in the NET Archive after four weeks (www.access.gpo.gov/su_docs/ locators/net/about_net.html).

Administrative Notes Technical Supplement—Library Programs Service's monthly newsletter, which updates various FDLP-related publications, directories, depository listings, (www.access.gpo .gov/su_docs/fdlp/pubs/techsup/index.html).

WEBTech Notes—an interactive, online resource for depository librarians to query ANTS (Administrative Notes Technical Supplement). The WEBTech Notes database is cumulated on a weekly basis and contains the information of the four main components of ANTS, specifically (1) Classification/Cataloging Update (2) Whatever Happened to ? (3) Update to the List of Classes, New Items; and (4) Update to the List of Classes, Misc. The data is updated weekly and is cumulative back to 1991 (http://www.access.gpo.gov/su_docs/ fdlp/tools/webtech.html).

U.S. Government Online Bookstore (http://bookstore.gpo.gov/)—the official online bookstore for U.S. government publications for purchase from the U.S. Government Printing Office.

The University of Michigan Documents Center—a central reference and referral point for government information (local, state, federal, foreign, or international). Its Web pages are a reference and instructional tool for government, political science, statistical data, and news (www.lib.umich.edu/govdocs/). Also see the page for "Government Documents Librarianship," (www.lib.umich.edu/govdocs/doclibs .html).

Government Documents Special Interest Section—AALL website that provides information on state bibliographies, section bylaws and business, a newsletter, and a government documents tutorial (www.aallnet.org/sis/gd/).

GODORT Handout Exchange—from the American Library Association, Government Documents Round Table, Education Committee. Provides links to electronic product guides and guides for documents staff and users (www.lib.umich.edu/govdocs/godort.html).

Secondary Sources, Manuals, Guides

"An Explanation of the Superintendent of Documents Classification System"—O'Hara, 5. Available online at www.access.gpo.gov/ su_docs/fdlp/pubs/explain.html.

Boyd, Anne Morris, and Rae Elizabeth Rips. *United States Government Publications*. New York: H. W. Wilson, 1949. A detailed review of government document series to the late 1940s.

Dwan, Ralph H. and Ernest R. Feidler. "The Federal Statutes—Their History and Use," *Minnesota Law Review* 22, no. 7 (1938): 1008–29.

Herman, Edward. *Locating United States Government Information: A Guide to Sources*. Buffalo, NY: W. S. Hein, 1997. "The purpose of this book is to provide a practical how-to guide for locating United States government publications. Emphasis is upon locating and using government information, rather than policy issues." (Preface)

Maclay, Veronica. "Selected Sources of United States Agency Decisions." *Government Publications Review* 16, no. 3 (May/June 1989): 271–301.

McKinney, Richard J. "An Overview of the U.S. Congressional Serial Set." Washington, D.C.: Law Librarians' Society of Washington, D.C.

Morehead, Joe. *Introduction to United States Government Information Sources*. Englewood, CO: Libraries Unlimited, 1999. An overview of the GPO and FDLP, general reference sources, and an overview of the publications, both print and electronic, of the legislative, executive, and judicial branches of government.

Schmeckebier, Laurence F. *Government Publications and Their Use.* Washington, D.C.: Brookings Institution, 1969. A thorough analysis of historical government document series.

Surrency, Erwin C. *History of the Federal Courts.* New York: Oceana Publications, 1987.

Surrency, Erwin C. "The Publication of Federal Laws: A Short History." *Law Library Journal* 79, no. 3 (Summer 1987): 469–84.

Treaties and Other International Agreements: The Role of the United States Senate, A Study. Washington, D.C.: Government Printing Office, 1993.

Zinn, Charles J. *How Our Laws Are Made.* Washington, D.C.: Government Printing Office, 2003. Also available online at Thomas, http://purl.access.gpo.gov/GPO/LPS4046, and http://thomas.loc.gov/home/lawsmade.toc.html.

Zwirn, Jerrold. *Congressional Publications: A Research Guide to Legislation, Budgets, and Treaties.* Englewood, CO: Libraries Unlimited, 1983.

State Documents: Finding Aids and Resources

Dow, Susan L. *State Document Checklists: A Historical Bibliography,* 2nd ed. Buffalo, NY: William S. Hein, 2000.

Government Relations Committee and Washington Affairs Office, *State-by-State Report on Permanent Public Access to Electronic Government Information.* Chicago: American Association of Law Libraries, 2003.

Hellebust, Lynn, ed. *State Legislative Sourcebook.* Topeka, KS: Government Research Service, 2006.

Hellebust, Lynn, ed. *State Reference Publications: A Bibliographic Guide to State Blue Books, Legislative Manuals and Other General Reference Sources.* Topeka, KS.: Government Research Service, 1999.

Hernon, Peter, John V. Richardson, Nancy P. Sanders, and Marjorie Shepley, eds. *Municipal Government Reference Sources: Publications and Collections.* New York: R. R. Bowker, 1978.

Manz, William H. *Guide to State Legislative and Administrative Materials.* Buffalo, NY: William S. Hein, 2002.

Parish, David W. *State Government Reference Publications: An Annotated Bibliography,* 2nd ed. Littleton, CO.: Libraries Unlimited, 1981.

Smith, Lori L., Daniel C. Barkley, Daniel D. Cornwall, Eric W. Johnson, and J. Louise Malcomb. *Tapping State Government Information Sources.* Westport, CT.: Greenwood Press, 2003.

State Bibliographies. AALL Government Document Series. Various authors. Chicago: American Association of Law Libraries, Government Documents Special Interest Section, dates vary. For more information, see www.aallnet.org/sis/gd/stateb.html.

Tulis, Susan E., and Daniel C. Barkley, eds. *Directory of Government Doc-ument Collections & Librarians,* 8th ed. Washington, D.C.: American Li-brary Association, 1974–.

Online State Resources

Council of State Governments—identifies issues common among state governments, provides directory of state government officials from all fifty states and territories, and lists research publications pro-duced by CSG staff (www.csg.org/CSG/default.htm).

LexisNexis Municipal Codes Web Library—includes links to Municipal Codes published through LexisNexis Municipal Codes Publishing and Ordlink Services (http://municipalcodes.lexisnexis.com/).

Municipal Codes Online at the Seattle Public Library—provides links to city and county codes available for unrestricted searching on the World Wide Web (www.spl.org/default.asp?pageid=collection_municodes).

Municode.com—a free online municipal code library (www.municode.com/resources/online%20Library.asp).

National Association of Secretaries of State—contains information on secretaries' responsibilities and such key NASS initiatives as election administration, voter participation, and electronic or e-government services. Provides biographies, contact information, and state Web links for all secretaries of state (www.nass.org/).

National Conference of State Legislatures—serves as a resource for those who draft legislation on the state level, providing a searchable database that accesses publications and court decisions on a variety of legislative issues (www.ncsl.org/).

State and Local Documents Task Force—American Library Association, Government Documents Roundtable. Provides professional develop-ment tools, links to state resources, and news on projects, issues, and initiatives (http://sunsite.berkeley.edu/GODORT/sldtf/index.htm).

State Government Information from the Library of Congress—contains general information on state and local government issues, state maps, and individual state Internet links (www.loc.gov/rr/news/stategov/stategov.html).

State Legislatures, State Laws, and State Regulations—provides a com-prehensive list of website links and telephone numbers, from the Law Librarians' Society of Washington, D.C. (www.llsdc.org/source book/state-leg.htm).

StateList—The Electronic Source for State Publication Lists. A joint proj-ect of the Documents and Law Libraries at the University of Illinois. Provides links to state publication checklists and shipping lists that are currently available on the Internet (www.library.uiuc.edu/doc/statelist/check/check.htm).

Top Ten List for New State Documents Librarians—From the State and Local Documents Task Force of the ALA-Government Documents Round Table, provides tips for new state documents librarians (http://dizzy.library.arizona.edu/users/arawan/top10statehandout.html).

REFERENCES

Aldrich, Duncan M., Gary Cornwell, and Daniel Barkley. "Changing Partnerships? Government Documents Departments at the Turn of the Millennium." *Government Information Quarterly* 17, no. 3 (2000): 273–90.

Boyd, Anne Morris, and Rae Elizabeth Rips. *United States Government Publications.* New York: H. W. Wilson, 1949.

Brown Jr., Garrett, E., Mark C. Cramer, and Mary Lee Carson. *Legislative Histories of the Laws Affecting the U.S. Government Printing Office as Codified in Title 44 of the U.S. Code,* 6 volumes. Washington, D.C.: Government Printing Office, 1982.

Eschenfelder, Kristin R. "Behind the Website: An Inside Look at the Production of Web-based Textual Government Information." *Government Information Quarterly* 21, no. 3 (2004): 337–58.

Government Printing Office: Actions to Strengthen and Sustain GPO's Transformation. Report to Congressional Committees. GAO-04–830. Washington, D.C.: United States General Accounting Office, June, 2004. Also available at www.gao.gov/cgi-bin/getrpt?GAO-04–830 (accessed June 22, 2005).

Hernon, P., and H. Relyea. "Government Publishing: Past to Present." *Government Information Quarterly* 12, no. 3 (1995): 309–330.

Jacobs, James A., James R. Jacobs, and Shinjoung Yeo. "Government Information in the Digital Age: The Once and Future Federal Depository Program." *Journal of Academic Librarianship* 31, no. 3 (May 2005): 198–208.

MacGilvray, Daniel R. "A Short History of GPO." First printed in "New Typeline" (1986–1987), reprinted in "Administrative Notes" (1986–1987). *FDLP Desktop.* http://www.access.gpo.gov/su_docs/fdlp/history/macgilvray.html (accessed January 28, 2006).

Martin, Kristin E. "Publishing Trends within State Government: The Situation in North Carolina." *Journal of Government Information* 30, no. 5/6 (2004): 620–36.

Matthews, Richard J., et al., eds. *State-By-State Report on Permanent Public Access to Electronic Government Information.* Chicago: Government Relations Committee and Washington Affairs Office, American Association of Law Libraries, 2003.

Morehead, Joe. *Introduction to United States Government Information Sources.* Englewood, CO: Libraries Unlimited, 1999.

O'Hara, Frederic J., ed. *Reader in Government Documents.* Washington, D.C.: NCR/Microcard Editions, 1973.

Relyea, Harold C. "E-Gov: the Federal Overview." *Journal of Academic Librarianship* 27, no. 2 (March 2001): 131–48.

————. *Public Printing Reform: Issues and Actions* (Washington, D.C.: Library of Congress Congressional Research Service, 2003).

Schmeckebier, Laurence F. *The Government Printing Office: Its History, Activities and Organization.* Baltimore, MD: Johns Hopkins Press, 1925.

Schmeckebier, Laurence F., and Roy B. Eastin. *Government Publications and Their Use.* Washington, D.C.: Brookings, 1969.

Slater, Robert. "Challenges and Changes: A Review of Issues Surrounding the Digital Migration of Government Information." *Science & Technology Libraries* 21, no. 1/2 (2001): 153–62.

Shuler, John A. "Beyond the Depository Library Concept."

Strategic Vision for the 21st Century. Washington, D.C.: United States Government Printing Office, 2004. www.gpo.gov/congressional/pdfs/04strategicplan.pdf (accessed January 25, 2005).

NOTES

1. For more information on the early history of government printing, see Laurence F. Schmeckebier, *The Government Printing Office: Its History, Activities and Organization* (Baltimore: John Hopkins Press, 1925), 1–16; and Daniel R. MacGilvray, "A Short History of GPO," *FDLP Desktop,* www.access.gpo.gov/su_docs/fdlp/history/macgilvray.html (accessed January 26, 2006).

2. *House Journal,* 1st Cong., 1st sess., May 15, 1789, 35.

3. Resolution of December 27, 1813, 13th Cong., 2nd sess., *Stats at Large of USA,* 3 (1813): 140–141.

4. Bruce R. James, "Message from the Public Printer," *U.S. Government Printing,* www.gpo.gov/factsheet/message.htm (accessed December 11, 2005).

5. Documents before 1817 are found in the *American State Papers.*

6. For more information on the Serial Set, see Joe Morehead, *Introduction to United States Government Information Sources* (Englewood, CO: Libraries Unlimited, 1999), 146–57; "Library Resources for Administrative History: Congressional Serial Set," *Archives Library Information Center,* www.archives.gov/research/alic/reference/admin-history/congressional-serial-set.html (accessed November 10, 2005); Richard J. McKinney, "An Overview of the U.S. Congressional Serial Set," *LLSDC's Legislative Source Book,* www.llsdc.org/sourcebook/sch-v.htm#over (accessed November 10, 2005); and Virginia Saunders, "U.S. Congressional Serial Set: What It Is and Its History," *GPO Access,* www.access.gpo.gov/su_docs/fdlp/history/sset/index.html (accessed November 10, 2005).

7. 15th Cong., 2nd sess., 1818, S. Doc. 29, serial 14, 1.

8. 15th Cong., 2nd sess., 1819, H. Doc. 139, serial 24, 3.

9. Public Resolution 6, 15th Cong., 2nd sess. (March 3, 1819), *Stats at Large of USA* 3 (1819): 538.

10. Schmeckebier, *The Government Printing Office,* 1–9.

11. Schmeckebier, *The Government Printing Office,* 1–9.

12. Schmeckebier, *The Government Printing Office,* 5.

13. Ch. 91, 32nd Cong., 1st sess. (August 26, 1852), *Stats at Large of USA* 10 (1852): 30.

14. Schmeckebier, *The Government Printing Office*, 7.

15. Ch. 91, 32nd Cong., 1st sess. (August 26, 1852), *Stats at Large of USA* 10 (1852): 35.

16. See, for example, Senate Committee on Alleged Abuses of Printing, 36th Cong., 1st sess., 1860, S. Rep. 205; House Committee to Investigate Alleged Corruptions in Government, *The Covode Investigation*, 36th Cong., 1st sess., 1860, H. Rep. 648; Senate Committee to Inquire into Expenditures from the Public Printing for the Support of Newspapers, etc., *Resolution of Inquiry Whether Certain Sums of Money Were Paid by Public Printer, or Any Party Who Executed Binding for 35th Congress [. . .] Testimony in Relation Thereto*, 36th Cong. 1st sess., 1860; House Committee on Public Expenditures, *Public Printing*, 36th Cong., 1st sess., 1860, H. Rep. 249.

17. *Joint Resolution in Relation to the Public Printing* 25, 36th Cong., 1st. sess. (June 23, 1860), *Stats at Large of USA* 12 (1860): 117.

18. MacGilvray, "A Short History of GPO."

19. MacGilvray, "A Short History of GPO."

20. For more information on the printing history of the *Congressional Record*, see Richard J. McKinney, "An Overview of the Congressional Record and Its Predecessor Publications," *LLSDC's Legislative Source Book*, www.llsdc.org/sourcebook/cong-record.htm (accessed January 12, 2006).

21. *Printing Act of 1895*, c. 23, *U.S. Statutes at Large* 28 (January 12, 1895): 601–624.

22. *An Act Providing for Keeping and Distributing All Public Documents*, c.22, *Stats at Large of USA* 11 (1859): 379.

23. *An Act Making Appropriations for the Legislative, Executive, and Judicial Expenses of the Government for the Year Ending the Thirtieth of June 1870*, c. 57, *Stats at Large of USA* 15 (1869): 283, 292.

24. Schmeckebier, *The Government Printing Office*, 15.

25. James Cameron, "GPO's Living History: Adelaide R. Hasse," *FDLP Desktop*, www.access.gpo.gov/su_docs/fdlp/history/hasse.html (accessed January 12, 2006).

26. For more information, see "An Explanation of the Superintendent of Documents Classification System," *FDLP Desktop*, www.access.gpo.gov/su_docs/fdlp/pubs/explain.html (accessed January 11, 2006); and "Gov Docs Online Tutorial, Module 3: The Superintendent Of Documents (Sudocs) Classification System," *AALL Government Documents Special Interest Section*, www.aallnet.org/sis/gd/tutorial/mod3a.html (accessed January 11, 2006).

27. MacGilvray, "A Short History of GPO."

28. Public Act 171, c. 103, 67th Cong., 2nd sess. (March 20, 1922).

29. MacGilvray, "A Short History of GPO."

30. MacGilvray, "A Short History of GPO."

31. MacGilvray, "A Short History of GPO."

32. MacGilvray, "A Short History of GPO."

33. MacGilvray, "A Short History of GPO."

34. Sheila M. McGarr, "Snapshots of the Federal Depository Library Program," *FDLP Desktop*, www.access.gpo.gov/su_docs/fdlp/history/snapshot.html (accessed November 7, 2005).

35. Senate Committee on Appropriations, *Second Supplemental Appropriations for Fiscal Year 1976: Hearings Before Subcommittees [. . .]*, 94th Cong., 2nd sess., 1976; House Committee on Appropriations, *Second Supplemental Appropriation Bill, 1976: Hearings Before Subcommittees [. . .]*, 94th Cong., 2nd sess., 1976.

36. MacGilvray, "A Short History of GPO."

37. "Depository Library Council: About," *FDLP Desktop,* www.access.gpo.gov/su_docs/fdlp/council/aboutdlc.html (accessed January 17, 2006).

38. For more information on the history of the *Federal Register* and *Code of Federal Regulations,* see Richard J. McKinney, "A Research Guide to the Federal Register and the Code of Federal Regulations," *LLSDC's Legislative Source Book,* www.llsdc.org/sourcebook/cong-record.htm (accessed January 12, 2006).

39. Joint Committee on Printing, *Analysis and Evaluation of Selected Government Printing Office Operations,* report prepared by Coopers and Lybrand, 95th Cong., 2nd sess., 1978, Committee Print, 280.

40. Joint Committee on Printing, *Analysis and Evaluation,* 280–81.

41. Joint Committee on Printing, *Analysis and Evaluation,* 283.

42. Morehead, *Introduction to United States Government Information Sources,* 155.

43. MacGilvray, "A Short History of GPO."

44. For more information on the transformation of government information during the "electronic revolution," see Morehead, *Introduction to United States Government Information Sources,* 1–14.

45. *Paperwork Reduction Act of 1980,* Public Law 96–511, *U.S. Statutes at Large* 94 (1980): 2812.

46. McGarr, "Snapshots of the Federal Depository Library Program."

47. McGarr, "Snapshots of the Federal Depository Library Program."

48. House Committee on Government Operations, *Electronic Collection and Dissemination of Information by Federal Agencies: A Policy Overview,* 99th Cong., 2nd sess., 1986, H. Res. 560.

49. Harold C. Relyea, *Public Printing Reform: Issues and Actions* (Congressional Research Service: Library of Congress, June 17, 2003), 3.

50. U.S. Congress, Office of Technology Assessment, *Informing the Nation: Federal Information Dissemination in an Electronic Age, OTA-C IT-396* (Washington, D.C.: U.S. Government Printing Office, October 1988), foreword.

51. Office of Technology Assessment, *Informing the Nation,* 10.

52. *Government Printing Office Electronic Information Access Enhancement Act of 1993,* Public Law 103–40, *U.S. Statutes at Large* 107 (1993): 112.

53. "Frequently Asked Questions," *U.S. Government Printing Office,* www.gpo.gov/factsheet/index.html#4 (accessed January 3, 2006). Since its inception, GPO Access retrievals have exceeded 2.45 billion. June 2005 was the busiest month ever, with more than 39 million retrievals. The total number of retrievals in FY2005 was 431 million. "Update for ALA," Government Printing Office, www.access.gpo.gov/su_docs/fdlp/events/ala_update06.pdf (accessed June 2006).

54. Harold C. Relyea, *Public Printing Reform,* 5.

55. Michael F. Di Mario, *Prepared Statement before the Committee on Rules and Administration, U.S. Senate,* Thursday, February 3, 1994.

56. Senate Committee on Rules and Administration, *Public Access to Government Information in the 21st Century*, 104th Cong., 2nd sess., 1996; Subcommittee on Government Management, Information, and Technology of the House Committee on Government Reform and Oversight, *The Government Printing Office and Executive Branch Information Dissemination*, 105th Cong., 1st sess., 1997; Senate Committee on Rules and Administration, *Title 44, U.S. Code—Proposals for Revision*, 105th Cong., 1st sess., 1997.

57. See, for example, *Requiring the Appropriate Committees of the House to Report Legislation to Transfer Certain Functions of the Government Printing Office, and for Other Purposes*, H. Res. 24, 104th Cong., 1st sess. (January 4, 1995); *To Improve the Dissemination of Information and Printing Procedures of the Government*, H.R. 1024, 104th Cong., 1st sess., (February 23, 1995); *Government Printing Reform Act of 1996*, H.R. 4280, 104th Cong., 2nd sess. (September 28, 1996).

58. Eric Peterson, "Concepts for Reform of Title 44," *Comprehensive Assessment of Public Information Dissemination: Reports and Directives*, www.nclis.gov/govt/assess/assess.html (accessed March 1, 2006).

59. *Wendell H. Ford Government Publications Reform Act of 1998*, S. 2288, 105th Cong., 2nd sess. (July 10, 1998).

60. Testimony of Robert L. Oakley, Senate Committee on Rules and Administration, *Wendell H. Ford Government Publications Act of 1998: Hearings on S. 2288*, 105th Cong., 2nd sess., 1998, 12–20.

61. Dupont Circle Group, "The Future of the Federal Depository Library Program," Washington, D.C., April 16–18, 1993, www.arl.org/info/frn/gov/dupont.html; and, "Chicago Conference on the Future of Federal Government Information, Chicago, October 29–31, 1993. Executive Summary [and] Report," *Documents to the People* 21 no. 4 (December 1993): 234–246. See also www.arl.org/info/frn/gov/chicago.html.

62. *Study to Identify Measures Necessary for a Successful Transition to a More Electronic Federal Depository Program: As Required by Legislative Branch Appropriations Act, 1996, Public Law 104–53* (U.S. Government Printing Office, June 1995).

63. *Study to Identify Measures*, 4–5.

64. *Study to Identify Measures*, 27.

65. "Progress Report on the Transition to a More Electronic FDLP 1996–1999," *Administrative Notes* 20, no. 8 (May 1, 1999): 26.

66. "Update for ALA," *U.S. Government Printing Office*, www.access.gpo.gov/su_docs/fdlp/events/ala_update06.pdf (accessed January 12, 2006), 11.

67. "Update for ALA," 11–12.

68. Schmeckebier, *The Government Printing Office*, 17.

69. "Frequently Asked Questions," *U.S. Government Printing Office*, www.gpo.gov/factsheet/index.html (accessed January 3, 2006).

70. *A Strategic Vision for the 21st Century*, 5–6.

71. Mary Alice Baish, "Washington Brief: GPO Plan to Reduce Print Distribution to Depository Libraries," *AALL Spectrum* 9 no. 6 (April 2005): 4.

72. John A. Shuler, "Beyond the Depository Library Concept," *Journal of Academic Librarianship* 27, no. 4 (July 2001): 299.

73. Shuler, "Beyond the Depository Library Concept," 300.

74. James A. Jacobs, James R. Jacobs, and Shinjoung Yeo, "Government Information in the Digital Age: the Once and Future Federal Depository Library Program," *Journal of Academic Librarianship* 31, no. 3 (May 2005), 205.

75. Depository Library Council, *The Federal Government Information Environment of the 21st Century: Towards a Vision Statement and Plan of Action for Federal Depository Libraries*, www.access.gpo.gov/su_docs/fdlp/pubs/dlc_vision_09_02_2005 .pdf (accessed February 4, 2006).

76. DLC, *Vision Statement*. The strategic documents of the Depository Library Council are located at www.access.gpo.gov/su_docs/fdlp/council/index.html.

77. DLC *Vision Future Scenarios Blog*, http://dlcvisionoutline.blogspot.com/.

78. "Update for ALA," *Government Printing Office*.

79. "Update for ALA," *Government Printing Office*, 2–10.

80. Bruce R. James, Introduction, *Public Printer's Annual Report, Fiscal Year 2003* (Washington, D.C.: GPO, 2003).

81. Schmekebier, *The Government Printing Office*, 15.

82. *FDLP Desktop*, www.access.gpo.gov/su_docs/fdlp/ (accessed February 20, 2006).

83. *FDLP Desktop*, www.access.gpo.gov/su_docs/fdlp/ (accessed March 10, 2006).

APPENDIX

Top Ten List of Things to Do for New Depository Coordinators

Last updated: November 28, 2005

Page Name: www.access.gpo.gov/su_docs/fdlp/mgt/top10.html.
PDF version at www.access.gpo.gov/su_docs/fdlp/mgt/top10.pdf.

1. Read the basic publications of the FDLP. In addition to the titles and websites listed in Resources for Federal Depository Library Administration, see: www.access.gpo.gov/su_docs/fdlp/pubs/reading .html.
   - GPO Access website, www.gpoaccess.gov
   - GPO Cataloging Guidelines, www.access.gpo.gov/su_docs/ fdlp/cip/gpocatgu.doc
   - FDLP Guidelines on Substituting Electronic for Tangible Versions of Depository Publications, www.access.gpo.gov/su_docs/fdlp/ coll-dev/subguide.html
   - Depository Library Public Service Guidelines for Government Information in Electronic Formats, www.access.gpo.gov/su_docs/ fdlp/mgt/pseguide.html
   - FDLP Internet Use Policy Guidelines, www.access.gpo.gov/ su_docs/fdlp/mgt/iupolicy.html

- Recommended Specifications for Public Access Workstations in Federal Depository Libraries, www.access.gpo.gov/su_docs/fdlp/computers/index.html
- Recommended Readings, www.access.gpo.gov/su_docs/fdlp/pubs/reading.html

Selected textbooks:

- Andriot, Donna, ed. *Guide to U.S. Government Publications* (Farmington Hills, MI: Gale Group, 2000). Annually identifies agency series and SuDocs class stems and provides publication history.
- Boyd, Anne M. *United States Government Publications*, 3rd ed. Revised by Rae E. Ripps (New York: H. W. Wilson, 1949, reprinted 1952). Guide to historical information about government printing and dissemination.
- Morehead, Joe. *Introduction to United States Government Information Sources*, 6th ed. (Englewood, CO: Libraries Unlimited, 1999). First edition in 1975 supplanted Schmeckebier (below).
- Robinson, Judith Schiek. *Tapping the Government Grapevine: The User-Friendly Guide to U.S. Government Information Sources*, 3rd ed. (Phoenix, AZ: Oryx Press, 1998).
- Schmeckebier, Laurence F., and Roy B. Eastin. *Government Publications and Their Use* (Washington, D.C.: Brookings Institution, 1969). Provides the history of documents, bibliographies, and catalogs.

2. Find out your depository library number and internal and external passwords. The number is on the inside flap of the shipment box. Send a message to the GPO Contact Center at www.gpoaccess.gov/help to obtain passwords if they can't be located. Update your library's directory entry at www.access.gpo.gov/su_docs/fdlp/tools/ldirect.html.

3. Find Item Lister of item selections at www.access.gpo.gov/su_docs/fdlp/tools/itemlist.html. Review item profile for additions and deletions, ideally along with a written government documents collection development policy in hand. Physically handle the material at your library and visit neighboring depositories to examine potential additions. Use the "Suggested Core Collections" at www.access.gpo.gov/su_docs/fdlp/pubs/fdlm/corelist.html and the Documents Data Miner features, http://govdoc.wichita.edu/ddm/GdocFrames.asp.

4. Locate Inspection Reports, Self-Study Submission, and Self-Study Evaluation reports (if applicable), and Biennial Surveys. Find any annual reports for the depository operation. If you can't locate this information, send a message to the GPO Contact Center at http://www.gpoaccess.gov/help and photocopies will be made from your library's permanent file and sent to you. Please note that

inspections and self-studies have been discontinued, but these files can still help you become acquainted with your library.

5. Contact your regional librarian for disposal instructions and advice. Find out whether there is a state electronic discussion list and how to sign up, whether there is a government documents group in the state or region and join it, and if there is a state plan. Contact neighboring depositories for networking opportunities, cooperative collection development, and promotion possibilities.

6. Subscribe to GPO-FDLP-L, gpo-fdlp-1@listserv.access.gpo.gov, as well as http://listserv.access.gpo.gov/, and other electronic discussion lists, such as GOVDOC-L at http://docs.lib.duke.edu/federal/govdoc-1/index.html, and DocTech-L at http://list.lib.usu.edu/mailman/listinfo/doctech-1.

7. Find out about the library's mission, vision, goals, and strategic planning documents so that you know how the depository operation fits into your setting. Who has purchasing power? Who are the techies? Find out whether there is a department budget for purchasing supplementary commercial reference tools, computer equipment, replacements for lost/damaged materials, travel/training, and so on. Communicate with your library administration.

8. Look for training opportunities on the local to national level. GPO offers several opportunities, including:
   - Interagency Depository Seminar, held annually for five and a half days in Washington, D.C. Preliminary agenda appears in Administrative Notes.
   - Federal Depository Library Conference, combined with the fall Depository Library Council meeting. Held annually in the Washington, D.C., metro area. Preliminary agenda appears in Administrative Notes.
   - Depository Library Council meetings, held semiannually. Fall meetings take place in the Washington, D.C., metro area; spring meetings are located in other parts of the United States. Preliminary agenda appears in Administrative Notes. Orientation sessions for new depository staff are held at both meetings, providing opportunities for networking and getting basic questions answered.

9. Find out if the library's depository operation has a Web presence. If it doesn't, to get started use the template at http://sunsite.berkeley.edu/GODORT/gitco/govinfotemplate.html. FDLP graphics are available at www.access.gpo.gov/su_docs/fdlp/pr/graphics.html.

10. Review other helpful websites, including:
    - ALA GODORT, http://sunsite.berkeley.edu/GODORT/index.html#comm (current news on variety of issues, e.g., appropriation

bills, NTIS, etc.; links to professional resources such as e-journals, electronic discussion lists, state documents groups; laws and legislation).

- Government Information and Depository Management Clearing-house, www.library.ucsb.edu/ala/clearing.html (contains information on cataloging, community advocacy, FDL management, etc.).
- Toolbox for Processing and Cataloging Federal Government Documents, www2.1ib.udel.edu/godort/cataloging/toolbox.htm (links to GPO products, GPO cataloging records at OCLC, vendors, PURLs; Web pages by depository librarians, etc.).
- ALA GODORT Handout Exchange, www.lib.umich.edu/govdocs/godort.html (submissions by documents librarians on a variety of topics, e.g., CD-ROM user guides, collection development policies, maps user guides and processing, staff policies and training guides, etc.).
- Documents Center (University of Michigan), www.lib.umich.edu/govdocs/federal.html (federal government resources on the Web. Comprehensive coverage including bibliographies, links to new and historic documents, broad subject access, agency directory, and search engine).
- Documents Data Miner (DDM), http://govdoc.wichita.edu/ddm/GdocFrames.asp (a search engine combining, from the List of Classes, the Item Lister's current item number selection profiles for depository libraries, and Federal Depository Library Directory. Includes information on inactive and discontinued items.
- National Bibliography Program, http://access.gpo.gov/su_docs/fdlp/cip/ (this program has the goal to develop a comprehensive and authoritative National Bibliography of U.S. Government Publications to increase the visibility and use of government information products, and to develop a premier destination for information services).
- Incentives Document—Progress Report 2; The Carrot Crop Is Still Growing, www.access.gpo.gov/su_docs/fdlp/pubs/proceedings/incentives_progress_oct2005.doc (list services/added benefits that GPO is considering to strengthen library partnerships).

Chapter 10

The World of Library Consortia: Collaboration and Resource Sharing in the Twenty-First Century

Tracy L. Thompson

Make no little plans; they have no magic to stir men's blood and probably themselves will not be realized. Make big plans; aim high in hope and work, remembering that a noble, logical diagram once recorded will not die, but long after we are gone be a living thing, asserting itself with ever-growing insistence.—Daniel Hudson Burnham[1]

DEFINING THE ENTITY

While Daniel Burnham's words were undoubtedly in reference to plans of the brick-and-mortar type, they apply equally well to the subject of libraries and consortia. Consortia, by their very nature, are "big plans." They are, in any sphere, individual entities or institutions with common problems or interests combining their individual resources toward some larger goal. Consortia are a means for the whole to achieve something beyond what the parts might. Not all formal definitions of the word capture that essence.

The Oxford English Dictionary[2] defines consortium as a "Partnership, association. An association of business, banking, or manufacturing organizations." Merriam-Webster OnLine comes closer to the word as it relates to libraries and educational institutions with "an agreement, combination, or group (as of companies) formed to undertake an enterprise beyond the resources of any one member."[3] But to get even closer to the meaning of the word with respect to libriarianship, we should consider some other words that may be used to describe the entity: Network, alliance, coalition, and association are all words that might be used to refer to the consortium relationship. A body need not include the word in its name in order to function as a consortium.

It is helpful to identify a few common characteristics of library consortia to further hone the definition and identify the enterprise. First, a consortium includes three or more institutions or libraries.[4] Second, member institutions usually join together voluntarily to create a consortium, although the creation and maintenance of a consortium may, in some instances, be mandated by state law[5] or required for the receipt of grant or government funding. Third, library consortia typically are composed of institutional members, distinguishing them from professional associations, which are usually composed of individual members. The final, and most significant, attribute of library consortia is that they are as dissimilar as they are numerous. They have different organizational and governance structures, different membership requirements, different missions, and different funding models, provide different services, and aspire to different goals. These attributes are examined in greater detail in this chapter. Yet beneath these differences the essential nature of a consortium, as a group united toward a common and greater purpose, a "big plan," shines through.

A HISTORY OF COLLABORATION IN HIGHER EDUCATION

As a species we thrive on collaboration. We have long recognized that there is strength in numbers. Early humans realized that cooperative living—living in tribes, clans, or kinship groups—would be more likely to provide personal safety than living in isolation and would be the most strategic route to a stable food supply. Collaboration led to survival.[6] The situation is not quite so dire for libraries in the twenty-first century. Still, we live in a world of ready access to an enormous array of electronic resources combined with an increasingly tech-savvy population of users; collaboration may in fact be necessary for the survival of the library and of librarians as a critical component in the education and research process, rather than as a quaint holdover from an earlier era.

While it is true that libraries have been collaborating in some fashion for many years, the electronic information era has spurred consortium activity. A survey conducted in September 2005[7] shows that, of the twenty-nine library consortia from around the world that responded, twenty-three of them have been founded in only the last twenty years. Of the six founded before 1985, two were started in the 1960s, three in the 1970s, and one in the first half of the 1980s. The earliest library consortium among the survey respondents dates back only to 1960, although one group pointed to agreements as far back as the 1930s prior to the existence of their formal consortium (see figure 10.1). While some of the impetus for library collaboration may be credited to Title II-C of the Higher Education Act of 1965,[8] this trend toward widespread growth of library consortia over the last two decades has it roots in collaboration on the educational institution level.

Colleges and universities in the United States[9] began to explore the economic and developmental benefits of collaborative action as early as 1925, with the founding of the Claremont Colleges in Sacramento, California. In 1923 James A. Blaisdell, then president of Pomona College, articulated the dream:

> My own very deep hope is that instead of one great, undifferentiated university, we might have a group of institutions divided into small colleges— somewhat of an Oxford type—around a library and other utilities which they would use in common. In this way I should hope to preserve the inestimable personal values of the small college while securing the facilities of the great university.[10]

Today, the thriving Claremont University Consortium (CUC) stands as a testament to Blaisdell's vision early in the twentieth century, "asserting itself with ever-growing insistence" as Burnham predicted.

Writing in 1974 about the consortium movement among colleges and universities, Franklin Patterson, despite the successes of the CUC beginning nearly fifty years earlier, characterized that movement as relatively recent.[11] They were seeing trends similar in growth on that broader scale of collaboration to what we are seeing today among libraries. Patterson noted that between 1925 and 1965, only nineteen consortia of higher education institutions had been established. Then, between 1960 and 1965

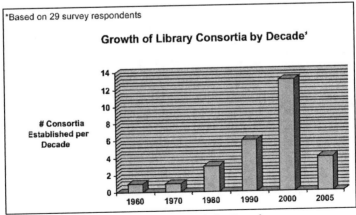

Figure 10.1. Growth of Library Consortia by Decade

thirty-two more consortia emerged. By 1973 there were a total of eighty consortia listed in the *Consortium Directory; Voluntary Academic Cooperative Arrangements in Higher Education.*[12] That growth has slowed dramatically in the intervening three decades. Today, in 2005, the Association for Consortium Leadership (ACL)[13] cites 125 higher education consortia in the United States (see figure 10.2). Patterson provides a comprehensive history of the higher education consortium movement from its inception in 1925 through the mid-1970s.

That period in history, the post–World War II era, saw the greatest expansion of the American higher education system, with enrollment swelling from 1.5 million to 15 million students in a fifty-year period.[14] The G.I. Bill, combined with a growing social awareness of the importance of a college education to the future of the nation, created an environment in which greater attention was paid to the state of our system of higher education. The demands on the system were escalating and it would become increasingly difficult to retain the status quo. "The old pattern of every college or university going it alone . . . would be eroded by the pressure of virtually unlimited needs on limited resources."[15] It made perfect sense for colleges and universities to pursue collaborative opportunities.

Collaboration during this period took many forms, including cross-registration, cooperative admissions programs, shared faculty, joint academic calendars, joint cultural programs, and cooperative faculty support. Of the fifty-five consortia upon which Patterson based his study, twenty-six had some shared library functions, including interlibrary loan

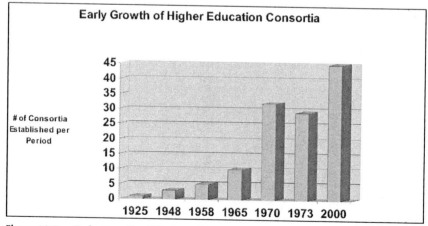

Figure 10.2. Early Growth of Higher Education Consortia. *Source:* Patterson, 1973.

(ILL), shared cataloguing, joint monograph purchasing, centralized journal deposits, and joint film libraries.[16] In fact, William Lanier, then director of one of the consortia that Patterson studied closely, the Greensboro Tri-College Consortium (GTC) in North Carolina, identified library cooperation as the most successful program carried out by his members.[17] It is following this period of dramatic expansion, growth, and cooperation at the higher education institutional level that we see the rise of the library consortium.

LIBRARY COLLABORATION TODAY

Before library consortia emerged as distinct organizations in their own right then, they were likely to have had a history of collaboration as departments within their parent institutions, which were participants in the higher education consortia boom of the postwar era. This gave libraries the benefit of having models to adopt or emulate in the development of their own consortia. Today, many library consortia operate as independent entities, responding to needs and interests distinct from those of the wider institution. This bifurcation is especially clear from the existence of two distinct organizations that exist to meet the needs of consortia.

The Association for Consortium Leadership (ACL), a nonprofit 501(c)(3) organization founded in 1975, supports the work of higher education consortia in the United States. ACL is a membership organization that holds an annual meeting, provides networking and mentoring opportunities, and publishes important work in the field of educational cooperation.[18] It lists sixty-five member consortia across the country.

A separate and more recent organization has emerged to support the work and world of library consortia. The International Coalition of Library Consortia (ICOLC) is a less formally structured[19] group that began meeting in 1997 to address issues of concern to library consortia, librarians, and other information professionals engaged in collaborative work. ICOLC, while most heavily populated by and geared toward academic library consortia, includes consortia that serve special libraries, school libraries, government libraries, and public libraries. ICOLC is international in scope and provides support for library consortia through two meetings annually (one in the United States and one abroad) and through a members' electronic mailing list. ICOLC focuses on "keeping participating consortia informed about new electronic information resources, pricing practices of electronic providers and vendors, and other issues of importance to directors and governing boards of consortia."[20] ICOLC, essentially a consortium of consortia, lists 188 participating consortia.[21] At the fall 2005 meeting of ICOLC in Poznan, Poland, the eighty-eight attendees represented twenty-two countries. ACL and ICOLC are completely unrelated, and despite the fact that both are dedicated to resource sharing in the consortium environment, there is no coordination between the two groups; each operates within its own sphere to address the concerns of its particular constituency.

Role of Library Consortia

So now the entity has been defined and placed into its historical context. But what exactly do consortia do? Why do they exist? Simply put, "the main reason for creating a consortium is to cut costs."[22] Cost avoidance in the consortium environment can take many forms. One of the most common ways in which consortia help member libraries cut costs is through group purchasing power.

With the skyrocketing cost of electronic information[23] in the twenty-first century, the economies that can be realized by a library's membership in a consortium are vital. Many library consortia play a key role in the acquisition of electronic resources for their member libraries. A group of libraries working together can offer significant savings to information publishers and vendors that are passed on to the member libraries. While this is clearly not the only collaborative role of library consortia, it is one of the most tangible benefits of consortium membership and the one most often relied upon to justify membership. In fact, electronic resource discounts were identified by nineteen of the twenty-nine survey respondents[24] as among the most significant benefits of consortium membership.

In a typical library consortium, many functions related to the acquisition of electronic resources are centralized and managed within the consortium rather than duplicated at each of the member institutions. For example, a consortium may work with an information publisher/vendor to establish a trial[25] of an electronic resource, and to negotiate pricing of that resource, for the entire consortium. Without the consortium, each library would work independently to set up trials and negotiate price, costing both the library and the information vendor significant investments of time.

Once an electronic resource has been identified as one that some or all members of the consortium wish to acquire,[26] the consortium may assume the task of negotiating the license agreement on behalf of the members. A license agreement sets forth the terms of use of an electronic resource and the rights and obligations of the parties to the agreement, the licensee (content user) and licensor (content supplier). Licensing alone is a task that takes an enormous toll on personnel and administrative resources. Endless workshops, seminars, working groups, online courses, committees, professional development programs, and electronic mailing lists are devoted to the intricacies of licensing electronic resources.[27] Many librarians, consortium staff members, information providers, and publishers participate in licensing listservs such as the liblicense list.[28] Licensing issues are also regularly addressed by members of the ICOLC listserv, but this list is open to members only. Delegating licensing, a relatively demanding yet low-return task, to the consortium can provide significant savings to the member libraries and free up professional staff at the library level for projects with more direct local impact.

Managing licensing at the consortium level also results in more continuity and consistency in the licensing process and the understanding of licensing terms and principles across the board, both on the library side and on the information-provider side. ICOLC has made great strides in this regard. They have issued several statements and guidelines[29] that have been widely endorsed by other consortia, individual libraries, and by information providers, covering such licensing issues as pricing, access, fair use, archiving, privacy, and usage statistics. In the years since the first release of ICOLC's "Statement of Current Perspective and Preferred Practices for Selection and Purchase of Electronic Information" in 1998, many of the recommendations cited in that document have been implemented by consortia and publishers alike. Added to the work of ICOLC are the initiatives of library associations like the American Association of Law Libraries (AALL) and the American Library Association (ALA). In 1997, AALL and ALA, in cooperation with four other library associations,[30] drafted the "Principles for Licensing Electronic Resources."[31] In 2004 that document was updated to reflect the changes in the licensing landscape in the intervening years.[32] The evolution of the license agreement, and more importantly of licensing principles, has been on a steady course since the 1990s, thanks in large part to such collaborative efforts. Licensing will continue to be part of the role of consortia for the foreseeable future.

Once a resource has been successfully licensed, the consortium may manage other centralized functions, such as billing, renewals, and customer service, again saving the time and resources of both the member libraries and the information publisher/vendor.

Consortia are engaged in a wide array of exciting and innovative activities and services that go beyond the purchasing and licensing of electronic resources. Consortia provide a forum for experimentation. They provide an opportunity for members to share both the costs and the risks associated with the implementation of new technologies or approaches to problems. Members may participate collaboratively in services, projects, and programs that they would be unwilling to tackle independently. Such projects may include a shared integrated library system (ILS); discounts on print materials, equipment, hardware, and software purchases; shared digital repositories; reciprocal ILL agreements; shared off-site storage; collaborative virtual reference; educational programming; consulting services; networking opportunities; and shared meeting space. Each of these was identified by one or more of the survey respondents (see note 7) as services currently being offered to their members (see figure 10.3).

Consortia also serve an important advocacy role. Libraries working together can have a significant impact with information providers and publishers. Project COUNTER[33] is a perfect example of the advocacy role reaping important results for libraries. COUNTER is a consortium of a unique composition, including among its members libraries, consortia, publishers, information providers, and associations. The focus of the U.K.-based group since its inception has been on the development of universally accepted standards for the recording and reporting of usage statistics for electronic resources. The project has been so successful that COUNTER-compliancy has become an industry goal for publishers and information providers. Compliancy is monitored and a list of compliant vendors is maintained on the Project COUNTER site.[34] So despite the common and justifiable emphasis on the role of consortia as discount brokers and licensing professionals, there are many other less tangible, but more enduring, consortium activities that could lead to even greater cost avoidance for members in the long run.

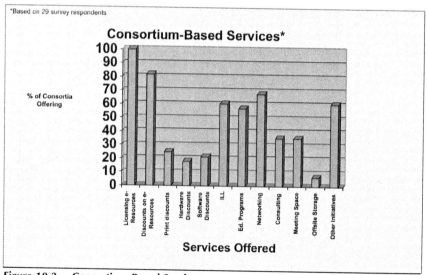

Figure 10.3.   Consortium-Based Services

Organizational Structure and Governance in Library Consortia

Library consortia may be established for a single specific purpose, such as the creation of a shared library catalog, or simply to take advantage of general opportunities for collaboration.[35] Library consortia may be formally or informally organized. Many begin as informal arrangements and evolve into formally recognized coalitions. The form an organization takes will depend on the forms available under their law and the reasons for their existence. In the United States many consortia are organized as nonprofit corporations as defined by Section 501(c)(3) of the Internal Revenue Code.[36] Meeting the IRC definition enables a consortium to enjoy tax-exempt status. Other forms include corporations, associations, government entities, ministries, and committees, departments, or other subgroups of a formally organized parent institution. In addition to attending to their tax status, a consortium may be accountable to a variety of local, state, and federal regulatory bodies.

There are a number of common governance structures, and undoubtedly multiple variations. The structure a group adopts will vary based on a number of characteristics, including the number of members, mission of the consortium, geographic boundaries, types of libraries included among the membership, and funding model. A good place to look for an organization's governance structure is in its bylaws or articles of incorporation. If a consortium is mandated by state or federal law, the governance structure may be set forth in administrative code or regulations.[37]

Many consortia have a board of directors, governing board, or council that provides direction and guidance, and has a fiduciary duty to the consortium. Members may be appointed or elected. Often, each member library has a seat on the board, which is commonly filled by the library director. Or, the board may be composed of regional representatives or representation by library type. In some cases, board responsibility rotates among the member libraries. This group tends to meet at least once a year to plan and check the progress of the consortium.[38]

An executive or steering committee usually works more closely with the consortium staff to implement the plans set out and supported by the board. At this level, the members are often elected from among the full board and serve for a specified term of office.

Serving the consortium on the front lines, administering the programs and services of the consortia to the membership, is the consortium staff. Typically, a library consortium is led by an executive director, who may manage any number of staffers.[39] Not all consortia have paid staff; some have a rotating directorship or presidency from among the board or council. It can be exceedingly difficult to move a consortium forward without a person in a position of full-time leadership of the organization. If leadership falls to someone for whom the task is simply one among many, a consortium can suffer from inertia.

The challenges of collaborative action are multiplied when no one is at the helm on a consistent basis. A crucial piece in the success of a consortium is regular, consistent, and reliable communication between the organization, the membership, and other key stakeholders. This is accomplished through an array of communication vehicles, including regular meetings, the maintenance of consortium websites, telephone calls, e-mail, electronic mailing lists, blogs, electronic and print newsletters, and videoconferences. Keeping the organization vibrant requires a continual evaluation of the effectiveness of the communication methods in use.

Communication to the membership is so vital because it can take many other bodies, beyond the governing bodies and the administrative bodies, to carry out the collaborative work of the consortium. Standing committees, task forces, ad hoc working groups, interest groups, and other action groups realize the plans and goals set forth by the governing bodies. This is where much of the magic of library collaboration takes place. It is also a consequence of membership that is often named by members as the most valuable benefit. Library staff members get the opportunity to work with their colleagues from other institutions. They share experiences and begin to understand the challenges their colleagues face and the strengths that they bring to the mix. This leads to the professional growth and development of participating library staff members, creative thinking and problem solving, and building strong relationships between and among member libraries. All of the synergies created at this level of the consortium feed back into the organization to enhance its effectiveness.

Membership Requirements

Membership in a library consortium may be defined by statute or regulation, or defined within the organization's bylaws or articles of incorporation. Membership may be limited by library type, collection size, geographic region, user population, or some other criterion. Some consortia are even composed of distinct libraries within a single system or institution, such as across multiple campuses or across libraries by discipline.[40] A consortium may offer several categories of membership, such as full members, associate members, affiliate members, and cooperative members. Each category of membership has distinct requirements, rights, and responsibilities.

Funding Models

As might be expected, the fiscal needs of a consortium vary widely depending upon the size, composition, reach, and mission of the organiza-

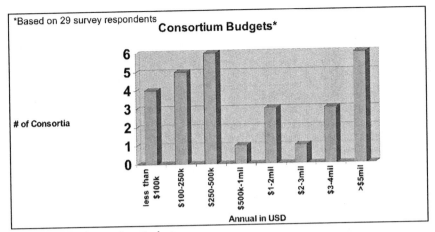

Figure 10.4. Consortium Budgets

tion (see figure 10.4). To fund their activities consortia may rely on any number of sources of income. Members typically pay some form of membership dues or assessment.[41] Dues may be apportioned equally to all members in a given membership category, or they may be proportional based upon some weighting factor, such as student or staff population measured by full-time equivalents (fte), library budget size or endowment, or some other agreed-upon criteria. In addition to dues, consortia may rely on funding from grants, service charges or administrative fees, government allocations, or funding from the budget of a parent institution or board of regents. None of these funding sources is necessarily exclusive, and consortia may rely on one or more of them as need dictates.

THE FUTURE OF LIBRARY CONSORTIA

It may be clear by now that consortia are, by their nature, nimble organizations that, in many ways, exist to manage change. With the rate of change accelerating in the library and information technology (IT) industry, the need for libraries and information providers to collaborate is likely to intensify before it declines.

When a group of consortium professionals was polled about the future, they unanimously reaffirmed the need for consortia to continue to function as key players in the acquisition of electronic resources for members. There is little doubt that a locus of expertise around negotiating and licensing will continue to emerge from within the world of consortia. However, the importance of the consortium as so much more than a buying club, the "big plans" perspective, comes through loud and clear in their comments: "consortia will continue to play an important role in negotiating licenses. But consortia can do so much more"; "focus must be on access to information"; "transformative technologies [and] organizations . . . constantly change the environment for libraries and consortia. [We] need to be agile enough to manage these changes"; "play a key role in the process of [the] transformation of the scholarly communications environment"; "collaborate to influence the market . . . generate positive changes in publishing practices"; "collaborative development of digital repositories . . . development of preservation initiatives."[42]

All of the issues currently facing libraries and information providers, from open access to digital archives, to the evolution of copyright, to the role of repositories, to the development of new authentication techniques, are fertile ground for collaborative efforts. In order for consortia to continue to participate, it will be important for consortium members and their funding institutions to see beyond the immediate and tangible benefits of group discounts to the enduring value of collaboration in these complex and dynamic matters.

It is no secret that people working together can usually accomplish more than an individual working alone. The same can be said of libraries. We are in the process of building on our relatively recent history of institutional collaboration, and we will continue to leverage our strengths into the foreseeable future.

REFERENCES

Dotolo, L. G., and J. Noftsinger. *Leveraging Resources through Partnerships: New Directions for Higher Education*. San Francisco: Jossey-Bass, 2002.

Dotolo, L. G., and J. T. Strandness. *Best Practices in Higher Education Consortia: How Institutions Can Work Together*. San Francisco: Jossey-Bass, 1999.

Kadlecova, I., and E. Simon. *Electronical Information: The Role of Consortia in Organizing Knowledge*. Berlin: BibSpider, 2004.

Kirkland, J. "Change and Continuity: The Case of the Association of Commonwealth Universities." In *Consortia: International Networking Alliances of Universities*, ed. D. Teather. Victoria, Australia: Melbourne University Press, 2004.

Kyrillidou, M., and M. Young. "ARL Library Trends 2003–2004." *Association of Research Libraries*, at www.arl.org/stats/arlstat/04pub/04intro.html.

Marchese, T. J. "U.S. Higher Education in the Postwar Era: Expansion and Growth." *Electronic Journal of the U.S. Information Agency* 2, no. 4 (December 1997), http://usinfo.state.gov/journals/itsv/1297/ijse/marchese.htm.

Patterson, F. *Colleges in Consort*. San Francisco: Jossey-Bass, 1974.

Patterson, L. D. *Consortium Directory; Voluntary Academic Cooperative Arrangements in Higher Education*, 6th ed. Kansas City, MO: Kansas City Regional Council for Higher Education, 1973.

NOTES

1. American architect and city planner Daniel H. Burnham (1846–1912) is best known for his comprehensive plan for the city of Chicago.

2. Second edition, 1989.

3. "Consortium." *Merriam-Webster Online Dictionary*. www.m-w.com/ (accessed October 10, 2005).

4. A consortium may consist of several libraries or several campuses under one institutional umbrella, as is true with the California Digital Library.

5. This is the case with consortia such as OhioLink (Ohio Rev. Code Ann. §3333.04 [2005]) and Texshare (Tex. Government Code Ann. §441.221-441.230 [2005]).

6. *The New Encyclopedia Britannica*, 15th ed., s.v. "Evolution, Human."

7. Author's survey (developed, collected, and analyzed using SurveyMonkey) conducted via the ICOLC electronic mailing list. The ICOLC website lists 188 consortia (www.library.yale.edu/consortia/icolcmembers.html) as participating members; twenty-nine responded to the survey. Complete results on file with author.

8. 20 U.S.C. §1041 (1965). This act established the Strengthening Research Library Resources Program, which encouraged library cooperation through the provision of special-purpose grants.

9. In the United Kingdom, the Association of Commonwealth Universities (ACU), "the oldest inter-university association in the world," dates to 1913. John Kirkland, "Change and Continuity: The Case of the Association of Commonwealth Universities," in *Consortia: International Networking Alliances of Universities*, ed. David Teather (Victoria, Australia: Melbourne University Press, 2004), 49–68.

10. Claremount College's Consortium website at www.cuc.claremount .edu/aboutcuc/history.asp.

11. Franklin Patterson, *Colleges in Consort* (San Francisco: Jossey-Bass, 1974), 3.

12. Lewis D. Patterson, *Consortium Directory; Voluntary Academic Cooperative Arrangements in Higher Education*, 6th ed. (Kansas City, MO: Kansas City Regional Council for Higher Education, 1973).

13. The Association for Consortium Leadership was founded in 1975 and is dedicated to providing "a forum for higher education professionals involved in cooperative programs." For more information, see their website at http://development.whro.net/acl/index.html.

14. Theodore J. Marchese, "U.S. Higher Education in the Postwar Era: Expansion and Growth," *Electronic Journal of the U.S. Information Agency* 2, no. 4 (December 1997), http://usinfo.state.gov/journals/itsv/1297/ijse/marchese.htm.

15. Patterson, *Colleges in Consort*, 2.

16. Patterson, *Colleges in Consort*, 11.

17. Patterson, *Colleges in Consort*, 87.

18. Two examples are Lawrence G. Dotolo and John B. Noftsinger, *Leveraging Resources through Partnerships: New Directions for Higher Education* (San Francisco: Jossey-Bass, 2002) and Lawrence G. Dotolo and Jean T. Strandness, *Best Practices in Higher Education Consortia: How Institutions Can Work Together* (San Francisco: Jossey-Bass, 1999).

19. To date, the ICOLC has not sought any official organizational structure. There are no membership dues, no governance structure, and no institutional affiliation. ICOLC continues to function, with a great deal of success, as a sort of grassroots undertaking.

20. From the ICOLC website at www.library.yale.edu/consortia/.

21. Complete list at www.library.yale.edu/consortia/icolcmembers.html.

22. Ivana Kadlecova and Elisabeth Simon, *Electronical Information: The Role of Consortia in Organizing Knowledge* (Berlin: BibSpider, 2004), 68.

23. "Not only have electronic materials expenditures grown sharply in the past decade, but they have grown at a rate far exceeding that of library materials expenditures overall. . . . [I]n every year of the last decade electronic materials expenditures have grown anywhere between three and ten times faster than materials expenditures. The average ARL university library now spends over 31% of its materials budget on electronic materials . . . and fourteen ARL libraries report that they spent more than 50 percent of their materials budget." Martha Kyrillidou and Mark Young, "ARL Library Trends 2003–2004," *Association of Research Libraries*, www.arl.org/stats/arlstat/04pub/04intro.html.

24. See note 7.

25. A trial provides a set period of free access to an electronic resource in order for a library to evaluate the content, interface, and functionality of the resource for acquisition purposes.

26. Most library consortia offer electronic resources to their members on an opt-in basis, with members paying only for those resources they select. However, some consortia move in lock-step, licensing resources for the whole rather than for individual members. The former model is the predominant one (twenty-six of twenty-eight survey respondents conform to this model; see note 7), but the latter all-or-nothing approach needs to be acknowledged to gain a clear understanding of the world of library consortia.

27. Among many others, the Association of Research Libraries maintains a list of resources at www.arl.org/osc/licensing/index.html.

28. For more information or to subscribe, please see www.library.yale.edu/~llicense/mailing-list.shtml.

29. The most recent of these are "Statement of Current Perspective and Preferred Practices for the Selection and Purchase of Electronic Information (Update no. 2: October 2004)," "Privacy Guidelines for Electronic Resources Vendors (July 2002)," and "Guidelines for Statistical Measures of Usage of Web-Based Information Resources (Update: December 2001)," all of which can be found at www.library.yale.edu/consortia/statementsanddocuments.html.

30. The Association of Academic Health Sciences Libraries, the Association of Research Libraries, the Medical Library Association, and the Special Libraries Association.

31. Available on the ARL website at www.arl.org/scomm/licensing/principles.html.

32. Available on the AALL website at www.aallnet.org/committee/LicensingPrinciplesElecResources.pdf.

33. COUNTER is an acronym for Counting Online Usage of Networked Electronic Resources. Their website is at www.projectcounter.org/.

34. See www.projectcounter.org/articles.html.

35. Of the twenty-nine survey respondents (see note 7), twenty-four were established for general collaboration and five for a specific purpose.

36. 26 U.S.C. §501 (2003).

37. This is the case with the Lithuanian Research Library Consortium (LMBA), which is funded by the Ministries of Culture, Education, and Research and governed according to statute.

38. Of the twenty-nine survey respondents (see note 7), twenty-seven met face-to-face at least once a year with their members.

39. Of the twenty-nine survey respondents (see note 7), three had no staff, nineteen had one to five staff members, three had six to ten staff members, two had eleven to twenty staff members, and two had twenty-one to thirty staff members. No respondent reported more than thirty staff members.

40. Of the twenty-nine survey respondents (see note 7), fifteen characterized their membership as being derived from a single system, network, or institution.

41. Of the twenty-nine survey respondents (see note 7), twenty charge their members a fee for consortium membership.

42. Excerpts from the responses to an open-ended question about the future of consortium, ten to twenty years out, posed in the survey (see note 7).

Index

AALL. *See* American Association of Law Libraries
AALS. *See* American Association of Law Schools
ABA. *See* American Bar Association
academic law libraries, 5–7, 15–16; administration of, 45–70; cooperation among, 82; goal statement of, 90; mission statement of, 89; new jobs in, 17; and print/digital balance, 96–97; scope of collection statement of, 92–93; tour of, 17–28
access, 83; for people with disabilities, 85
access points, 120, 151
accreditation, collection development and, 110–12
acquisitions, 20–21, 89–116, 118–20. *See also* collection development
administration, 45–70; definition of, 46–50
Administrative Notes Technical Supplement, 187
advancement, in law libraries, 28–29
AI. *See* artificial intelligence
ALA. *See* American Library Association

Alexandria, Library. *See* Library of Alexandria
A.L.I.C.E. AI Foundation, 154
alumni, relationships with, 50
American Association of Law Libraries (AALL), 1–2, 5; on competencies, 86–88; Computing Services Special Interest Section, 160–61; and consortia, 207; Government Documents Special Interest Section, 188; listservs, 44n50; Special Interest Sections, 10–11; standards on collection development, 112
American Association of Law Schools (AALS), 6; standards on collection development, 112
American Bar Association (ABA), 6, 16; library report to, 54, 126; Standards, 45, 53, 61n61, 110–11
American Lawyer 100 (AmLaw 100), 32
American Library Association (ALA), xv, 207
American Memory, 186–87
American Society of International Laws, 134–35
Ames, John G., 178
Andriot, 183
Anglo-American Cataloging rules, 120

About the Contributors

Roy Balleste is the law library director and assistant professor of law at the Charles N. and Hilda H. M. Mason Law Library at the University of the District of Columbia, David A. Clarke School of Law, in Washington, D.C. He formerly served as associate law library director at Nova Southeastern University, Shepard Broad Law Center, Law Library and Technology Center, in Fort Lauderdale, Florida. He also served as head of public services at St. Thomas University School of Law Library, in Miami Gardens, Florida. He received his BA in political science from Jacksonville University, Florida; his JD from St. Thomas University School of Law, Florida; his master of arts in library science from the University of South Florida; and his LL.M. (cum laude) from St. Thomas University School of Law, Florida. His research interests include Internet governance, Web design technologies, knowledge management, artificial intelligence, and reference services. He teaches law librarianship for the University of South Florida School of Library and Information Science program. At Nova Southeastern University he taught computers and the law. Balleste is a member of the American Association of Law Libraries, the American Association for the Advancement of Science, the Southeastern Chapter of the American Association of Law Libraries, and the Supreme Court Historical Society. He has served as a member of the AALLNET Advisory Committee.

Robert C. Berring Jr. is a professor of law at Boalt Hall Law School, Berkeley. He is a past president of the American Association of Law Libraries and a former dean of the School of Library and Information Studies at Berkeley. He has also served as interim dean of Boalt Hall Law School. Berring worked at the law libraries of the University of Illinois, the University of Texas, Harvard, and the University of Washington before coming to Boalt as a professor of law and director of the Law Library in 1982. He holds a BA (cum laude) from Harvard College, 1971; a JD from Boalt Hall Law School, 1974; and an MLIS, University of California, Berkeley, 1974. He has published widely on the topic of legal research and legal information.

Lisa Smith-Butler is the assistant dean and director and an assistant professor of law at the Nova Southeastern University, Shepard Broad Law Center, Law Library and Technology Center. She received her BA (magna cum laude) from Hastings College, her JD from Creighton University (cum laude), and her MLS from Clark Atlanta University. Before entering the field of librarianship, she practiced law in Georgia. In the librarianship field, she has worked as reference/operations librarian for the Atlanta firm of Powell, Goldstein, Frazier, & Murphy. At Georgia State University, she was the head of public services. Before becoming the assistant dean at Nova, she served as the associate law library director. She was president of SFALL (South Florida Association of Law Libraries). At Nova, she teaches advanced legal research and juvenile law.

Vicki L. Gregory is the director and professor of the University of South Florida, School of Library and Information Science. She earned her PhD in communications, information, and library studies from Rutgers, the State University of New Jersey, and an MLS and MA (history) from the University of Alabama. Before beginning her teaching career, she was the head of Library Systems and Operations at Auburn University at Montgomery. She is active professionally, serving on the boards of the American Society for Information Science and Technology and the Florida Library Association. She is the ALA councilor from the state of Florida. Her current research is divided between licensing and other intellectual property issues dealing with electronic resources and social informatics issues dealing with online virtual communities. She has written three books and numerous articles in library and information science journals as well as presenting at state, national, and international conferences.

Karl T. Gruben is the law library director and associate professor of law at St. Thomas University's School of Law Library in Miami Gardens, Florida. He has also worked in law firm libraries, as well as in a court law library. He holds a BA and an MLS from the University of Texas at Austin, and a JD from the South Texas College of Law in Houston, Texas. He has served as president of the Houston Area Law Librarians and on the executive committee of the American Association of Law Libraries' Private Law Libraries SIS. He has also served as an officer, the secretary, and board member on the executive board of the American Association of Law Libraries. Among his publications are *A Reference Guide to Texas Law and Legal History* and contributions to *Law Library Journal*.

James S. Heller is director of the law library and professor of law at the College of William & Mary School of Law. He formerly served as director of the law library at the University of Idaho College of Law, director of the Civil Division Library of the U.S. Department of Justice, and head of Reader Services at the George Washington University Law Library. Heller has a BA from the University of Michigan, a JD (cum laude) from the University of San Diego School of Law, and an MLS from the University of California at Berkeley. He has served as president of the American Association of Law Libraries and both the Virginia and Southeastern Chapters of the American Association of Law Libraries.

Anne Klinefelter is associate director of the law library and clinical professor of law at the University of North Carolina at Chapel Hill. Klinefelter began her library career as a reference librarian at the University of Alabama Main Library. She was a senior reference librarian at Boston University Law Library and later served in the positions of head of reference, head of public services, associate director, and acting director at the University of Miami Law Library. She teaches a privacy law seminar at the UNC School of Law and Law Libraries and legal information at the School of Information and Library Science at the University of North Carolina. She is active in law library associations and is a speaker and writer in the areas relating to libraries and copyright, licensing, and privacy.

Sonia Luna-Lamas is the associate law librarian and head of technical services at St. Thomas University Law Library. Her previous positions include foreign and comparative law cataloger and serials librarian at the University of Miami School of Law Library. She holds a BA from the University of Miami and an MLS from the University of South Florida. She is active in and has held various positions in county, state, and regional library associations, as well as chaired various SIS and technical services–related network groups, and organized and helped present various workshops and institutes in the library field.

Roy M. Mersky is a member of the University of Texas law school faculty and the director of its law library since 1965. He holds the Harry M. Reasoner Regents Chair in Law and the Hyder Centennial Faculty Fellowship in Law. He is also a professor in the university's Graduate School of Information where he teaches courses and is involved in the development of the legal information/law librarianship program.

Mersky is a pioneer in law librarianship. Under his leadership the Jamail Center for Legal Research has become one of the most important legal research institutes in the United States. He is known for his innovative approaches to library management and services and his strong commitment to improving library resources, services, and facilities. He received the American Association of Law Library's 2005 Marian Gallagher Distinguished Service Award.

He is widely published and a frequent lecturer, particularly in the areas of legal research, language and law, and the history of the U.S. Supreme Court. He is coauthor of Fundamentals of Legal Research, now in its 8th edition, the recognized authority on legal research and the standard textbook used in first-year legal research courses across the United States. He recently coauthored *The First 108 Justices* (2004), which examines and evaluates the character, intellect, and statesmanship of current and former U.S. Supreme Court Justices, as well as *Landmark Supreme Court Cases: The Most Influential Decisions of the Supreme Court of the United States* (2004). He also coedits a multivolume series, The Supreme Court of the United States: Hearings and Reports on Successful and Unsuccessful Justices by the Senate Judicial Committee, and collaborates on the Documentary History of the Legal Aspects of Abortion in the United States, with the most recent volume in that series published in 2003.

Mersky has also made significant contributions to the field of law, is active in national law and library organizations, and is a member of the State Bars of Wisconsin, Texas, and New York, and has been admitted to practice before the Supreme Court of the United States. He serves as a consultant to many academic institutions and law firms, as well as private corporations seeking to establish or organize collections of law-related materials. Active in both state and civic organizations, Mersky is an executive board member of the Wisconsin Non-Resident Lawyers Division, past president of the Texas Humanities Alliance, and an executive board member and treasurer of the Texas Supreme Court Historical Society. He received his BS in 1948, a JD in 1952, and a master's degree in library science in 1953 from the University of Wisconsin, Madison.

Jennifer Bryan Morgan has been the documents librarian at the Indiana University School of Law–Bloomington since 2001. She earned her BA from Saint Mary-of-the-Woods College in 1990 and her MLS from Indiana University–Bloomington in 1995. As documents librarian, Bryan is responsible for providing specialized reference service in the use of U.S. government documents and directing the law library's U.S. government depository program. She teaches legal research in the Legal Research and Writing Program and provides guest lectures on specialized legal research in other law school classes. Serving on local and national committees, she is a member of the Indiana University Librarians Association; the American Association of Law Libraries and its Government Documents Special Interest Section, INDIGO (Indiana Networking for Documents Information and Organizations); and the Ohio Regional Association of Law Libraries. Bryan's research interests are in the areas of legislative history and electronic access to state and local government information.

Mary Rumsey is foreign, comparative, and international law librarian at the University of Minnesota Law Library. She holds a BA from the University of Wisconsin, a JD from the University of Chicago, and an MLIS from Dominican University. She is vice chair/chair-elect of the Foreign, Comparative, and International Law Special Interest Section of the American Association of Law Libraries. Among her publications are contributions to *Law Library Journal, Legal References Services Quarterly,* the EISIL project of the American Society of International Law, and other periodicals.

Tracy L. Thompson serves as the executive director of the New England Law Library Consortium, Inc. Prior to assuming that post in 2001, Thompson was international reference librarian at the Lillian Goldman Law Library at Yale Law School. She is an active member of the American Association of Law Libraries, having served as treasurer and then chair of the Foreign, Comparative, and International Law Special Interest Section, chair of the Special Committee on Licensing Principles for Electronic Resources, and is currently a member of the Committee on Relationships with Information Vendors (CRIV). Thompson is a graduate of the University of South Florida and the Yale Law School. She resides in Keene, New Hampshire, with three busy boys, a demanding dog, a songbird, and some nice quiet fish.